# Endorsements

"Dr. Griffiths presents a manual from your child's newborn to preteen years, including important chapters on brain development, attachment, emotional needs. Parents are also given information on how to support learning and respond to behavior challenges. She presents personal and professional knowledge, along with comprehensive research supporting guidance recommendations, in a clear and direct format."

**Amelia Miller, M.A. Child Development,**
**Infant Mental Health Certification**
**Infant Mental Health Specialist at LaRabida Hospital**

"Chapter One on the biology of the brain is absolutely fascinating. Some people may not have the patience for the details, but I thought it was great."

**Elisabeth Trost, M.Ed., M.A., Ed.S.**
**Educator, District Administrator, Chicago Public Schools**

"As a therapist, and as a parent myself, I appreciate how Dr. Griffiths identifies children born with a problematic temperament style and gives helpful tips on how to address the issues of ADHD while positively supporting the child's self-esteem.

I appreciate learning about morality vs kindness—the difference between them, how to encourage those behaviors and discourage unkind or immoral behaviors.

I was surprised to see discussion of the issue of physical punishment. I understand that some parents choose to use physical punishment and so it does make sense to identify what is appropriate versus what is harmful or abusive."

**Deborah Birch Gaytan, M.S.W., LCSW**
**Therapist, Private Practice**

"I enjoyed reading about the history of the 'self-esteem movement' and recalled how my own children didn't want sports team 'participation' trophies, regardless of where they had placed, because they knew it wasn't deserved."

**Lisa Ferguson, Master of Arts in Teaching/**
**Early Childhood Education**
**Erikson Institute, Early Math Collaborative**

"Dr. Griffiths' style is very informative in a curiosity-encouraging and sometimes playful manner. The reader is invited to adopt this style in learning evidence-supported parenting tips with good research support. Dr. Griffiths strongly emphasizes the importance of facilitating individualized growth for both child and parent(s)—and the joy that accompanies those efforts."

**Bruce Johnson Bonecutter, Ph.D.**
**Retired Public Health/Clinical Psychologist**
**Formerly Clinical staff of Stroger Hospital**

"My son is seven weeks old as I am writing this, and once I started reading the chapter on Infancy, I finished it the same day. I like what the author said about spoiling at this age—that it's not possible to spoil him with *too much* love.

I was particularly interested in the part where she explained how to build a healthy Self; the book explains the way to say "no" and not to damage the Self."

**Marketa Placha Galek, M.B.A.**
**New Mother**

"As a former teacher of school age children, I truly appreciated the treatment Dr. Griffiths gave to the topics of ADHD and Learning Disabilities. Parents and teachers will benefit from learning about these difficult-to-understand issues which she covers in a clear and concise format. Her vast and long-term experience allows her to be practical and effective in helping families cope with these problems so very common to childhood."

**Ann Beran Jones, B.A.**
**Retired Educator**

# PARENTING
## WITH A
# PSYCHOLOGICAL
## PERSPECTIVE

*How Research and Theory*
*Can Enrich the Parenting Experience*

Margaret O'Connor Griffiths, Ph.D.

Parenting with a Psychological Perspective:
How Research and Theory Can Enrich the Parenting Experience
by Margaret O'Connor Griffiths, Ph.D.
FAM034000 FAMILY & RELATIONSHIPS / Parenting / General
PSY004000 PSYCHOLOGY / Developmental / Child
FAM039000 FAMILY & RELATIONSHIPS / Life Stages / School Age
ISBN: 979-8-88636-015-8 (paperback)
ISBN: 979-8-88636-016-5 (ebook)

Cover design by LEWIS AGRELL

Printed in the United States of America

Authority Publishing
11230 Gold Express Dr. #310-413
Gold River, CA 95670
800-877-1097
www.AuthorityPublishing.com

# Dedication

To my grandkids, Gavin, Payton, and then Connor (who came along just in time to contribute to the Infancy section).

# Acknowledgements

How can you acknowledge a great career? That's what has led to the writing of this book. I have been immersed in the field of Psychology from 1966 (graduate school) to my retirement in 2020. That's fifty-four years! My long career encompassed being a graduate student in Clinical Psychology at the University of Texas (starting the September after Charlie Whitman shot people from the Texas tower), teaching a short time at the University of Kentucky's Department of Psychology, working as a Staff Psychologist at Children's Memorial Hospital in Chicago in the Child Psychiatry Department, and then a twenty-five-year experience at Cook County Hospital (now Stroger Hospital), in Chicago, also in the Child Psychiatry department. And for thirty years, I was the sole practitioner of a private practice of Psychology in the Lincoln Park neighborhood of Chicago. These experiences, all the colleagues I worked with, and all the patients I treated made up a grand career for which I am grateful.

When I retired, I felt that hanging up my shingle was tantamount to letting all that information blow away in the wind. I didn't want that to happen. So, I embarked on this book, putting my experience in writing so that parents and other professionals working with children could have the advantage of my learning. While I set out to write about the average child, I did cover some common problems. Mental health professionals reading this book will recognize some useful tips.

I am indebted to many for furthering my career in Psychology—from the counselor at the University of Minnesota who encouraged me as a sophomore to follow a psychology path—that I was capable of getting that Ph.D.. My graduate school professors shepherded me through the long years of learning and training and helped quell my fears that getting a Ph.D. would put me out of the marriage market. (Yes, this was the '60s.) Jim Bieri, as my chair, was a big help. And then I discovered in the writing of this book that Norm Prentice was the big researcher in the Santa Claus area! In Chicago, there were many on the staff who helped me into the clinical realm, especially Bernie Suran, who agreed to an instant interview (I was in town for other reasons), hired me, and supervised my work to get me up to snuff. Those children and staff at Children's Memorial gave me the wherewithal to become a decent clinician.

Cook County Hospital is a public hospital, where patients were from lower income backgrounds and primarily African American. Those parents taught me so much, and my respect for their parenting in the face of difficulties grew. How many grandmothers or aunts became "parents" for their young children? My experience was chiefly working with families where children were failing in school; that niche led me to become very familiar with the problems of Attention Deficit Hyperactivity Disorder and Learning Disabilities. The staff at this hospital continues to be a community, meeting unfortunately sometimes at funerals, and other times for convivial times. We really enjoy each other's company, and I respect all of them tremendously.

Cook County Hospital is where I met Dr. Deborah Matek, who became the Chair of the Child Psychiatry Department, and who agreed to help me in the writing of this book. She read the initial manuscript carefully, noting typos as well as conceptual problems and agreed to write the Foreword. Her effectiveness as a therapist is exceeded only by her kindness (not only to me; to all).

Others helpful in the writing are friends and colleagues Rickie Cowin, Dr. Tomi Henek, Debbie Block, and Laura Barrett, who read early versions of the manuscript and encouraged me in the beginning stages.

My son Clark, his wife, Kim, and their three children have been inspirations for me as well. What a privilege to be Nana to Gavin, Payton, and Connor. Having grandchildren was the icing on the cake—as I could view them with a "developmental" eye, intercede when helpful, and certainly write about them as they illustrated points I was making. Kim and Clark are excellent parents, and I have learned from them as well.

My many friends and former colleagues encouraged me to write the book, and I thank them for that. They kept me sane—with cultural adventures, biking treks, and sports as well.

*(I was not the only person in my family with ties to this hospital. My mother whose name at that time was Elsie Mladick, did a nursing rotation there. Also, my two cousins who were surgeons trained there as well—Richard and Edward Mladick.)

# Foreword

Dear Reader:

Perhaps you are walking alone on an early spring day and you see the new leaves against the clear blue of the sky and it is just so breathtakingly gorgeous that you wish you could share it with someone. Maybe you are watching the sun set in a blaze of oranges and pinks and it is so striking that the urge to take and send someone a photo comes over you irresistibly.

The urge that led Dr. Margaret O. Griffiths to write *Parenting with a Psychological Perspective* is a version of that feeling. She knew she had something worth sharing. She had worked directly with children and their parents for decades. She had worked in a variety of settings including the inner city and the urban enclaves and in the field of psychology, she saw the need to create a work that presents modern parenting and the foundation for those parenting ideas in a friendly and warm manner that treats readers as intelligent and eager to do what the evidence shows works best. She worked hard to put this together over many months, returning repeatedly to the research and writing and re-writing.

The resulting book contributes greatly to the literature available currently. *Parenting with a Psychological Perspective* is an enlightening and important text and furthermore easy to read. In addition, the book is a deep enough resource to turn to when questions arise, as they inevitably do when striving to raise children to the best of your ability. As an experienced Child Psychiatrist, I can enthusiastically recommend this book.

**Deborah Matek, MD**
Board Certified in Child and Adolescent Psychiatry
Child and Adolescent Psychiatrist and
long-time colleague and friend of the author

# Table of Contents

Introduction. . . . . . . . . . . . . . . . . . . . . . . . . . . . . . . . . . .xvii
A Letter to Parents, Guardians, Educators,
   & Psychology Professionals. . . . . . . . . . . . . . . . . . . . . . xxi

## SECTION I
### The Brain: What Starts Development in Your Child

Chapter 1  How the Brain Grows and How You Help . . . . . 3
Chapter 2  Intelligence and How to Increase It. . . . . . . . . 18
Chapter 3  Can You Raise a Smarter Child? . . . . . . . . . . . 29
Chapter 4  Emotional and Behavioral Style, Including
                Attention Deficit Hyperactivity Disorder . . . . . 41

## SECTION II
### Theorists Attempt to Explain What's Going On

Chapter 5  Theories of Personality Development:
                The Why's of Behavior . . . . . . . . . . . . . . . . . . . 59
Chapter 6  Theories of Intellectual (Cognitive)
                Development. . . . . . . . . . . . . . . . . . . . . . . . . . . 77

## SECTION III
### Five Pillars of Personality Development

### Pillar #1
### Love: Relationships

Chapter 7  Nurturing the Loving and
                Emotionally Well-Adjusted Child. . . . . . . . . . 89
Chapter 8  Developing a Secure Attachment
                and Healthy Emotional Expression . . . . . . . . 101

## Pillar #2
## Responsibility: Giving Your Child The Capacity To Work

Chapter 9   Using Positives to Develop Work Habits..... 115
Chapter 10  When Positives Don't Work—
            The Principles of Punishment............. 130

## Pillar #3
## Creating a Healthy Self

Chapter 11  Self/Other Balance and Self-Esteem........ 143
Chapter 12  Building True Self-Esteem and
            Healthy Expression of Emotions........... 159

## Pillar #4
## Teaching Your Child To Be A Moral Person

Chapter 13  Morality and Kind Behavior:
            Inborn or Taught?..................... 171
Chapter 14  How Morality Develops in Children and
            When There are Lapses................. 182
Chapter 15  Religion and Santa Claus as
            They Relate to Morality ................ 198

## Pillar #5
## Raising An Independent Child

Chapter 16  Concepts of Independence, Separation,
            and Some Cultural Differences............ 211

## SECTION IV
## Ages and Stages

### Infancy Age (0 to 15 Months)

Chapter 17  Early Infancy (0 to 3 Months)............. 229
Chapter 18  Middle Infancy (4 to 9 Months) ........... 240
Chapter 19  Late Infancy (9 to 15 Months) ............ 246

## Toddler Age (15 Months to 3 Years)

Chapter 20  Development in the Toddler Years . . . . . . . . . 255

## Preschool Age (3-6 Years)

Chapter 21  Relationship Building and
            Teaching Adaptive Behavior . . . . . . . . . . . . . 273
Chapter 22  Continuing Pillars of Adaptive Behavior, Self,
            Morality, and Independence . . . . . . . . . . . . . 286

## School Age (6 to 11 Years)

Chapter 23  Education and Brain Growth,
            Including Learning Disabilities and ADHD . . 307
Chapter 24  Physical Care, Relationships,
            Communication/Screen Time . . . . . . . . . . . . 316
Chapter 25  Elements of a Healthy Self & Moral Values . . 325
Chapter 26  Moving Toward Independence . . . . . . . . . . . 333

## SECTION V
### Appendix

Appendix A – Discussion of the Issue
             of Physical Punishment . . . . . . . . . . . . . . . 349
Appendix B – Examining Morality in Various Cultures . . . 364
Appendix C – The Issue of Independence in Other Cultures:
             Family-Centered vs. Individualistic . . . . . . . 368

# Introduction

When I took down my shingle and closed out my career as a Clinical Psychologist, I determined that the many ideas, techniques, approaches, and aspects that I had learned over the decades would not go to waste. For parents who would like more, not less, information about the childrearing process, I wrote this book.

Choosing the content and order was a challenge. While I wanted to share the research and theory behind child-rearing strategies, I also wanted to give some hands-on advice. How to accomplish that? The notion of two major sections—one conceptual and the second more practical—was the answer. So, this book is really two books in one. And that's why it's so long.

The order of material was the next decision to make. Putting the "Brain" chapter first was a conundrum, as it is highly technical and has been found by some to be overly challenging. If you started with the first chapter, it could be a turn-off. Simplifying that chapter some was possible, but for those who really wanted that information, I didn't want to water it down too much.

The first section, "The Brain," contains the mechanics of nerve transmission and brain growth, the notion of intelligence, and the inborn personality characteristics called "temperament." For those parents whose children struggle with a portion of academic learning, the material on Learning Disabilities will be helpful. And for those parents of overly active children, the last chapter is a helpful guide to the diagnosis and treatment of Attention Deficit Hyperactivity Disorder.

The second section, on "Theory" is a review of personality theorists whom I deem helpful to understanding child development. Freud and neo-Freudians lead the pack. In the area of cognitive theory, Piaget is a giant, but I do mention Lev Vygotsky as an addition. This material might be daunting to the reader, but all parents are theorists of some sort—trying to figure out how their input will affect their child's personality—and so you might as well see what the professionals have to say!

Personality development is covered in the third section. When I taught medical students at Cook County (now Stroger) Hospital, I used two "Pillars" to divide the lecture: (1) Building Relationships and (2) Teaching Adaptive Behavior. When he was asked what a psychologically healthy person could do well, he answered, "*To love and to work.*" Those are the first two pillars of Section III.

However, there is so much more in the field of Child Development than those two. So I added three more Pillars: the Self, Morality, and Independence. I had the most fun in the Morality section when I learned that a former professor of mine was the "expert" on the issue of Santa Claus.

When I got to Independence, I got side-tracked on cultural and anthropological issues in how people relate to one another as families. The material was so interesting, and my familiarity with Arab culture was so compelling that the chapter got very, very long. My editor and I eventually formed Appendices to accommodate chapter length. So the issue of Independence is treated in two areas.

Once the conceptual basics were covered, I turned to the "Ages and Stages" section. Dividing chapters by age, I accomplished two tasks in each. First, I reviewed the most salient aspects of brain development and each pillar for each age group. Then I collected helpful hints on how to handle typical issues that emerge again in each age group. My experience helping families with problems was useful here. Since my career spanned pre-cell phone years, the issue of technology in childhood was especially challenging for me.

Throughout various chapters, when punishment strategies were discussed, I mentioned my take on physical punishment (usually the act of spanking). I tried to be careful to articulate the fact that while physical punishment was not a necessary part of child-rearing, it is so frequently used by parents that a discussion of "best practices" would be helpful. (My foil here was my friend and colleague, Dr. Deborah Matek, who wrote the foreword for this book. She disagrees with me.) Because it is an important issue, and couldn't be covered in the book's chapters, I researched the issue and wrote Appendix A.

Appendix B continues the discussion of cultural aspects of Morality, and Appendix C, as mentioned above, continues material covered in the chapter on Independence. My friends of Palestinian/ Arab backgrounds were invaluable in giving me perspective on family relations—which I can now relate to you.

Now that I have finished the writing task, I will learn what the publishing world does to get the word out. New learning is what life is all about. My career in Psychology allowed me to learn every day. And now, as I volunteer in numerous charities, I can continue learning to do things totally outside the world I know. Those that know me well know I am a very curious person. Who knows what I will get up to next?

I wish you a happy journey of learning as you read this book. It is not an easy read, but I truly hope you will find it worth your while.

# A Letter to Parents, Guardians, Educators, & Psychology Professionals

Dear Parenting Persons, Mental Health Professionals, and Educators:

Becoming a parent is one of the most exciting and sometimes the most fearful experiences in our lives. Having your little one in your arms is one of the most important moments of your life. There are hundreds of questions about how to care for them, nurture them, develop them, teach them, discipline them, and love them. At times, it is frightening to be fully responsible for the life of another human being. However, you can do this—I promise. Billions of us are raising children, working with children in education and in behavioral health capacities, and billions more will take on these roles just like you.

A friend and fellow author, Barb Yokum, introduced me to the following phrase: "We're not raising children; we're raising adults!" Keep this mantra in mind. It is "the big picture." And as you view the eventual adult with whom you will want to spend time, it will help you choose your parenting strategies.

Your child, no matter which age they are today, is continuously developing their physical, intellectual, and psychological capacities. In this new phase of your life with your first child or your next child, *you* are also developing. The absolute best way to learn how to become the best person in this child's life you can be, is to learn and become informed. Congratulations! You are already doing it by picking up this book!

Throughout this book, you will learn about your child's inherited characteristics, also known as the "givens," which are the characteristics that are *given* to your child when conceived. Your little one has been gifted with a brain and all its manifestations, including their temperament or "emotional style." I'll also share theories from child psychologists and experts in child development that support, debate, or negate various areas of development so you can better understand the who, what, where, why, and how of child development from conception through school age.

These chapters will give you insight on how and what to recognize in your child as they develop and allow you to begin to consider why each child, even those in the same family, develop with entirely different personalities.

Through my forty-plus years as a child and family psychologist, I've researched, practiced, and published in numerous areas of development, and shared everything I know to be helpful to those practicing the art of raising children.

There is no one way to parent, care for, or work with a child. It is my great hope that this book provides the level of knowledge you will find most helpful to understand your child's "inner workings" as they grow into human beings. In doing so, you will be better able to properly set expectations, understand their milestones, and nurture your child with more intentionality.

Each of us is unique in our parenting journey, as unique as each child. As you read through this book, you'll be better able to understand the theories and information I share so you can determine which of the theories, approaches, and styles fits your desired style of parenting.

As they say: "When we learn more, we know better. When we know better, we do better." May your parenting journey be informed, enlightening, and enjoyable!

Margaret Griffiths, Ph.D.

# SECTION I

## The Brain:
## What Starts Development in Your Child

Chapter 1    How the Brain Grows, and How You Help
Chapter 2    Intelligence and How to Increase It
Chapter 3    Can You Raise a Smarter Child?
Chapter 4    Emotional and Behavioral Style Including Attention
             Deficit Hyperactivity Disorder

# Chapter 1

## How the Brain Grows and How You Help

Our brains are the basis for all life, and parents who appreciate the amazing physiology of the brain may be in a better position to make decisions on how to interact, engage, discipline, and love their children. Did your high school Biology 101 class have a section on "neurogenesis"— the creation of the nervous system? Whether your answer is "yes" or "no," you are not to worry. To appreciate the physical changes in your child's brain during pregnancy and their first year, this chapter will cover brain anatomy and nervous system development. Once you better understand the most important physical development of your child's brain and nervous system, you may see how your child's development results from brain maturation. This knowledge may give you ideas or offer explanations on how you, as parents, can understand, respond, and act with your child to help their development along in a new way. Once you understand the delicate structure of our brains and nervous system, your task will be to respect your child's brain and to facilitate its continuous development. At the very least, once we learn and are aware of this insight many are humbled to appreciate the enormous miracle of brain development, which will be the most all-important area of development in your child.

# THE NATURE VS. NURTURE DEBATE

If you took a high school or college psychology course, you may remember the concept of "Nature vs. Nurture." Since before the sixteenth century, philosophical concepts continue to be discussed and researched regarding brain development. The greatest "debate" remains whether an infant is born with characteristics, beliefs, behaviors, and/or emotions that are natural to who they are, or if they learn these attributes through their environment as they are nurtured. Hence, the debate, "Nature vs. Nurture." Which philosophy do you believe?

1.  Does the brain contain inborn traits and capabilities when a child is born, which they received from "nature?"
2.  Is the child's brain a "blank slate" with nothing written on it except that which the environment (you) put into it as you "nurture" them?

The "Nature" issue has been discussed since Plato. René Descartes (1596–1650) wrote, among many other things, that some ideas are inborn. He noted that understanding truth, thought, and what a thing is, appeared to be *"inborn" or as the term used by psychologists, "a given,"* which means that nobody had to teach it. This idea first appeared in his famous work, *Meditations on First Philosophy*[1]. Somewhat later, the English philosopher, John Locke (1632-1704), defined the philo side of "Nurture," which subscribes to the theory that the brain does not come with inborn traits, but is nurtured by parents and the environment to learn, adapt, mature, and develop. Locke put forth the idea that babies come into the world with the capacity to think but have no other predispositions. His notion of a *"tabula rasa"* (Latin for "blank slate") was that education and experience will give the child all it needs to develop[2].

In the 1960s, advancing knowledge about the brain proved that Locke was wrong and that indeed babies are not born with a "blank slate." The field of behavior genetics emerged in psychology to show which traits have inherited beginnings. Babies come into the world with various mental skills and predispositions, and there is actually a programmed sequence of brain development which continues well into when your child is in their twenties. This is the "Nature" view of the argument. However, education and experience are absolutely necessary for brain advancement, and that is up to you, as parents and psychology professionals.

---

**SPOILER ALERT!**

**Both notions of nature and nurture are valid as the environment (which you control as parents) works hand in hand with your child's physical brain structure to develop to its optimal potential.**

---

So, as parents, during this adventurous journey of brain development, you will be vigilant, watching for steps of brain maturation ("motor milestones") in your developing child, such as when they roll, crawl, walk, and run. Then, you will see advancements in thinking, such as learning to read by age six, multiplication at eight, and algebra at thirteen, or so. By virtue of their questionable judgment and sometimes foolish behavior, anyone who knows teenagers knows that their brains do not reach full brain maturation until around age twenty-five, which means you have a fair amount of waiting ahead of you, as far as brains go, until they are fully developed human beings. So, let's dive into "Neurogenesis" and the miracle of brain development.

## NEUROGENESIS: THE BUILDING BLOCKS OF THE NERVOUS SYSTEM

We now return to Biology 101. Our bodies are composed of cells, and among them are nerve cells that conduct electricity and "talk" to one another through chemical messages across a tiny gap that separates them[3].

The nervous system consists of the brain, the spinal cord, and the network of nerve cells (neurons) that transmit and return impulses from a stimulated part of the body to the brain. We'll look at the neuron first and then at "electrical" transmission mechanisms.

## The Neuron

The basic unit of the nervous system is called a "neuron." Ten billion of these cells build the brain. Each neuron is a living cell with a nucleus, dendrites (short fingers that receive impulses), and an axon (a long fiber projecting away from the cell body). Those axons are located in the spinal cord and may vary from very, very small lengths to two or three feet in length. "Nerves" are actually bundles of neurons, perhaps around 1,000 that allow us to do the mental and physical work of living. Neurons are not directly connected to one another. Rather, an impulse (explained next) travels across a small space called a "synapse" from one neuron to another by means of molecules interacting with the neuronal membrane.

---

### A SHORT COURSE ON THE BRAIN

We won't go into great detail on brain structures for the purposes of this book. But it may be helpful to know the basics.

- The lower-brain structures are almost completely developed at birth and control physical functions such as breathing, movement, and reflexes.
- The cerebrum is our higher brain, known as the cerebral cortex, and is the largest part of our brain. It's the seat of our conscious experience, intentional behavior, and reasoning.

Both parts progressively contribute to development.

---

## Nerve Impulses

In a manner that defies belief, nerve impulses only move in one direction from dendrite to axon to dendrite of another cell. While you are reading this, your neurons are transmitting seamlessly. It is an amazing feat we take for granted. How does it happen?

All of our behavior is due to *electrical activity* of one impulse traveling from one neuron to the next over the synaptic gap. The formation of electricity in the human body is electrochemical, and it's similar to that formed in normal batteries by a difference in the charge of two elements. Perhaps, you made a battery with a potato in elementary school? In the body, electricity travels from two to 180 miles per hour[4]. That's why it seems to take no time for your eyes to see this WORD and wonder why it is capitalized. The chemical changes take place on a minute scale. The energy involved in firing a neuron is around a billionth of a watt, with ten billion neurons in the human brain. Assuming every neuron in your brain is active at the same time, the whole brain can operate on a power supply of about ten watts[5].

Those of you who engage in heavy exercise and perspire a lot are told to keep yourselves "hydrated" and keep the "electrolytes" up. Have you ever wondered, "Why?" The electrolytes, potassium and sodium, are important for neuronal transmission. Let's look at this in more detail so you will know the importance of these elements.

---

**PICTURE THIS...**

**Picture looking inside your child's brain.**

- **Look at the nerve cell as a tiny, polarized battery.**
- **Inside the cell is the negative pole.**
- **The outside of the cell is the positive pole.**
- **When the axon is stimulated, the electric potential of the protoplasm inside the axon is LOWERED below its normal negative 70 millivolts.**

---

- With a reduction of that potential, the cell membrane CHANGES in that its permeability increases.
- With more capacity to accept new material, the membrane allows sodium ions (Na+) to flow into the cell and a smaller number of potassium (K+) ions to flow out.
- This interchange results in a voltage difference, and the process is repeated down the nerve.
- Each impulse causes the chemical change at the synapse, and travels to the end point.
- Amazingly, no energy is lost in the transmission.
- The impulse is just as strong when it starts as when it ends.
- The resting potential negative of 70 millivolts is restored in the neuron by the outward flow of the K+ ions.
- Now you know how important potassium and sodium are for neuronal transmission.

Absence of these "electrolytes," also called "ions," results in the impairment and eventual shutdown of the nervous system. Heat stroke results when this happens and death can occur. Gatorade and similar "sports drinks" contain potassium and sodium and therefore correct any deficiency. So, you Gatorade drinkers are actually helping the physiology of your nervous system

An added helper to speed the impulse is the "myelin sheath," which develops over time. Myelin is a fatty substance that coats the axon and seals the leaks. The sheath allows the nerve impulse to jump along the fiber from node to node and makes that fast transmission possible, which we all take for granted.

Without myelination, the nervous system transmission is hampered. Ions of potassium and sodium can leak out of the cell membranes, resulting in a loss of efficiency. Unfortunately, children whose brain does not develop the sheath have demyelinating diseases such as multiple sclerosis, which is caused when a patient's own immune system destroys the myelin and results in severe sensory and motor deficits.

# THE BEGINNING OF YOUR CHILD'S BRAIN DEVELOPMENT

Now that you are more familiar with the building blocks of the nervous system and the fact that our brains have ten billion neurons, let's examine how the brain starts with zero nerve cells and increases to ten billion.

## Neural Development – Getting the Neurons On Board (Prenatal through 4.5 Months Gestation)

Prenatal neural development begins even *before* pregnancy can be detected and *before* the fetus is in the embryonic stage. Let's have a brief review of the physical development during pregnancy. After initial conception and a bit of cell division, a blastocyst, which has thirty-two cells, develops. Of these thirty-two cells, some will become the fetus and the rest, the placenta (I know you always wondered about that thing). The blastocyst transforms into an embryo (less than 1/100th of an inch) one week after fertilization. The embryo then implants on the uterine wall. At sixteen days, it will develop a vertical axis and two types of cells give rise to the Neural Plate, the origins of the nervous system. Ectoderm will become the future brain and spinal cord. This "neurulation" begins only nine days after fertilization and before pregnancy is detected. The rapidity of growth of neurons is beyond amazing. Around three weeks post-fertilization, the embryo is 1/10-inch in size (about the thickness of eight stacked pieces of paper) and a neural tube connecting the higher and lower brains are fashioned. At the top of the tube will be the eventual higher brain; at the lower end will be sensory/motor brain development.

**CAUTION FOR PARENTS-TO-BE!**

Parents-to-be are keenly aware of the importance of the mother's health *during* pregnancy; however, early development begins before knowing there is a pregnancy. That is why prenatal planning with your doctor is important and why prenatal vitamins are prescribed. There are implications for mothers who are not cautious with their nutrition and who consume toxic substances like alcohol, legal marijuana, illegal drugs, and even prescribed medication before pregnancy occurs.

It is an amazing fact that neurogenesis starts at three weeks of fetal development, increases in speed at seven weeks, and is mostly completed by eighteen weeks. These cells are permanently in the brain. The speed is mind-boggling.

In the fifth week in utero, five areas of brain enlargement emerge and the neural tube closes. The cells that divide to make the neurons are then trapped inside. Chambers of the nervous system appear: four chambers of the brain and one running along the spinal cord. The walls of these ventricles begin the cell division at warp speed to convert neuroepithelial cells into neurons, which is the process of "neurogenesis." In order to produce the ten billion neurons in the brain, they must divide at a rate of 250,000 PER MINUTE (Myers). For some "growth spurts," cells are produced at 500,000 per minute, unlike cells in other organ systems, which can continue to divide while neurons cannot. The brain is special in that if it is damaged, cells will not repair lost circuits. But can they function? Developing brain structures is the next task of physical maturation.

# Brain Structures – Development Begins
# (6 Weeks through 9 Months Gestation)

In the sixth week in utero, the cells differentiate into what will become major brain structures. Cranial nerves appear. After eight weeks, the embryo is referred to as a "fetus" and is about two inches long. At three months gestation, the fetus is five inches long, and has fairly well-developed lower-brain structures. But the cerebral cortex that gives us our unique human intelligence is undifferentiated. In the next few weeks, the two cerebral hemispheres grow, and their connection to the corpus callosum is seen.

By twenty-four weeks, the fetus is fourteen inches long, and lungs are prepared to breathe air. The brain stem can support life outside the uterus, but the cerebral cortex is just beginning to add neurons for advanced mental function. And develop, it will! A smooth brain surface just won't work, so the brain develops "grooves" that allow for a larger number of neurons. The number and depth of these grooves expand during the prenatal period and continue into the first year of life. The number and depth of grooves will determine how many neurons and their connections get made with implications for mental development; the more grooves and connections, the higher the mental capacity will be.

At nine months gestation, the process of myelination begins. The process is slow and uneven, and the rate of progress determines how well that brain region's function will work. Genes determine the timing, but environmental factors such as malnutrition may affect the process. Myelin requires fat in the diet, so the need for myelin is why pediatricians recommend a sufficient level of it in children's diets until about age two.

So, by the time of birth, brain development, especially of the cerebral cortex, is not complete. In the first year, a child's brain will nearly triple in size, growing from about one-quarter to three-quarters of an adult's brain weight. In addition to the difference in size, at the microscopic level, the child's brain remains very different from an adult brain.

**PICTURE THIS**

Picture the skull as containing an amorphous (undefined shape) and gelatinous (wiggly) mass of "gray matter."

- The cells are alive but separate and are not capable of transmitting any impulses yet. Which means, lots of neurons with no place to go.
- Now, genetic coding takes over.
- The genetic coding directs the action so axons send out a length of cell matter with an enlarged tip called a "growth cone."
- The cone sends out tentacles in all directions and picks up signals such as chemicals and electrical fields to find appropriate targets.
- All of these changes are genetically coded axons that meet up with molecules of another neuron, which attracts it (think magnet) to complete a connection.
- When the contact is made, a synapse is formed!

Remember, these synapse connections allow your child's brain to function.

## Synaptogenesis – Organizing Synaptic Connections

Once the cells are formed during neuronal development, they are useless unless they have some organization. They may migrate to a particular area of the brain, but without a synaptic connection, they do nothing. The synapse begins forming between two cells. At its peak, some 15,000 synapses are produced on every cortical neuron, which corresponds to a rate of 1.8 million new synapses PER SECOND[6]. "Synaptogenesis" continues all through gestation into the second postnatal year.

During that first year of life, the cerebral cortex triples in size as a result of all that dendritic growth. The brain will overproduce synapses, about twice as many as it will ever need. An estimated quadrillion synapses exist in the brain. However miraculous the process, the neuron is still useless, because the wiring does not have a purpose. But what about the wiring—how does that take place?

## The Battle of the Synapses & the Role of Experience

So now we have a brain with zillions of useless neurons and synaptic connections with nowhere to go. What gets the brain moving once the child is born? The brain needs experience from the outside physical world to make those connections. Touch, smell, taste, vision, hearing; all of these experiences will build those synaptic connections, which are so important to brain function. The neurons will become organized such that the experience is conscious and recorded in the brain. This is called *learning*.

The richness of an environment will stimulate certain neurons to develop, and an unstimulating environment will not. Laboratory animals, such as rats, monkeys, rabbits, etc., that were reared in rich or empty environments have been compared. Those reared in the more stimulating environments have larger brains, and thicker cortexes, which means more neurons, more dendritic branches, and more synapses. Those animals also learn faster.

Again, our brains are given way too many neurons/synapses, and they must be winnowed out for the brain to actually function. Experience forces the synapses to compete with each other. The most used synapses will survive while the lesser synapses do not develop and will eventually die out. Children lose approximately twenty billion synapses per day between early childhood and adolescence. This is not bad news, nor is it making your child less able, but it makes mental processing more streamlined and coherent, and allows learning to take place. The synapses that are used (meaning transmitting impulses from one to the next) will develop into a channel for motor or cognitive activity. Some parents focus on giving their unborn child prenatal experiences such as listening to classical or rock music with hope that synapses are formed. Whether or not providing prenatal "experiences" like classical music or rock music forms potentially meaningful synapses remains a question and will be discussed in more detail in Chapter 2.

## How is Brain Activity Measured?

Before learning about how experiences play a role in brain development, it's worthwhile to share some of the modern techniques that are used to measure brain maturity. Again, some areas of the brain are not mature until the mid-twenties. Until recently, age sixteen was thought to be the year when the brain ceased to make qualitative changes.

Recent techniques such as MRI (Magnetic Resonance Imagery), EEG (Electroencephalogram), and PET (Positron Emission Tomography) have been used to measure a baby's brain activity and glucose use. Glucose is a basic sugar and is the energy of life. Parts of the brain that are active and in use will use more glucose. PET exams are used to measure the brain for glucose up-take for strict medical diagnosis for brain injury or understanding Attention Deficit Disorder, which will be discussed in Chapter 4. The test is performed by inserting a radioactive form of glucose in the bloodstream. Active areas of the brain will show "red" and less active will show "blue." Glucose use means that the area of the brain in question is working. PET tests done by UCLA researchers showed that around three months after birth, glucose metabolism increases in several cortical areas, notably in visual perception at the rear of the brain. After six or eight months, the frontal lobe containing the cortex begins to rise in glucose use. These are the first signs of higher cognitive function[7].

## Critical Periods In Brain Development – The Role Of Prenatal Experiences – Or Not

As time passes, the brain grows, but it needs stimulation. The level of stimulation has to be appropriate, or the child will turn away to protect themself from over-stimulation. Introducing new challenges to your child is a matter of timing. "Readiness" is a useful term. Some things are just common sense. You cannot have a child walking at three months, nor counting to five before one year, even if they're a genius. Ideally, every child should be allowed to learn and function at their own pace. Social timetables are based on average brain maturity, which is the reason for school entry beginning at five or six years of age. Math concepts are also timed to the norm like multiplication tables in third grade, or at eight years old.

Looking at different types of stimulation, or lack of it, may shed some light on the nature/nurture issue that was reported in the 1960s and 1970s. There are some studies of development with humans and animals where they were placed in deprived, usually extreme, circumstances. For instance, tests for children raised by wolves, in isolation, or in substandard care facilities such as orphanages show variously that some brain function can be recovered, but some loss is permanent.

Examining how different cultures handle the issue of stimulation may help us understand its role in brain development. Appendix C provides cultural differences in more detail, but one study will be described here to show the role of nature, nurture, and the roles of stimulation, critical periods, and brain maturation.

In 1972, Jerome Kagan, an eminent scholar in child development and author of "Cross-Cultural Perspectives on Early Development"[8], challenged the Lockean notion by philosopher and scholar John Locke that experience is everything (nurture) and posited that maturation/biology (nature) was chief. He studied indigenous children in an isolated village, in San Marcos, Guatemala. During the first ten to twelve months, the San Marcos infant spends most of his life in the small dark interior of thatched huts with a dirt floor. There are no books, pencils, paper, or pictures. The culture presumes the outside sun, air, and dust are harmful. The infant is rarely spoken to or played with. The only objects available for play are his clothing, the mother's body, oranges, ears of corn, and pieces of wood or clay. When the child becomes mobile around age one, they leave the hut and play with other children. Observations of these children were that interactions occurred only 6-12% of the time compared to 25-40% in US middle-class homes. At age one, San Marcos children appeared motorically passive, fearful, and very quiet. Many would not orient to a taped source of speech, nor smile or babble to vocal overtures, and would hesitate over a minute before reaching for an attractive toy. They walked at eighteen months and talked at three years. At ages five and eight, they lagged behind children raised with stimulation; however, by age eleven, measures of attention, recall, and perceptual inference showed <u>no difference</u> from children reared with stimulation. He posits that genetic maturation is chief in determining functioning, and relative "retardation" is not permanent.

Suffice it to say, you are not about to deprive your children of necessary experiences. You are reading this material to *optimize* your child's experience. Be aware that not all children suffer permanent damage when their environments are less than what many would consider optimal.

Whether a child is raised in San Marcos or the US, stimulating experiences such as times when the child is attentive and interacting, are necessary for the synapses to form. The educational experiences of preschool have been discovered to be positive in terms of overall brain function. Many countries that recognize the importance of early learning have introduced early childhood education. This experience for children is particularly important in families which may provide less stimulation because preschool programs have the ability to provide the essential ingredients for brain maturation. Since 1965, the US government funded Head Start programs to serve children ages three to five to support their education and development. Later, in 1993, Early Head Start programs began intervention with children zero to age three.

## SUMMARY (Chapter 1)

Understanding how the developing brain matures allows us to appreciate the growth and development of our child. Having awareness of various milestones and phases helps set expectations of abilities during various ages. You may be surprised to know that throughout the years of raising or treating a child, development occurs when the child's brain has matured enough—not when the caregivers decide.

# Chapter 2

## Intelligence and How to Increase It

### INTRODUCTION

No explanation of brain development would be complete without touching on an area of great concern—your child's level of intellectual ability. You are looking at a child's future in terms of their ability to navigate learning challenges from preschool to graduate school and may equate their future chances of "success" in terms of their cognitive abilities. I suggest you be careful in how you judge "success" because it is poorly correlated with intelligence. In this section, I will try to give you the basics of how psychologists have viewed and measured "intelligence."

### Individual Differences

Not all brains are created equal. This is standard knowledge. Naturally, a loving parent wants their child's brain to function optimally, and parents watch carefully as their child's brain matures and grows while the child demonstrates new capabilities. Starting with physical development, parents are concerned about the "advancement" of their child through developmental "milestones," which mark progress of development from rolling over to academic achievement.

Psychology began by looking at how people differ in terms of certain abilities. Individual differences in human brain functioning have long been apparent, and we know how different people can be with respect to their speed of acquiring new information by learning. There are fast learners, average learners, and slow learners.

Through infant development to adulthood, brain functioning is understood in relation to other children in the same age group. There is a wide spectrum of function from far below the average to far above the average. Persons functioning in the lowest two percent are diagnosed as having an intellectual disability, formerly known as mental retardation[1]. Those above the highest two percent are classified as superior in intelligence, or "genius." The rest are in between. But how is intelligence defined, and how is it measured?

## What is "Intelligence?"

What do YOU think it means to be "smart," "bright," or "intelligent?" The word "intelligence" is derived from the Greek word for "understanding." In the 1800s, a serious interest in the concept of "intelligence" developed and started the study of individual differences, otherwise known as "psychology." Take a moment to think about what it means to you. When I asked pediatrics residents in a class I taught to define "intelligence," they usually gave another synonym like "bright," "smart," or "good at learning."

Here are some attempts at a definition.

- One of my old textbooks states: "Learning is a process in which past experience or practice results in relatively permanent changes in an individual's repertoire of responses"[2].
- Jean Piaget defined intelligence as "acquisition of operations that facilitate adaptation."
- Another way of looking at intelligence is the "ability to benefit from experience, and the ease with which a child learns new ideas or behaviors"[3].

- Psychologist Robert Sternberg[4], a recent writer in this era, sees "successful intelligence" as composed of the following three elements:

  - analytical intelligence (problem-solving abilities)
  - creative intelligence (using prior knowledge and skills to deal with new situations)
  - practical intelligence (the ability to adapt to a changing world)

You could consider that an easy, common sense, and very general descriptor of these definitions pertains to how one adapts to the environment.

But how and when did interest in "intelligence" develop?

As European cultures evolved in the eighteenth century with advancement in work and education, people started differentiating from each other. (Apparently everybody seemed pretty much the same in preindustrial times.) The science of psychology developed from the impetus to understand individual differences in learning. First efforts in the mid-1800s in Germany were led by Wilhelm Wundt[5] to measure individual adults' responses to stimuli—the faster you were, the smarter you were. Wundt's lab defined "intelligence" as the speed of response to various stimuli.

Later psychologists invented other measures to assess whatever they thought learning was. They went beyond Wundt and chose varying mental "tests." In defining "intelligence," they posed the question, "Intelligence for what?" Interestingly, the concept of "adaptation to the environment" recognized the following areas for measuring intelligence:

- Language and writing
- Orientation in space
- Mathematical thinking
- Conceptual abstracts

- Common sense "judgment" or "people skills"

Is there one "intelligence" or many "intelligences?" The study of various branches of psychology is ever-evolving as people pursue answers to "What is my purpose in life?" which is followed by the second greatest query: "How does the brain work to determine how people work, think, and act?"

Several psychologists posit various numbers of "intelligences"[6]. Based on a series of fifty-six tests, Thurstone found six major areas that constituted "primary mental abilities." People being tested would get separate scores for each subtest. The subtest topics included:

- Perceptual Speed (was Wundt on the right track?)
- Numerical Ability
- Word Fluency
- Verbal Comprehension
- Spatial Visualization
- Memory
- Reasoning

Despite the knowledge that there are so many variants in brain function, including music, creativity, and emotional intelligence, the notion that there is one type of intelligence persists. That is called "g" for "general," and subtopics would be called "s" for "specific." The argument for one general trait is that scores on these tests tend to group together in any individual. That means that if one scores high or low in one, there is a tendency to score high or low in most. So an individual tends to be at one level across the board. And we still use the terms "smart," "bright," "quick learner," and "intelligent" because we presume intelligence is only one trait. So, to sum up, these "tests" define intelligence.

Kagan offers his opinion that intelligence tests mostly predict academic performance. After all of this work, I'm sorry to say there is no definitive definition of intelligence; it is an abstraction (construct) made by people trying to invent a useful tool. Intelligence is what intelligence tests measure! In jest, you could say, depending on how you score on these tests, could form your opinion on whether the intelligence tests really are "intelligent."

We all have an opinion on this subject. Different tasks are required to function in one's "environment" and must be included in the definition of "intelligence." Thinking about "intelligence" has clearly advanced beyond speed of response to stimuli!

## Current Tests in Use for Children and the Concepts Of Mental Age & IQ

Now that we have tried to define "intelligence," we can examine how those early psychologists tried to measure it. In France in the late 1800s, a measure was sought to differentiate those children who could profit from attending school to learn language and mathematics from those who lacked the ability to learn traditional school material. A French educator named Alfred Binet[7] undertook that task. Binet's definition of intelligence was "judgment," which is a fairly broad, but very interesting, concept.

---

**IMPORTANT NOTE**

**It should be emphasized that tests must be of something the child has *not* typically learned before. The task should be a *new* experience such that all test takers are in the same position. Only in small parts of tests would prior knowledge or education be involved.**

---

Binet devised a series of tasks for preschool through school-age children such as building with small blocks, finding a missing object under a small box, counting to five, and defining words.

One of the tasks clearly geared to the definition of judgment was "Foolish Pictures" such as a person using a saw upside down. Other tasks required language, number skills, and/or spatial skills. The variety of tasks showed that Binet respected the fact that brain function is varied.

Binet gave these tasks to numerous children of preschool through school age and saw which tasks were generally solved by a certain age. That task became a measure of "Mental Age" (MA) at a particular age. For example, let's say a seven-year-old took the test of various skills. A child's score was the total of tasks solved. Thus, a child's performance on this test showed them to be functioning at a certain mental age, such as the MA of seven, which means they were performing like the average seven-year-old.

---

**IMPORTANT NOTE**

Note: These tests which are devised to determine the average are only as good as the group measured. Ideally it should be a random selection of many, many individuals of various backgrounds.

---

The concept of the *mental age* of a child is probably the easiest way to look at development. You are probably aware that there is an "average" rate of development that is measurable. Parents watch their child for those known developmental milestones such as sitting, crawling, walking, speaking, drawing a line or circle, knowing colors, and so on. You will know the drill from your pediatrician.

After age five, school achievement is generally used as an estimated measure of MA. If a child is reading and doing math at a certain grade level, that would be presumed to be their MA. It is fairly easy to understand what is meant by a child as "having a mental age of eight." Keep in mind that the child may be five or ten years old, or any chronological age (CA).

Binet developed the concept of the Intelligence Quotient (IQ), which was a division of the MA by the CA times 100. (The act of division gives us the term, "Quotient.") The IQ yields a measure of the *rate of growth* of the capacity for learning. For example, if the MA of a child was four years old and they were four years old, their IQ would be 1.0 times 100 with a result of 100, indicating that the brain is growing at the same speed as their age. If the MA was six and the child was eight, the IQ would be 6 over 8 or .75. Then .75 is multiplied by 100 to get an IQ of 75, which means the brain is growing at a rate ¾ of the age; if the MA was measured to be ten and the child was eight, the IQ would be 10 over 8 or 1.25 x 100 or 125, which means the brain is growing at a rate 1¼ times the age.

Rate of development is a concept that is workable only until the teen years, after which the quotient simply does not work. Test developers issued new norms based on new tests; but the Stanford-Binet is still used[8]. New series of tests were based on norms based on the performance of children at various ages.

The concept of MA is somewhat useful in predicting what mental level a child will reach at adulthood, particularly if that child is seriously below average in rate of mental capacity. The measured MA will predict approximately the MA any person will reach by age sixteen. For example, a person with an IQ of 50 will reach a MA of 8 by age 16 (16 times .5); a child with an IQ of 100 will reach a MA of 16 at 16. Computations above 100 aren't accurate because brain growth slows.

After age sixteen, the meaning of IQs will no longer relate to MA, but rather to a relative place among the population, based on percentage. There is a statistical curve with an average of 100 and a spread ranging for 98% of the population from 70 to 130. For example, a person with an IQ of 130 will have scored 2% lower and 98% higher than the population. A person with an IQ of 85 will be placed ahead of 15% of the population and 85% of the population will be higher than them. The middle 50% of the population scores between 90 and 109.

---

## MORE ABOUT THE IQ SCORE

When considering the scores of IQ tests, imagine a bell shape. The curve and both of its sides represent the majority of the population. The ends constitute the highest IQs and the lowest IQs. The "bell-shaped curve" is everything in between. Those with intellectual disabilities and superior abilities are known as the "outliers" and constitute approximately 2% of the general population; 99% of the population is inside the range of 70 to 130. Approximately 50% of us fall within the average range between 90 and 109. Scores between 20 and 69 are considered in the intellectually disabled category, while those scoring above 130 fall into the very superior to "genius" ranges.

---

IQs can be estimated if we consider developmental milestones as mental ages. For example, Julius Caesar at three years old was observed to be reading on his own, which is considered an accomplishment for a five- or six-year-old. His IQ would then be computed (6 divided by 3 x 100) to be around 200, which is genius level. Delays may give an estimate as well. If a two-year-old child without physical deficiencies is observed to sit up at one year old when that milestone is expected at six months, is walking at two years old when that milestone is expected at one year old and is speaking one-word utterances at two when those utterances are expected at one year old, the child may have a mental age of one year old. Hence an IQ of 50 (1 divided by 2 x 100) would require considering that the child has an intellectual disability.

**SENSITIVITY NOTE**

To be more mindful and respectful of people with disabilities, I share with you some insight into our vernacular when speaking of people with disabilities. When people score in the lowest 2% level on intelligence tests, you may hear terms such as "cognitive disability," "learning disability," or other disabilities. The terms "mental retardation" and "handicapped" are no longer used as they are considered biased and problematic when talking about another human being. However, one parent I worked with at a Chicago hospital was very clear about wanting to know what was holding her child back from learning. When I mentioned "mental retardation," this very straightforward woman said, "Now I know what's wrong! I didn't know from all those other words! Thank you!" For more information about bias-free language for people with disabilities, view the American Psychological Association APA Style Guidelines at https://apastyle.apa.org/style-grammar-guidelines/bias-free-language/disability[9].

Psychology continued to evolve with later efforts to measure intelligence, for example the Wechsler tests[10] divided intelligence into 50% verbal and 50% nonverbal tasks, with a total of both yielding an overall score. That score was compared with scores of children the same age to find their IQ. Note that none of these intelligence tests are geared to measure specific abilities such as music, visual arts, creativity, or other specialty talents which your child may demonstrate. Other tests have been developed to measure these skills.

## Advice for Parents on Learning Disabilities & Using These Concepts

We began this section with the beginning efforts of Binet to find those children for whom academic learning would be suitable. The tests that were developed have been found to predict ability for school success. As noted in a previous section, Jerome Kagan suggested that these be viewed as tests of "Academic Potential" rather than "Intellectual Potential" (Kagan). So Binet got what he was looking for in his original purpose to find which children would benefit from schooling!

Not all children learn the same academic subjects at the same speed, and some children's academic progress lags behind their general intelligence, a situation which can be very alarming and confusing for families. Starting in the 1950s, educators began identifying certain "learning disorders," which today are called "learning disabilities" that explain the particular problem. They discovered, by means of brain studies and autopsies, certain deficits in brain structure caused these learning disabilities. Intelligence tests along with tests of academic skills have been useful in identifying specific deficits in reading, math, and written skills which affect school progress.

---

**STAY POSITIVE**

*Success—however you define it—is not what intelligence tests measure.* If your child has a learning disability, anything is still possible, no matter the score. There are people all around you who live with learning disabilities in your neighborhood—your children's classmates, your colleagues, employers, friends, family, and even celebrities. They are examples of tremendous success, of thriving, surviving, or failing. Famous actors, musicians, CEOs, financial moguls, and everyday people are known to have dyslexia, ADHD, autism, Asperger's, and other learning disabilities. Anything is possible, and all is not lost, especially when the child has an involved parent, such as yourself, who cares enough to learn about their development. If you find yourself in this position, seek out more local resources from your pediatrician, school district, community, church, or psychological specialists for assessments and therapy for both the child and the parent(s). Success stories are shared every day when we overcome the challenges laid before us.

---

These deficits occur in children with otherwise normal ability to learn (intelligence). The subject of learning disabilities will be more fully discussed in the Part IV, Ages and Stages section.

## SUMMARY (Chapter 2)

In this section, we covered how the brain develops, works, and how psychologists measure and predict mental growth. A little knowledge can be a dangerous thing, so let's make sure you have perspective. The concepts of testing for intelligence, mental age, and IQ can take on a life of their own, and some parents may over-focus and see this aspect as all-important. Let's face it. As parents, we are frequently tempted to compare the development of our own child to the development of others. I don't expect that will ever change, but you should be aware that the ability of an intelligence test to predict future overall functioning beyond school is limited. In addition, be aware that your child's motivation to achieve in school may override their intelligence—both in under-achievement and overachievement! So, these tests may be best at predicting school achievement. Keep in mind that achievement is affected by many factors.

I will repeat, "Success, however you define it, is *not* what intelligence tests measure." Genetics gives us limits on how fast or slow we learn, which we will cover in Chapter 3, but a well-known maxim for "success" is that we live up to our "potential." But "potential" is just that; other qualities are necessary for "success." For example, intelligence is helpful in the workplace, but if good work habits are not present, like showing up on time, and completing assignments, the person in question will lose their job. Your child's happiness will depend on various components—personality, temperament, emotional expression, spirituality, and others—not just IQ. Remember, your child is more than their IQ, and their successful development relies on your commitment to nurturing all aspects of their being.

# Chapter 3

## Can You Raise a Smarter Child?

### INTRODUCTION

Now that you are more familiar with concepts of intelligence, you would most probably be interested in learning which inputs will help your child to maximize the potential of their brain. You now know that environmental stimulation produces more connections between neurons. What does environmental stimulation include? Let's explore.

### The Flynn Effect: Increase in Intelligence

Again, common knowledge has it that we are all given a certain intellectual limit based on our genes. This "given" has been challenged by the so-called "Flynn Effect"[1]. Since intelligence tests have been around, and thousands of persons tested, Flynn observed that the performance on the questions given has increased. Spatial, verbal, abstraction, and math performance is higher than it was decades ago. The (tested) world has increased in its ability to perform on an IQ test. There is still the "average," so the test will place an individual relative to their age peers. So, despite your better performance, your IQ (statistic) won't go up because everyone else's goes up.

Reasons for the increase have been speculated to be a more stimulating environment, more familiarity with testing and school procedures, better nutrition, relative absence of infectious diseases, and a reduction of inbreeding ("heterosis").

This effect apparently has had its end according to some research on and by Norwegians. Scientists looking at IQ scores of Norwegian army conscripts from the 1950s to 2002 saw a leveling off of scores[2].

Referring to the nature/nurture issue, genes contribute a good portion of intelligence—estimated at 50/50 as our IQs are generally similar to those of our parents. What in the environment has caused the increase? Here are some thoughts which may aid you in providing the best chance to optimize your child's brain development.

## PRENATAL BRAIN DEVELOPMENT

**Nutrition.** I feel confident that you know full well that a healthy mother-to-be is important to a healthy baby, but I will briefly review some aspects regarding nutrition, toxins, and stress, and how they affect brain development. Regarding nutrition, in modern life the diet of mothers is carefully monitored to include the necessary thirty-eight elements (Eliot). You may recall the description in Chapter 1 of the necessity of the myelin sheath in neuron development. South Asian mothers are traditionally advised to "eat lots of ghee." Ghee is butter, which is fat, which is necessary to construct the myelin sheath. In past times of famine, scientists have followed up on subsequent births. Studies from the time of starvation in World War II (Dutch Hunger Winter of 1944)[3] showed increased risk for mental illness. The authors felt deficiency in many nutrients could alter brain development, or maternal stress secondary to famine could have neurotoxic effects[4]. Malnourished fetuses will develop smaller brains, fewer neurons, and less myelination. Brain size does correlate with intellectual function, and that is why head circumference is a part of well-baby visits. IQ scores are higher in babies with higher birth weights (over an optimal size, birthweight is a detriment due to difficulties with the birth process)[5].

**Toxins.** Toxins such as PCBs or methylmercury have been linked to neurocognitive deficits. As a result of research on maternal health and birth, pregnant women now ingest fewer pathogens (harmful input) such as alcohol, drugs, nicotine, and lead, and inhale less pollution. However, if you recall from earlier in this chapter, the neuronal development begins *before* women realize they are pregnant. Beginning at four weeks after conception, the brain is sensitive to nutrients, so women intending to get pregnant are counseled to keep their body free from toxins at all times.

## NUTRITION NOTE

**One of my former patients was six months pregnant when sadly, the fetus died in utero. She developed a mild case of what felt like the flu, but it was discovered that a bacterium called Listeria caused her illness, which resulted in fetal death. This bacterium is found on various raw vegetables, and does not do much damage other than to unborn babies. My patient only ate cooked vegetables when she, thankfully, became pregnant again and delivered a healthy baby. Unfortunately, the presence of this pathogen is not widely known. Now you know.**

**Stress.** Another major factor in maternal health is the experience of stress, which can have effects on the neurodevelopment of the fetus. Keeping stress to "normal" levels will allow the brain to grow optimally. Research has shown that with excess stress there can be long-term emotional or cognitive problems in later childhood. Clinical studies link pregnant women's exposure to a range of traumatic experiences (e.g. earthquakes), as well as common life stressors (i.e. bereavement, family dysfunction including marital "fights") to significant alterations in children's neurodevelopment. These studies are, of course, correlational, as you can't have a controlled study which induces stress![6,7]

**Stimuli.** What is the effect of stimulation in the prenatal months? The sound, motion, voices, and maternal heartbeat are all normal stimuli for the growing fetus. Some parents play music to their unborn child, presuming that stimulation of the growing fetus will have a positive effect on neuronal development. A fetal response to sound begins at twenty-five weeks gestation. If the music is intense, fetal heart rate and motor activity tends to increase, and vice versa for soft music, such as lullabies[8].

There is no earthly way that neuronal development can be adequately measured with live and growing life forms, so it seems to be conjecture whether playing music to your baby-to-be translates into more or better neurons. It certainly can't hurt, and if you like the music, so much the better.

# BRAIN DEVELOPMENT

## For Infants and Toddlers

Exploring and language stimulation are important in both the infant and toddler years. To some parents, the infant and toddler stage is the cutest stage of children, and for certain, it is the fastest growth period of life. Within the first two years, babies grow exponentially, and parents document each month with pictures to commemorate this quickly changing infant who will soon become a toddler. For the first few months, it may look like there isn't a lot going on with your child because they just sleep, eat, cry, and poop, but I assure you that every sound, light, smell, taste, touch, and interaction you have with them significantly contributes to their developing nervous system and brain.

How a parent interacts with a child emotionally is as important as stimulation in brain development. The trust and emotional development that results from parents' interactions in these years is critical. Children's attention and focus, motivation, persistence, and in a word, "curiosity" are available only in a setting where emotional stability presides.

From the first moment a baby is born, the brain requires stimulation to build the synaptic connections between its cells. Stimulation is derived from the environment of people and objects. One area where parents provide appropriately stimulating environments is giving toys to the infant and toddler. An infant may have a pacifier, teething ring, rattle, or floor gym while the toddler may have a favorite stuffed animal, puzzles, trucks, dolls, and more. Sometimes, it seems the more toys the better, but not necessarily. Overstimulation or chaos in the household can be a detriment, as infants and toddlers will pull back from the confusion and noise. It's extremely important for your child to explore different environments in those toddler years because doing so will support their neuronal development.

Certain toys will provide necessary stimulation, but again, too many may contribute to a messy home or overstimulate the baby. One suggestion (Eliot) to make the environment even more interesting with a lesser number of toys may be to rotate toys, or to put them in different places to encourage exploration and manipulation. New experiences in visiting museums, zoos, restaurants, and with other families are appropriate as well for babies and later stages of development.

Language begins developing from the earliest days when your infant hears sounds. Relationship development is covered in Chapters 7 and 8 but suffice it to say that "tuning in" to the baby's and especially toddler's level of verbal communication is critical in speech development. You can encourage and nurture this stage by repeating their sounds and anything you say to encourage them to respond, as using language stimulates receptive and expressive speech.

With all the toys and activities available to children now, it begs the questions, "Are homes more stimulating now than in the early 1900s?" and "Are we making our children smarter?" It would be interesting to know if that would explain why our brains perform better now[9]. How do modern families differ from those in the earlier part of the 1900s? Is there more exploration permitted, and more language and communication going on? It's difficult to guess, but the advice to parents is clear: stimulate and talk, even when you don't want to answer the 10,000[th] "Why, Mommy?"

---

**IMPORTANT NOTE**

A gap in language performance between children of higher and lower socio-economic-status (SES) is evident by eighteen months, and by age two years, children living in lower SES homes were six months behind children who lived in higher SES homes. This gap is explained by how much parents speak directly to their children. Some children experienced 12,000 words per day and some only 670[10].

---

## For Preschoolers

The beginning and flourishing of "preschool education," named by educators as "Early Childhood Education," began in the mid-1800s and flourished at the turn of the century. Prior to that time, some credit goes to Martin Luther in the 1500s, who promoted reading education so that children could begin to read the Bible. John Locke, whom we covered earlier, subscribed to his philosophy of "nurture" and viewed children as needing molding and shaping through education. Fast forward to the US in 1837, when the first public kindergarten was started in St. Louis. Later, Susan Blow brought a public school to her town, and by the early 1900s, there were 400 public kindergartens. Maria Montessori (1870-1952) pioneered educational techniques for young children which respected the child and promoted hands-on learning techniques. In 1965, the US government began the Head Start program for low-income families administered now through 1,600 agencies.

Today, there remains a growing interest in providing preschool education, and now many, if not most public schools provide classes for pre-kindergartners. Brain development is definitely challenged in these group educational settings. "Quality" preschools, where children are given opportunities to learn in a nurturing environment and with an optimum teacher/student ratio, are shown to increase mental function when compared to children in "lower quality" schools (Eliot). Research has shown that cognition and language development are generally more advanced in children in nursery schools than those in home care or cared for by babysitters. On the positive side, the US government continues to pass laws to promote education, the latest being the "Preschool For All Initiative" in 2013 whereby from birth to five years of age have access to high quality early education to continue success. Stay tuned for future changes to promote education in all socio-economic levels

## MARY CRANE CENTER, CHICAGO

I happen to be more than familiar with early childhood education because of my association with the Mary Crane Center, which was founded by Jane Addams in 1908, as part of her Hull House service for immigrants. She was a pioneer in early childhood education, and convinced a donor, Richard T. Crane, to donate a building for this purpose. The center has grown to serve children from over 350 families in four Chicago neighborhoods, as part of the Head Start program for low-income families. Key ingredients to a successful preschool experience include learning pre-reading (literacy) skills, a social experience of children working in groups, following teacher instruction, and their joy of curiosity and mastery. The child-centered curriculum at Mary Crane Center follows children's interests, rather than a pre-set lesson structure. Free play is an essential part of learning. Those children love to come to school. Instilling a love of learning in children and encouraging parents to work collaboratively with educators sets the stage for their future academic success.

---

**NOTE ON DAYCARE & PRESCHOOL**

Choose carefully the daycare or preschool that provides your child the best stimulating environment and just as important, promotes a love of school and learning.

---

## For School Age Children in Formal Education Setting

When children enter kindergarten, they embark on "formal education." Reading, writing, and math involve symbols, whereas other kinds of learning like tying shoes, do not. (The difference of the types of learning will be covered in more detail in the Ages and Stages section of this book.) Over the past 120 years, it's likely that the introduction of mandatory formal education to age sixteen has provided the "Flynn Effect." When children enter a school, they are challenged in ways the home cannot manage. (Home-schooling is an exception.) Brain development is definitely increased by our use of symbols (those letters and numbers—which are arbitrary. Think of what is meant here: i.e. any squiggle can become a letter or number). It depends on which meaning is attached to it. We, in the US, just happen to use the Roman alphabet. Many others are available. Squiggles are just that.

As discussed in a previous section, we are able to do more with our brains than we were in the early 1900s. And if learning stops for some reason, brain development may slow down as well. During a war or when education is interrupted for several years, studies do show declines of IQ scores. The "Flynn Effect" will be covered in Chapter 6, and you will encounter an educator named Vygotsky who felt that intelligence was affected by academic training. This notion offers additional insight into the "Flynn Effect."

Elementary schools have improved in their ability to deliver education beyond the past century. If they have the option, parents may choose a school which they feel optimizes their child's progress and success. Much research, discussion, and stress go into school choice. Even the option of home-schooling or via computer may be discussed as the recent pandemic showed everyone how children learn remotely.

---

## THOUGHTS ON HOME-SCHOOLING

My opinion on home-schooling is that children learn not only academics but social habits in group environments (school). Those overly protected from other children will ultimately lack social skills and suffer more. If problems in peer relations are present, mental health professionals should be consulted to address the issues.

---

As children begin formal schooling, which usually starts in kindergarten, parents enter a different stage of parenting, as well. Competition with age-mates is apparent, and children's skills and preferences are demonstrated. You get to know your child better as they set out to master the various challenges in language and math-related subjects. And you may get to know yourself better as you stress out with those science projects.

Parents frequently delay starting kindergarten school when their child is "young" for their grade in terms of learning delays or emotional immaturity to give the child an advantage. This strategy is controversial; studies of learning success showed no difference; and younger and older children in a grade learned at the same rate. When parents delay entry, Eliot makes a point that the little bit a child gains by being the oldest in kindergarten is more than offset by how much they lose from missing a full year. However, some children benefit from a year of brain maturation; the "embarrassment" of being held back can be more than offset by the feeling of success, rather than frustration in learning. This decision is a big one for parents.

On the other side of the spectrum, some parents will wish to push their child *ahead* a grade if the child is academically advanced. In this case, socio-emotional maturity will be an issue as the child will be "behind" in that respect. Gifted programs in the public schools are available for those children academically ahead by at least two years, and they don't have to skip a grade. And some children will benefit from being taught at their advanced level. School personnel will be instrumental in grade selection, taking into consideration advantages and disadvantages. For your child to gain maximally, collaborate with schoolteachers and work as a team should problems arise.

Whether homes are better at fostering learning now than in earlier years is not known. Parents can benefit from these conjectures about why our brains do better now, and how your children's brains can function better. In the following section, a controversial idea will be proposed as to how a brain can be trained to think better in adult years.

## CAN A BRAIN BE ENHANCED TO BE SMARTER?

This chapter has discussed how parents can contribute to maximize their child's brainpower. We presume that genetics gives an upper limit. Still, the question remains whether procedures or training will help a brain advance OVER what is thought to be its capacity. Some psychologists have experimented with raising brain function. Bryan Roche, a behavioral psychologist at the National University of Ireland, Maynooth, advances the "Relational Frame Theory," originally proposed by Steven Hayes in 1985, to which Roche posits that understanding relations between objects or concepts is the foundation of intelligence; for instance, understanding the difference between less/more, opposite/same, before/after, etc. The results from Roche's studies show that training to understand those relationships better can increase scores on IQ tests in adults from average to above average[11].

Recently, "adult training" to improve brain function has been supported by the many offerings of games and apps available for cognitive and short-term memory like Sudoku, Wordle, word finds, etc., where adults concentrate on a task to solve the puzzle. Psychologists developed another game called Dual N-Back. The game is intended to raise adult IQ scores by a type of "brain training" which is not available in children, and not available in game stores. The thought is that training on short-term memory tasks is presumed to raise general intelligence as measured by IQ tests[12,13]. I cannot speak from experience about these developments, but they are presented here for you to research should you want more information.

## SUMMARY (Chapter 3)

In this chapter, we have looked at the physiology of brain development, how to measure brain capacity, and which factors enhance cognitive growth. Enhancement of your child's brain is a very important part of your parenting. Optimal stimulation inside and outside the home will be hallmarks of best practices. School choice and support of academic learning will be essential parts as well.

Keeping a level head about your child's intellectual potential is important. Mental capacity is a very sensitive issue in individual differences, and from the perspective of the child, it is important for parents to understand realistic expectations for each of their children. Parents frequently and unfortunately see themselves reflected in the abilities of a child, and when a child shows deficiencies in mental development, parents may need support and coaching to help their child reach potential as a fully functioning human being. These are challenges that many parents face with children who have Down syndrome, and any children whose capacity for learning happens to fall below average. Children are not "blank slates," as Locke presumed. Children far above average also present parenting dilemmas to keep the child academically challenged, yet connected socially to children at their emotional level.

Parents' attitudes toward a child's mental level is key. In addition to keeping a level head about the extent of your child's cognitive gifts, it is important to keep a perspective that intellectual function is only one part of human existence. It is helpful for you to see your child as a "whole human being" with social, spiritual, and creative abilities beyond their and your "desire" to go to an Ivy League college. Remember, as much as we may want to believe that our children should turn out like ourselves, your child is a separate person. Your goal and purpose as their parent is to enhance your child's brain development—not to replace it with one you select. The additional benefit of having children is that you, too, will grow psychologically as your child grows!

# Chapter 4

## Emotional and Behavioral Style, Including Attention Deficit Hyperactivity Disorder

### INTRODUCTION

This book provides information based on research and child-rearing principles that apply to children in general. However, raising a child based on recommendations from others will never quite suit your needs as every child is unique. Understanding a child's uniqueness may be helped by understanding inherited characteristics in "style" that have been described in children. It is the "how" of behavior, apart from the "why." Psychologists call this aspect of behavioral style "temperament." By being aware of some of the characteristics of temperament, you can better understand your child, appreciate their uniqueness, and tailor your approach to best fit your child.

> **TEMPERAMENT (noun):** the basic foundation of personality, usually assumed to be biologically determined and present early in life, including such characteristics as energy level, emotional responsiveness, demeanor, mood, response tempo, behavioral inhibition, and willingness to explore. - APA Dictionary of Psychology[1]

In addition to the growth of intelligence, the brain is responsible for how children differ in various ways. At birth, the spectrum of "emotional excitability" ranges from reactive, intense, and fidgety to easygoing, placid, and quiet[2]. As children age, some become aggressive, some quiet, some fearful, and some bold. Parents have known for centuries that children differ in major ways because those with multiple children see them differing from one another despite essentially similar environments (parents). Ancient theorists and philosophers have shared this idea, but amazingly, psychologists caught up only about seven decades ago, in the 1950s.

## A LITTLE HISTORY ABOUT HOW THE ANCIENTS UNDERSTOOD HEALTH

The relative importance of how much nature and nurture affect personality development has been debated since time immemorial. I will digress a bit here to review some key principles that guided ancient minds in this issue, and then we will come up to date.

How the body works and how it affects behavior came to be better understood only within the last two centuries. Since illness and disease including behavior issues have been part of life since forever, healers have tried to figure out what will help. In India thousands of years ago, theorists postulated that health was an orderly relationship between natural environment and personality. Three substances of the body were spirit, phlegm, and bile, and they were influenced by air, water, and geographic location. If the substances were out of balance, poor health resulted.

Ancient Chinese medicine saw one's character and health affected by Yin (dark and influenced by the Earth) and Yang (active, light from the heavens). These forces combine to affect health and regulate the flow of fluids in the body.

---

**EASTERN HEALING TECHNIQUES: WHAT'S OLD IS NEW**

Acupuncture was developed to influence the flow of fluids, which was the essence of good health. This technique, as well as other Eastern healing methods, have gained popularity in recent years.

---

Westerners were thinking of how the body influenced health as well. Galen, a Greek physician, philosopher, and writer lived around the second century CE (Common Era or AD) and is thought to be the "Father of Western Medicine." He formulated a theory that health (and mental health) is an equilibrium of four "humors" including melancholic (sad), choleric (anger), phlegmatic (relaxed), and sanguine (cheerful)[3]. The thinkers also thought the liver was the seat of the soul. That theory influenced healers throughout the Middle Ages. All this thinking which became known as "physiology" represented efforts to understand health and behavior through mechanisms of the body.

In the latter part of the nineteenth century (1801-1900), scientists began studying the mental qualities and behavior of humans. In the Western part of the world, curious explorers studied the human body systematically and discovered anatomical features, the circulatory system, germ theory, and all the bases of modern Western medicine.

# THE BEGINNING OF HUMAN/CHILD DEVELOPMENT STUDIES

When the Industrial Revolution (1760-1840) occurred, the economy of humans changed from survival and the prospect of early death to at least having some leisure time and a longer life. Children tended to survive childbirth and infancy more. If they lived, they were still part of the labor force with the addition of factories to farming until the early 1900s. As such, they were seen as "little adults" and were subjected to authoritarian parenting. You've heard the expression: "Children should be seen and not heard."

We have seen the early study of intelligence, beginning in the mid-1800s and blossoming in the early 1900s. In the middle part of the 1800s, the first psychologists and educators began studying mental qualities and behavior of humans. As the disciplines of Psychiatry and Psychology grew, so did the focus on child development. Economic growth increased, and the middle classes emerged where families began changing their philosophy over the decades. In the late 1800s, psychologists began studying children.

In the early 1900s, Freud was one of the first to posit that early experience resulted in various types of character development. In the study of adults and children, the issue of nature versus nurture arose. Was behavior determined by the chemistry of the body or by the experience with the world after birth? Was biology a destiny? Or could the environment mold the individual?

Neurobiology is the study of how physiology affects behavior. For example, gender differences in behavior are affected by the y and x chromosomes and the hormones they produce. You may recall an early experimenter in animal behavior, Ivan Pavlov (1849-1936) who studied how animals learned (classical conditioning). He is well-known for showing that dogs could learn from certain principles of reward. Pavlov identified two types of nervous systems: 1) easy to train and 2) resistant to training, which were both based on inherited or inborn behavioral styles. Well, this seems fairly straightforward, especially for those of you who own dogs.

In the 1950s, some psychologists theorized about personality development and looked at temperamental characteristics of adults. These were thought to be hereditary characteristics that were somewhat resistant to environmental influence. Two noted theorists added their ideas.

- Gordon Allport (1897-1967) emphasized emotional differences in personalities.

- Raymond Cattell[4] noted differences in whether people act impulsively or think before they do.

Despite these ideas, parenting models continued into the 1960s to see the environment (i.e. parents) as responsible for all of children's behaviors. In other words, if the child was deviant, the parents made them so. Parents were faulted for severe behavior problems such as autism, childhood schizophrenia, excess hyperactivity—and everything else. Children were seen as those "blank slates." However, parents of multiple children knew their children were not just blank slates. Their children behaved differently from each other from early infancy. Parents treated them the same, yet psychologists insisted that the environment—"the parent(s)"— was the cause of how the children turned out as adults. Innate or inborn differences were ignored. Parents knew better and eventually psychologists caught on.

## THE BEGINNINGS OF THE STUDY OF TEMPERAMENT IN CHILD DEVELOPMENT

In 1963, Alexander Thomas and Stella Chess, researchers at the New York University Medical Center, recorded early behavioral styles in infancy, based on reports from 141 parents. They determined that the environment (parents) had not had enough time to "cause" the behavioral differences and pointed the "causes" toward inherited characteristics. The findings that children who had differences in patterns of behavior from early on were at odds with the "environmentalists." And these findings were repeated in other studies (5).

Findings from Thomas and Chess (6) were that infants and toddlers differed on nine different dimensions, which tended to cluster in three different styles.

## Nine Personality Dimensions

1. Activity level
2. Approach to and withdrawal from a new stimulus
3. Confidence in approaching new experiences
4. Ease of adjustment to new situations
5. Intensity of response
6. Type of positive or negative mood
7. Attention span
8. Distractibility from task
9. How much stimulation is needed for response

## Three Styles of Personality

1. ***Easy or Flexible*** (about 40%) regular in biological rhythms, adaptable, approachable, positive in mood, and mild to medium intensity of emotion
2. ***Difficult or Feisty*** (about 10%) biological rhythms variable, very intense crying response to new stimuli, slow to adapt, disagreeable mood, and prone to temper tantrums
3. ***Slow-to-Warm-Up or Fearful*** (about 15%) shy, discomfort with new experiences, slow to adapt, biological rhythms regular, mildly intense

## Further Research on the Longitudinal Effects of Temperament

Temperament differences typically persist, some even to adulthood (7). Research was performed in controlled settings, and parent reports tended to agree with how infants were seen in the behavioral lab. These children were studied for several years to see what happened over time. Longitudinal data reported by psychologists

Arnold H. Buss and Robert Plomin showed four dimensions that persisted to be characteristic "styles" to age four.

1. **Emotionality** – Do they cry at every new situation? Do they get upset if someone else picks them up? When a situation changes, do they respond negatively?
2. **Activity** – Are they squirming and squiggling in your arms or running around that seems in excess?
3. **Sociability** – Do they like to look people in the eye and respond to communication? Will they play with other children?
4. **Impulsiveness** – Are they quick to react without pause?

Most reactive newborns continued to be reactive at nine months (8). Inhibited two-year-olds were still shy at eight years (9), (10). Also, more emotionally intense preschoolers tend to be relatively intense young adults (11).

In addition to these "styles," parents of toddler age children and older experienced "activity level" as another dimension of temperament. Chess and others did not include that category since they studied infants, and infants can't run around.

Another adjective that may be applied to toddlers is "impulsive." Practically 100% of children this age are impulsive, but some more than others. While others "mellow out" during preschool, some will maintain this fast-paced, quick-to-respond quality; much to the occasional despair of parents. High activity level and high levels of impulsivity can be characterized as a maladaptive and potentially diagnosable entity known as Attention Deficit Hyperactivity Disorder. Parents and teachers are well aware of this constellation which affects around 10% of the population from mild to severe degrees. Here is a history and a description of diagnosis and treatment in short form.

# ATTENTION DEFICIT HYPERACTIVITY DISORDER—AND HOW THE NAME GOT THAT WAY

Attention Deficit Hyperactivity Disorder (ADHD) was noticed by the medical field in the 1940s when adults with brain injury showed behavioral changes in that they became more impulsive. The phenomenon was also seen in children with traumatic brain injury when they became more impulsive and more active. However, there were children who manifested these traits of poor self-control and who had no history of brain injury. The medical professionals presumed there was some damage to the brain and postulated "minimal brain injury" as the cause of the behavior. Then, after figuring that there was no trauma to the brain, the "brain" label was dropped. The disorder was then described as "hyperactivity."

## Diagnostic Criteria for ADHD

- High activity level (adjusted for age)
- Short attention span (likewise)
- Impulsivity (likewise)

In the meantime, as children with the above-mentioned traits of problems with attention, activity, and impulsivity were observed, the psychological spirit of "experience causes all behavior" was popular. Hence parents were seen as the cause of the behavior; mental health professionals believed the "bonding" of parent to child had not been successful and so the child was "abnormal." Can you imagine the tremendous guilt these parents felt since these children were typically causing havoc wherever they went? Relatives and strangers looked askance at these parents who were without support or help for their lively (to put it mildly) children.

Over time, the quality of "inattention" was seen as the chief cause of the disorder, and it became re-named "Attention Deficit

Disorder"—or "ADD." Then, the quality of "hyperactivity" was so noticeable that the disorder was again re-named Attention Deficit Hyperactivity Disorder (ADHD).

Clinicians also discovered (by accident in the 1940s) that stimulant medication (related to adrenaline but not the same) reduced the amount of activity and impulsivity and increased attention and focus. This medication became a treatment for ADHD. In the 1960s, the cause of the behavioral traits was again seen as a brain-based issue. Parents were relieved of their guilt, and treatment became available for serious cases.

ADHD is considered a hard-wired (inborn) disorder, and in order to be diagnosed, these traits must be observed prior to age twelve or age seven, depending on which diagnostic manual is used. Generally, they will be observed prior to age seven (mostly they can't be missed!), but for some children, only when they go to first grade, where they must sit still for prolonged periods, the symptoms are noticed because they are harmful to school functioning.

Again, this trait is displayed to some degree by 10% of children; 2% of children are considered seriously enough handicapped to qualify for medication. If one figures thirty children in a class, there should be three displaying some traits of ADHD and maybe one with a serious problem (for teachers and hence the classroom). These children are continually out of their seats, not listening to the teacher, unable to focus on class written assignments, touching others, talking out of turn, etc. In other words, breaking all the rules of the classroom and annoying others.

Before we get to treatment, it is important to describe a separate classification of ADHD that consists solely of inattention *without* hyperactivity. These children demonstrate a serious lack of focus on tasks and are at risk of many of the same issues as the ADHD kids. However, they are not overly active nor impulsive (annoying) and frequently get missed. Additionally, diagnosis needs to separate medical issues from temperament since some of these children have a type of seizure which can be misinterpreted as lack of attention.

It should be noted that the diagnosis of either ADHD or ADD must be made by a physician, who frequently will work with mental health professionals. Physical reasons for the behaviors must be ruled out.

## SIDE NOTE

**The more subdued ADD child, who doesn't focus, appears to be daydreaming in class. When I gave a talk about ADD, I titled it "The (Impossible) Dreamers" after Don Quixote in *Man from La Mancha*, for those of you who are Broadway aficionados.**

## Classroom and Home Modifications to Support those with ADHD and ADD

The first method of treatment for ADHD and ADD children are classroom and home modifications. There are numerous ways clever teachers and parents accommodate the high energy and poor focus of their students and there are numerous books to give you ideas. Here are some changes that can help.

## Classroom Modifications to Support Those with ADHD & ADD

1. Give the child space to move—e.g. they can stand at their desk and work without any problem.
2. Break big tasks into smaller ones—e.g. divide 30 math problems into 3 sets of 10.
3. Seat the child optimally so that the child is least distracted or can be re-directed easily by the teacher.

# Home Modifications to Support Those with ADHD

## DO

1. Provide mattresses in the basement for jumping.
2. Send kids outside to run around as much as possible.
3. Have jumping jack sessions when needed.
4. Go to playgrounds and parks as much as feasible.
5. Use timers during homework to break time into ten minute (or so) intervals; then they get a break.
6. For homework, keep distractions at a minimum.

## DON'T

1. Go to fancy restaurants that require waiting.
2. Overdo reminders to "sit still" or "keep your mind on your work," which will be less effective.
3. Use the word "bad" in relation to your child, as it will affect your child's self-esteem.

If you are a parent of a child who has ADD or ADHD, remember that others may see you as "inadequate" or "failing to set limits." They are ignorant of the fact that you are helpless to calm a hyperactive child. But if your child is acting in ways that annoy others, be sure to get treatment or modify the environment so that your child (and you) are not seen as pariahs.

## Medications When Necessary

When classroom modifications have too little effect, most children accurately diagnosed with ADHD respond positively to stimulant medication with few or no negative side effects. Parents generally fear that medication will turn their child into "zombies" who are spaced out and unresponsive. Accurate doses of medication will not cause this effect. When successfully treated, children are able to meet goals of acceptable behavior as they are more able to pay attention, sit for reasonable periods, and wait their turn. When the medication wears off, in about four to eight hours, their old behavioral traits appear, and they are jumping around, inattentive, and impatient. The medication typically wears off just in time for after school when their parents get to deal with the ADHD behavior.

Successfully treated children appreciate the effects of medication because as they mature, they realize which days and times they benefit from taking medication and when they don't really need it. Children tend to think of the two behaviors. When they are on medication they believe, "I'm good," and when they're off the medication, "I'm bad." Parents need to remember and to remind the child that the medication does not cause "good behavior." The child is in charge of their behavior, and the medication allows them to perform "expected behaviors." As mentioned above, the important issue is to avoid a label of "bad" as that word can have significant "bad" effects on the self-image.

## What Causes Problems in Attention and Activity? The Big Question

What is the cause? Well, before it was "bad kids." Then it was "bad parents." In the 1980s, when the technology of Positron Emission Tomography (PET) was invented, brain scans of children with ADHD were compared to those that were considered normally functioning[12]. The PET scan can show where oxygen is being taken up in the brain, where the blood flow is ok, which brain centers are working, and which are not working. The anterior prefrontal cortex is the part of the brain associated with self-control and for those with ADHD, it shows little uptake of oxygen. That lack of oxygen means that part of the brain was *underfed* by the blood vessels that take oxygen to it. The "normal" children's brains showed that part of the brain as getting necessary oxygen. When the ADHD children had stimulant medication in their system, their brains reversed with the self-control part (anterior prefrontal cortex) of the brain getting oxygen. More recent research with Functional Magnetic Resonance Imaging (fMRI) found similar results in that stimulant medication improved activation in the part of the brain that is the bilateral inferior frontal cortex (13).

## UNDERSTANDING ADHD

**Given this body of research, I see ADHD/ADD as a kind of plumbing problem. For some reason (most probably chemical), the capillaries going to the critical part of the brain are not getting enough blood/oxygen; and for some reason the stimulant medication enlarges or does something to the blood vessels to get the blood and energy flowing. So, the ADHD child's brain is working fine for the time that the stimulant medication is doing its job. Again, it's a plumbing problem! Nobody has to feel guilty!**

## CHILDREN'S STYLE OF DELAY OF GRATIFICATION AND FUTURE SUCCESS

Impulsivity versus self-control as a trait is certainly important in future personality development. It is one of the diagnostic hallmarks of ADHD, but it may stand alone as well. Self-control or self-discipline are desirable traits that parents wish to instill in their child. Making sacrifices such as saving money, studying, and keeping to a healthy lifestyle for a future gain is a hallmark of maturity, and one that most parents "preach" to their children.

Since the 1960s, there has been an interest in child psychology to find out to what extent childhood impulsivity is related to "achievement." Perhaps you have heard of the "Marshmallow Test." Picture a child sitting at a table in a laboratory with one marshmallow in front of them. The experimenter tells the child they may eat the marshmallow immediately, but if they can wait a few minutes (seven minutes maximum), they will get an extra marshmallow to eat. If you search YouTube on this subject, you will see children in mental limbo, excruciatingly looking at, licking, or touching the marshmallow as they wait. For those that aren't able to wait or control their urge, they eat it promptly. Follow-up research found the ability to wait was related to academic achievement at preteen age (SAT scores), which determined the longer the wait, the better the scores. The nation paid attention to these findings from the chief experimenter, Walter Mischel, who was even interviewed on public television (14).

Based on these findings, the question of whether delay of gratification could be increased with training was posed. Some schools even added "delay of gratification training" to school curricula. The issue is still up for discussion (15).

Where does parenting fit in here? Certainly, the process of setting goals and achieving them is a hallmark of success. Parents are motivated to help children achieve such traits as patience, completing tasks, and planning for the future. As a parent, you will coach your children in various situations where their patience is tested. There are many opportunities for that such as keeping to a schedule, praising them for successful completion of tasks, helping them to save money for a future goal, and so forth. Of course, the problem of those children diagnosed with ADHD is more difficult, but they can be helped to understand their limitations, adjust situations such that they are more tolerable, and succeed despite the frustrations of their diagnosis. High activity and energy can be a distinct plus!

## SUMMARY (Chapter 4)

When a child is born, that infant is born with numerous traits, styles, assets, and potential challenges. Parents can be aware that biology, while it may not be destiny, has important implications for your child's development. Parenting techniques that maximize the positive, and do not attempt to erase totally the natural style of the child will be most successful in the end. Many fears surrounding ADHD and ADD and their treatments should be minimized by education and competent clinicians. Parents can do their utmost to reduce their child's symptoms, but the difficult behavior never goes away. Parents need support from groups and each other to deal with the inevitable blaming looks from others.

# SECTION II

## Theorists Attempt to Explain
## What's Going On

Chapter 5    Theories of Personality Development
Chapter 6    Theories of Intellectual (Cognitive) Development

# Chapter 5

## Theories of Personality Development: The Why's of Behavior

### INTRODUCTION

This chapter and the following one divide theories into two kinds. The first covers those theorists who specialize in emotions and behavior, and the second focuses on intellectual or cognitive maturation. We'll start with those that try to explain how childhood experiences affect how we act and feel (personality).

### PERSONALITY THEORIES

As parents, you may have questions pertaining to what constitutes a "good" or "healthy" personality in your child(ren). As a parent, sometimes we see problems in our child when there are none. To be successful parents, it's important to understand the limitations of our child's thoughts and behavior.

This section will introduce you to a basic understanding of four personality theorists who, in my opinion, have a great deal to say about personal growth and development. No one theory can encompass all of human behavior. Several theorists will be presented here for your review.

There have been times in my practice when I have noted "Freud lives!" when I see examples of his theory in action. My ultimate hope is that you will see in your own child some of the concepts that others have put forth in their renowned theories. You are free to pick and choose the theories of development that are best for your child and your family. Some will come from some of these theoretical concepts and/or some will come from your own observations.

To measure how well a developmental personality theory works, it is critical to measure *"how"* it predicts what sort of personality will come after environmental input, and it will also explain the *"why"* of developing that personality.

- Why does a person choose one action over another?
- What motivates the child to adapt, with age, into a "successful" person?

## History of The Study of Personality Development

In "early times" (prior to eighteenth century), people were seen as pretty much alike, notwithstanding differences in severe retardation or mental illness. Survival mode prevailed as for most social classes; one had to work diligently to survive, and all participated in getting enough food to eat. As technology and sanitation conditions improved over the 1800s, people lived longer and no longer had quite the day-to-day stress of survival. "Personhood" differentiated from strict adherence to roles as dictated by survival mode to individual variations in how people acted, thought, and contributed in various ways to their social milieu.

## How Did People Get the Way They Were?

- Why were some people careful and tidy, others tolerant of messes?
- Why were some people aggressive and belligerent around authority and others compliant?

- Why were some people quiet and others direct and plain-spoken?
- Why were some fearful and others bold?

Differences in intelligence began to be observed in the 1800s, and the measurement of "all things human" became the rage. In Chapter 2, we learned that in the 1850s, Wundt developed a laboratory in Germany where reactions to stimuli such as light or sound were measured for speed (and interpreted as intelligence). Sir Francis Galton was an English Victorian-era expert on many subjects including psychology, anthropology, and geology. As a British scientist around the time of Darwin in the late 1800s, Galton began to measure people's height, weight, arm length, and reaction to sensory differences (1). He found that these measurements fell in a pattern with more in the middle and fewer at the extremes, and in so doing developed the concept of the normal curve.

## SIGMUND FREUD

We will begin our review of theorists with the one who is a household name. Sigmund Freud was an Austrian neurologist and founder of psychoanalysis. In the mid- to late-1800s, he trained in medicine in Vienna and shifted his interest from the physiological underpinnings of neural functioning to the "why" of behavior. As mentioned in the Introduction, when he was asked what a psychologically healthy person should be able to do well, he replied, "to Love and to Work" (*zu Lieben und zu Arbeiten*, actually).

## Psychoanalysis

Freud developed his theory through his treatment of patients with various symptoms of phobias, amnesia, and anxiety. He used hypnosis to uncover reasons for the symptoms. As a result of his experiences, he gradually devised the "talking" cure, which he called "psychoanalysis." A ground-breaking discovery of the unconscious was made during these treatment sessions. An unknown life, hidden from consciousness, reveals true emotions. Releasing these unconscious notions was the essence of the healing process. (We all know the "Freudian slip," where the truth comes out in an "oops" moment.)

Current strategies of addressing psychological problems known as "psychotherapy" evolved out of his technique. But the basic principles remain; give credit where credit is due.

## Instincts and Drives

Freud spent some time trying to understand the "whys" of human behavior. He dubbed "instincts" or "drives" as motivating forces. He differentiated between the instinct to preserve the Self (Pleasure Principle) and the instinct to keep the species alive (Libido). Our current society uses the word "libido" in a sexualized sense, but Freud meant it in a larger sense, which included the drive to reproduce. He saw childhood where certain bodily activities led to pleasure, and the integration of those experiences would lead to the capacity to have an adult sexual relationship. (That is one measure of a successful person—the Love part). Can you imagine how this theory went over in the Victorian Age when sex was thought of as "nasty" and women couldn't show so much as an ankle?

## Life Instincts & Death Instincts

His theory called "Psychodynamic Theory" implied that human behavior was motivated by two driving instincts: "Life Instincts" noted above and a new one, the "Death Instinct." Basic needs for survival are known as "life instincts" and include reproduction and pleasure such as food, shelter, love, and sex. "Death instincts" were based on his belief that all humans have an unconscious wish for death and thus express such wishes through self-destructive behavior. He changed his theory several times during his lifetime.

---

**MORE ABOUT FREUD**

Freud also noted "ego-instincts" such as hunger, thirst, and escape from pain were concerned with self-preservation. On the other hand, libido is concerned with preservation of the species. Freud debated whether hostility and aggressiveness as sources of energy and motivation were instinctual or a means of self-preservation. Later, after experiencing two world wars, he came to believe that hostility was part of a separate instinct. He theorized that the death instinct accounted for aggression and hostility and lay at the root of destructive activities.

---

## Parts of Personality: ID, EGO, SUPEREGO

The theory of drives and the discovery of the unconscious were indeed ground-breaking, but currently his concepts of the three parts of the personality are frequently used to understand the question of how instinctual energy channeled into adaptive behavior. Freud developed the concepts of the id, ego, and superego to answer this question.

## ID

The difference between a socialized adult and an unsocialized child is a matter of difference in regulating mechanisms or how they control their drives and wants. Young children are impulsive, emotional, and want what they want instantly. Can you see that trait in your young children? Freud called these free expressions of feelings the "Primary Process."

As infants, our personality begins in the unconscious *id* because it is the most primitive part of personality that functions on the

Pleasure Principle. Think of their crying as on-demand requests for their basic needs and self-preservation. It's pretty obvious that it's the infant's pleasure and not yours that is going on here. And, don't forget, your Pleasure Principle was during your "babymoon," if you are lucky enough to have had one! The id is manifested at an early stage of development and it is never totally outgrown. The irrational, impulsive part of adult personality persists forever, and can be used productively by artists in their creations whereby, "id acts in service of the ego." (You wondered where artists get their ideas!)

## EGO

The second system to develop in the child's personality is the *ego*. The ego is the rational part of personality that controls the drives by delaying and restraining them in the interests of achieving their wants and needs in a realistic manner that is both safe and socially acceptable. With maturity, the *ego* rules the *id*, but there are conflicts between them. The child needs to inhibit behavior (drives) and find detours to gratification. For example, it's not appropriate to eat in church (or another place of your choice). As your child matures, they realize that the former on-demand drive to satisfy their hunger is no longer appropriate, and must wait until after church to eat their snack or meal. Therefore, the *ego* component of personality will:

- Restrain inappropriate behavior
- Guide behavior to acceptable goals
- Control the access of ideas to consciousness (defenses) and logical thinking
- Learn to recognize when to change behavior

These operations are called "Secondary Processes." As you teach your child to "wait" and correct your child for impulsively grabbing the candy or hitting a sibling, you are working toward advancing the development of the "Secondary Process" and hence the *ego*.

## SUPEREGO

The third system to develop in your child's personality is the *super-ego*, also known as their conscience. It develops out of the ego's experiences with social reality and the "rules." Social rules are taught to the young child but they are only taken into the child's person, internalized, in such a powerful way around seven years of age. Then, the child has a conscience. Prior to this development, doing "wrong" was understood as displeasing others, and punishment may be expected, but with a conscience the individual punishes him or herself! The important role of age seven and the development of the conscience will be described in detail in Chapters 14 and 25.

While the id, ego, and superego parts of your child's personality develop through the years, understanding this development should hopefully guide your expectations about meeting and managing their needs, and teaching them to behave in the standards you set.

## PSYCHOSEXUAL DEVELOPMENT

In addition to discovering the unconscious and describing *id, ego,* and *superego*, Freud was the first to strongly believe that early childhood experience can affect the essence of the adult personality. He presented five stages of Psychosexual Development, theorizing that a child's body focused pleasurable energy on particular parts which were critical to survival. As discussed earlier, he called that energy "libido." He labeled the stages Oral, Anal, Phallic, Latent, and Genital according to where the libido seeks to find pleasure. It's important to note that if a child has a "fixation" at any stage, it will lead to arrested development, and the personality will be affected throughout their life.

- The *Oral Stage* (1-2 years) in infancy focuses on giving pleasure to the mouth much like a pacifier, bottle, food, ice cream, etc. Later in life "oral" personalities are supposedly gratification-seekers and people-pleasers.

- In the *Anal Stage* (2-4 years), Freud believed the pleasure energies of the anus needed to be satisfied. The success of this stage is associated with toilet training. People who are fixated in this stage due to overly harsh experiences become more resistant to outside influence and tend to be stubborn, and sometimes overly so. For example, excessive emphasis on being clean (and toileting properly) in early infancy and toddlerhood would yield an "OCD" or obsessive-compulsive person, whose behavior is characterized by excessive cleanliness, obstinacy, or stinginess, and might show repetitive and ritualistic behaviors. This is the "anal" character, and this way of labelling people is well in fashion today.

- The *Phallic Stage* begins around five years old and is named for the focus of energy boys have for their penis. Girls got rather short shrift in this stage; Freud tried to include them, but those efforts are too detailed for this chapter. This stage entails the Oedipal complex, which is covered in Chapters 21 and 22. It's a time where children (both boys and girls) learn their realistic place in the world versus believing they control their parents.

- The *Latent Stage* is the period when the libidinal drives are more or less dormant. Kids just want to be kids, and don't have any particular body urge conflicts. Peer group issues abound.

- The *Genital Stage* is adolescent and adulthood where people fall in love and have babies, ensuring the survival of the species, which this book will not cover.

As you cater to the needs of your infant, which become less and less as they mature, it's important to be supportive and understanding as you notice signs through each of these stages. For instance, during the phallic stage, our immediate reaction to masturbation (for both boys and girls) may be to become alarmed, raise our voices, slap their hand away, or say "no" when our child touches themself what in a way we deem "inappropriate." However, they don't know any better. It may be the way they self-soothe, just like a pacifier or you rubbing their head to sleep. Try not to be alarmed. Obviously, if they are doing that in public, find a gentle way to whisper a calm explanation that it's something to be done in the private space of their bedroom, and not in the living room or at the store. Definitely do not shame them, ever, and indicate that touching themselves is "bad" or say that their "private areas" are "yucky." That type of response will be hard, if not impossible for them to recover from. It's best to try to avoid judging, blaming, or shaming and remember, they are kids who are developing, and nature has a part in their development, as well as how we nurture.

## Psychological Defenses

Another of Freud's ground-breaking concepts is the notion of *psychological defenses*. This, too, is a concept that has entered our everyday goings on when we use the label "defensive" to describe a person who makes excuses for their mistakes, blames others, and in general doesn't seem to "get it." Let's give Freud his due. He presumed that the conflict between id, ego, and superego is ever present in personality throughout our childhood and adult lives. When an "id urge" conflicts with the superego's "morals and standards," the unconscious can trigger a defense mechanism. Forgetting or repressing is one such mechanism. Then the experience is "gone," and anxiety disappears. Note: the term anxiety can mean trembling in fear or nervousness. The "anxiety" referenced here by Freud is internal to the Self when a forbidden thought rises up to consciousness and must be pushed away.

We all live with defenses, some adaptive, some maladaptive. To give a clearer picture of how this works, I will present a detailed picture. See if you can find your favorite defense.

American psychiatrist and professor at Harvard Medical School, George Eman Valliant reported a longitudinal study that assigned classified psychological defenses into four major classes: psychotic, immature, neurotic, and healthy (2).

1.  ***Psychotic defenses*** distort the reality of the situation. For example, a four-year-old who wanted to play outside denied it was raining despite the clear evidence for such. In some families, *denial* can be a convenient defense ("I never said that!" "Yes, you did!") and lead to different perceptions of reality, which makes for difficult conversations. More serious and harmful than the argument of whether it is raining or not, is when people deny an addiction even when it's very obvious.

2.  ***Immature defenses*** include several responses of which you may be familiar.

    •   Projection is an attribution of an undesirable characteristic that embarrasses or shames a person to another person. "That woman has a terrible temper." Again, "projection" is a common term useful in everyday attempts to understand irrational behavior. For example, Shakespeare's "He doth protest too much," is an accurate observation of a projection defense.

    •   Passive-aggressive behavior is also seen as an immature defense. Daniel K. Hall-Flavin, MD, defines passive-aggressive behavior as "a pattern of indirectly expressing negative feelings instead of openly addressing them. There's a disconnect between what a person who exhibits passive-aggressive behavior says and what he or she does" (3). It can be more or less deliberate, but permits individuals to avoid the anxiety of overtly expressing their resistance. It is irrational because it continues the conflict without resolution. For instance, when one agrees to wash the dishes and doesn't, the family partner can become upset. Then, the shirker can blame the family partner for being upset.

- Acting out or doing something against the "rules" can also be seen as an avoidance of anxiety. This behavior may be childish and immature and often antisocial as teenage vandalism.

3. *Neurotic defenses* were first described by Freud as he saw repression, displacement, reaction formation, and intellectualization as he worked with his patients.

- Repression is the cornerstone of all defenses because the incident doesn't come to consciousness. It is forgotten.

- Displacement is the defense mechanism by which an instinct is satisfied by a behavior somehow linked to the original impulse. An example of displacement would be to punch pillows when a child is angry at their teacher.

- Reaction formation is where repressed motivation is replaced by its diametrically opposite motivation. The defense protects against the acting out of the undesirable drive. You may notice this behavior when someone who is inwardly rather hostile may act super nice on the outside.

- Intellectualization is a defense to protect unwanted emotion where the individual removes the emotion from consciousness and replaces it with comments on the cognitive content of the problem, not the emotional aspect. A person facing a weight gain issue might give a lecture on the uselessness of eating healthy rather than admit his true feelings.

4. *Healthy defenses:* Yes, there actually are such things as healthy defenses. One such defense is healthy denial, which comes in handy when one is facing major surgery or when one boards an airplane. It is far more adaptive to "forget" the catastrophic things that could take place in a potentially risky endeavor.

   - The Sublimation defense is a mature behavior to put an instinctive drive into socially useful action. For instance, if you choose boxing as a sport, you can relieve aggression in a healthy way.
   - Suppression is when one faces an anxiety-arousing experience and tries to reduce or avoid or "cover up" the anxious episode. If one can "compartmentalize" and put the problem aside, anxiety is lessened.
   - Anticipatory anxiety or fearfulness which is healthy allows one to anticipate "the worst case" outcomes and to make decisions that maximize success.

In summary, Freud's Psychoanalytic Theory puts forward that physiological instincts "drive" behavior. As the person matures and learns from experience, more realistic thinking replaces the pure emotion of the id, and the conscience develops later. If there are conflicts in any of the stages of child development, personality structure may be affected in a negative way. Freud's major contribution, for our understanding, is that internal anxiety is avoided by the development of psychological defense mechanisms.

## NEO-FREUDIAN THEORISTS

Freud collected a number of eminent scholars as followers. These neo-Freudian theorists were also psychologists and thinkers who followed Freud's work and changed some of the tenets of his studies to adapt their own version. The neo-Freudians of interest to us here are those that see that personality development was not so much a biological orientation as much as orientation to *social* phenomena. Instead, their position was that personality development was seen as a result of interactions. Since we are looking at a developing child who is a member of a family by necessity, it seems important to note those social influences and the theorists who took the effect of relationships seriously. We will now make a brief introduction of Alfred Adler, Harry Stack Sullivan, and Erik Erikson.

## ALFRED ADLER

Alfred Adler (4) was also from Vienna and originally trained as an ophthalmologist before becoming a psychiatrist. In 1911, he broke with Freud's theory over the issue of biological drives versus social drives, and called his theory "Individual Psychology." He settled in the US in 1935 and was an academic.

Adler assumed human motivation was fueled by social urges, and he posited that "social interest" is inborn but had to be nurtured by guidance and training. A big predictor of social relationships is the culture and society into which the person is born, and he felt that the sexual instinct is less important than the social instinct. Adler felt that consciousness was the center of the personality, rather than centered around the unconscious urges proposed by Freud. Humans were capable of planning actions with expectations of the future. Aggression was dealt with in the sense of "striving for superiority" in the sense of self-actualization or self-improvement. In children, movement from one level of functioning to another is motivated by this striving for superiority. My impression of this striving is better labeled "mastery," and observations of young children persisting and persisting in solving a problem is an example. He also called this striving the "will to power," which I feel is an apt description for children of toddler and preschool age. I'm sure all of you will agree!

Adler's Individual Psychology Theory proposes that individuals may feel "inferior" in some respect and may compensate for it by striving for completion. We use the term "inferiority complex" in our current efforts to understand some irrational behaviors. Individuals are motivated by feelings of inferiority, which is not a sign of abnormality but can stimulate growth. A sense of incompleteness is the driving force of mankind. Perfection, not pleasure, is the goal. These goals are primarily social in character.

Adler advocated for social justice; he saw adult development complete only if the person was contributing somehow to society's betterment. Neurotic persons are more focused on themselves while healthy psychological development produces efforts for the good of humankind.

In terms of child development, Adler sees parenting styles as important contributors to psychological health. Indulged children do not develop social feeling and rather expect society to conform to their self-centered wishes. Child neglect by parents affects children negatively and may lead them to take revenge on society. If parents see a child struggling with "inferiority" in some area, they will help them to compensate for it. A style of personality is formed by age four or five, and a "creative Self" is the center for growth. Heredity and experience form a personality where life is given meaning by social improvement. Altruism, cooperation, creativity, and uniqueness give a sense of dignity to human function; people determine their own destiny and are not victims of fate.

## HARRY STACK SULLIVAN

Harry Stack Sullivan (5) is a theorist who, in my opinion, has contributed the most to understanding how we get to be who we are. His theory posits that healthy or problematic functioning in adults and families is characterized by the style and pattern of interpersonal relationships. His articulation of the "Self" and "Self-esteem" has much to contribute to parents who want their child to be a balanced, reasonable, and resilient adult who can handle ups and downs in life. Chapter 11 will elaborate on these concepts in detail.

Sullivan was an American psychiatrist educated in Chicago, who presented his Interpersonal Theory of Psychiatry in the mid-1930s. He saw heredity and brain maturation as important to development, but what becomes most distinctly human is the product of social interactions. Remember we mentioned this early on? We revisit the notion that babies are born into families which are the very essence of interaction. He defines "personality" as a pattern of processes which characterize how the person interacts with others.

As in any encompassing theory, the energy of growth must be put forth. For Sullivan, he defined a "dynamism" as a unit of energy that is any form of seen behavior, unseen behavior, or thought. Like Freud, he saw that basic needs of the body must be satisfied, and continued to ask, "What propels behavior?" For Sullivan, like Freud, dynamism results from "Anxiety," which may be from unmet bodily needs or threats to one's psychological security. Anxiety feels unpleasant to the individual, which is why a person seeks to avoid it—and in so doing may avoid seeing reality. What is the source of anxiety? Well, for an infant, toddler, child, or school-age child, it would be in the basic interpersonal unit, their family. Anxiety is transmitted by persons parenting the child unknowingly through disapproving cues such as looks, tone of voice, demeanor, reactions, and behaviors. An infant senses the caregivers' anxiety by an empathic process and takes these cues in building awareness or lack of such. By your own observations, babies can "catch" these feelings and respond by showing distress. The opposite of an anxious interaction is one that is relaxed, accepting, and satisfying. Parents who feel anxiety, struggle with their own anxiety, or make other people nervous, including their children, may want to seek therapeutic support.

Unlike Freud, Sullivan did not believe that personality was set at an early age, but did theorize and presume there are stages of personality development which can happen at any time and can change throughout. His names and definitions of these stages are vastly different from Freud's because he focused on the interactions with others and the skills required to interact with others.

- "Infancy" (years 0-2) is the name for the first stage of development, like Freud. Relations with caregivers prevail.
- Childhood (years 2-6) emphasizes relationships with various caregivers and "imaginary playmates."
- The Juvenile era (age 6-8.5) stresses the need for playmates. Language promotes the development of the "Self-System," which is an important contribution and will be discussed at length in Chapters 11 and 12.
- Preadolescence starting at 11, 12, and 13 is characterized by the need for intimate friendships, a "best friend" in whom one can confide and collaborate in solving life's problems. This new relationship signals the beginning of genuine (intimate) relations with others and is within a balanced view of the self and another human being.
- In Adolescence, the beginning of romantic attraction and interest begins, and a full complement of interpersonal relations is developed.
- Adulthood is the final stage, which is another whole book.

Sullivan does not believe personality is set at an early age. He theorized that personality may change at any time as new interpersonal (between two or more people) situations arise. Dealing with challenging situations at work with a new boss or exploring the ins and outs of a romantic relationship may cause change. For today's therapists, this notion is very helpful in planning strategies while working with clients to modify maladaptive patterns of behavior. Change can occur when substituting an open, accepting manner of the therapist as an alternative to the stereotypes and presumptions built in prior family relationships. Mental health professionals refer to the "therapeutic relationship" as part of the healing process because it is a non-judgmental and safe environment.

# ERIK ERIKSON

Erik Erikson was born in Germany and taught at an elementary school. Without any formal degree in medicine or psychology, he was trained in Freudian psychoanalytic methods by Anna Freud, Sigmund Freud's daughter. He moved to the US in 1933 and taught at several major universities and has had major impacts in the field of early childhood education. (For example, the Erikson Institute in Chicago is an esteemed center for training students in child development.)

Erikson was a neo-Freudian who accepted many of the central tenets of Freud's theory such as defense mechanisms but added his own ideas about how experiences in childhood affected personality development. His book *Childhood and Society* was published in 1950 and revised in 1963 (6). He, like Sullivan, believed that personality developed in a series of stages by virtue of social experience.

Erikson proposed that a balance between the two descriptors of the psychosocial "conflict" (as listed below) was achieved by optimum parenting. The balance is important. For example, one should not be overly trusting; some mistrust is necessary. Beginning from infancy, his theory stretched past adolescence and into old age. For purposes of this book, our interests are the first four stages:

- **Trust vs. Mistrust** (birth to 18 months) (development of hope): For example, meeting a seven-month-old baby's needs signals the availability of "good stuff" in the world; how long an infant has to wait for their needs to be met will determine that mind set of "Is the world a good place or not? Can I trust it to be there for me?"
- **Autonomy vs. Shame and Doubt** (18 months to 3 years) (development of will and determination): For example, if

a parent hovers anxiously while a child explores, that sense of foreboding will affect the toddler. A healthy balance of "hands off" will allow a child to explore freely and with support from an attentive parent.

- **Initiative vs. Guilt** (3 years to 6 years) (develop sense of purpose): For example, a child's production of a painting or project may be met with criticism or praise. Over praise and excess criticism will both have drawbacks.

- **Industry vs. Inferiority** (6 years to 12 years) (Act and plan to achieve goals): Children this age will achieve in school and will also venture out with new projects such as lemonade stands. How parents support efforts to help their child achieve a realistic sense of their strengths and weaknesses will allow that child to reach a satisfactory level of success.

# Chapter 6

## Theories of Intellectual (Cognitive) Development

### JEAN PIAGET

Jean Piaget was a Swiss psychologist (1) known for his study of intellectual development with his theory of cognitive development. He worked his whole life in Geneva. For those of you who studied education or child development, the name Piaget will ring a bell. Unlike Freud, Adler, Sullivan, and Erikson, Piaget did not posit an entire theory of personality development. Rather, he charted the way in which *thought* matures in children, beginning from infancy through adolescence.

His work is best characterized as "genetic epistemology," or a division of philosophy concerned with the basis of how we think of a real external world. He had a background in biology (it seems like all of them did!) and used evolution as a template for children's cognitive growth. His first publications were in 1921, with interests in the 1930s and then a re-activation of interest in the 1950s.

We all know that the infant's brain starts with no information (inborn brain structures covered in Chapter 1, but really no actual information). With sensory input, a picture of the external world, space, time, and logic is built. Piaget painstakingly studied the changes made in brain growth and assumed that children have an inborn predisposition to use space and time as a framework and that their experiences with real life gradually teach them there is an external world. With time and experience, children develop a notion of reality as predictable, stable, and logical.

By virtue of his observations of how children see time and space, Piaget saw the child dealing with problems of understanding what was going on. Ideas develop continuously to deal with the new experiences; for example, a child trying to figure out a puzzle will be frustrated that they don't fit until they figure out how to turn pieces around. Once they get that idea, they can apply it to new puzzles or situations. They have advanced. Piaget saw continual fitting of old ideas into new functions and named that unit of knowledge a "schema." The schema may be a simple or a complex set of connected ideas, and it is the basis for cognitive development. It is not quite the same as an "idea" but rather a pattern that guides thinking. It is the schema that changes over time with new experiences. Parents of young children see their child working out a set of problems with every new toy. The work done to that toy is mentally represented by what Piaget named an "operation." Children are constantly coming up with new operations within a schema to try to make sense of what's going on.

Why do children keep trying new things? As discussed just above, theories must have a "why" to explain behavior. In previous discussions of Adler and Freud, we have seen "mastery" or "will to power" or the need to reduce tension/anxiety as a motivation, which might also explain why children keep trying new things. Does Piaget have such a concept?

Piaget does use a dynamic principle, although not to the extent of the theorists discussed previously. The child adapts their conceptions by means of *"Assimilation"* and *"Accommodation."* These processes explain how one gets from "Point A" to "Point B." The child may have a schema which has worked to understand some aspect of reality. That old schema may be applied to a new situation and may work perfectly well. For example, the grasping schema will work with lots of different small objects. However, once the ability has been acquired, there may be more opportunities to use that schema, but they may not always work. No doubt, Piaget saw the struggle children had exhibited and had to explain the "why." Piaget understood that the child must <u>want</u> to work out a new schema and must be challenged by the new situation. If the situation is not completely "assimilated" or "fully understood" by the old schema, Piaget saw the situation as providing "aliment" or "food for thought" such that the situation requires a change of schema, or in other words, an "accommodation." If the task is too easy, it is not motivating. The child's mind pushes forward, step by step, assimilating and accommodating. You can see these processes at work in your child. Despite these observations, Piaget's theory did not include a concept that explained motivation.

Piaget's work was on aspects of the physical world. However, in the 1960s the field of "social cognition" emerged, which studied children's understanding, or "cognition" of other people. Social issues, such as different points of view, friendship, and moral issues such as fairness and justice were discovered to emerge in "stages." The field of "role-taking" developed, and discovered stages where the child's thought developed to understand that others are different from themself. In the toddler age, children think that everyone sees the same thing they are seeing. Piaget's original experiments looked at how the ability to understand that others saw a picture different from oneself changed over time. In experiments, younger children were given tasks to "hide" a doll from an undesired doll. It appeared that with age they could anticipate what the seeking doll could "see" (2). In fact, my dissertation dealt with the connection between preschool children's social behavior and their understanding that others saw things differently from them. Both Piaget and Freud live! This connection will be further explained in Chapters 21 and 22.

By Piaget's observations, he grouped certain schemas/operations in stages to determine if development proceeds at a steady rate, or is it somewhat steplike, taking jumps as one stage is left and another entered? I'll present a brief review of the cognitive stages here and, later, I'll provide more details in Section IV, Ages and Stages. When certain mental tasks are conquered, parents can see entry into the next more mature stage as depicted in the following descriptions.

## Stage 1. Sensory—Motor—Birth through 2 Years

- Infants learn that an object, even when not in sight, is still there. When an object is hidden, and the infant searches for it, they build that schema.

- Infants seek stimulation by banging, kicking, and making interesting things last. These actions are NOT accompanied by any mental representation, though the movements make up a pattern which is learned.

- Goal-directed behavior that indicates "intention" is seen, much to the pleasure of parents. "Look what the baby is trying to do!"

## Stage 2. Preoperational

## Phase 1: 2 Years through 4 Years

- The child continues to be egocentric and is unable to take the viewpoint of others ("role-taking" mentioned above).

- Behavior seems more stable and integrated; however, the child cannot think of two things at once. For example, if a child is presented with a set of blue circles and red squares and asked to say whether all the blue ones are circles, the child cannot.

## Phase 2: 4 Years through 6 or 7 years

- Schemas become organized into internal systems called "Operations."
- The child can think in terms of classes such as colors and shapes and can think of two things at once to solve a task such as the one described above.
- The child continues to be influenced by the "look" of things. For example, if a clay ball is divided into smaller balls, the child will think there is more clay. With this reasoning, the physical environment is changeable and unstable, and the child doesn't understand that things don't change unless they're added to or subtracted from.
- In experiments that change the looks of some substance, the child will be convinced that the substance has changed just because its physical shape has changed. You may recall the famous experiments where a liquid is poured into a shape which makes it taller, and the child is asked whether the amount is the same or different. Also, as mentioned above, if a clay ball is divided into numerous smaller clay balls, the amount of clay has not changed in amount but the child will think there is more. Understanding this sense of permanent reality characterizes movement into the next stage.

---

**CAN YOU HURRY THE BRAIN?**

There have been attempts to teach younger children to understand the conservation of mass by training (3). While the trained child in the experimental setting could solve the problem of which vessel has more water, they soon reverted to their previous developmental level in a short time. Their brain was simply not ready for that understanding. Piaget lives!

---

## Stage 3. Concrete Operations

## 7 Years through 11 Years

- There is a big difference in a child's functioning when this stage is reached—observed in many ways which will be mentioned later. Age seven is a hallmark of development in moral reasoning which Piaget didn't cover, but we will.
- Now, children's thought processes have become more stable and reasonable. They can understand class, order, and the fact that a class cannot have fewer members than any subclass; rudimentary conception of Time, Space, Number, and Logic.
- Parents' experience of this stage is that these children are more reasonable, learn from explanations, and are capable of many adult-like functions.

## Stage 4. Formal Operations

## Adolescents

- Where abstract thought is possible.
- This book will end with childhood, so you are on your own in learning about this interesting stage.

---

**LEV VYGOTSKY, An Additional Cognitive Voice**

Lev Vygotsky was a Russian psychologist (1896-1934) who proposed a theory that use of *language was critical in developing thought*. While this notion seems non-controversial, it opposed Piaget's idea that language is only an *expression of thought*. Vygotsky promoted education as fostering mental development; hence education was crucial in developing advanced mental processes. He saw children as motivated to attain advanced thought processes that they saw in older children, and labeled a "zone of proximal development" as that stage just before growth. Educators use that concept in strategizing new material; children have to be "proximal" or near that information to acquire it or it is too "over their head" (Stuart-Hamilton).

---

## SUMMARY (Chapters 5 and 6)

In these two chapters, I have attempted to describe in brief the basic thoughts some major theorists have put forth in their attempts to explain the complexities of human behavior. The ground-breaking leader in the analysis of personality, Sigmund Freud, led to others expanding his views to include social input. Jean Piaget, in the cognitive realm, educated us in how children develop in their understanding of the physical world and morality. No one theory will explain the whole of personality development, that is, how we get to be the persons we are. But I hope that you who have plowed through this chapter feel more a part of this process, even though you might be more confused!

## Reminders:

- When your child tries to out-power you, think of Adler's "will to power."

- When your child doesn't understand that what they do impacts another, think of Piaget's egocentrism.
- When your child refuses to acknowledge they made a mistake, think of anxiety and defense.
- When your child "forgets" what you told him, think of Freud's defense mechanisms. That is, if it's not an outright lie. We'll get to moral behavior later.
- When they struggle with a task as a preschooler, think of Erikson's stage of initiative/guilt.
- When they have an inaccurate understanding of the world or think others all think like them, think of Piaget.

Knowing the limitations of childhood development may help you understand that your child is not a "little adult" and cannot be expected to act as such.

# SECTION III

## Five Pillars of Personality Development

Pillar #1      Love: Relationships

Chapter 7      Nurturing the Loving and Emotionally
               Well-Adjusted Child
Chapter 8      Developing a Secure Attachment and Healthy
               Emotional Expression

Pillar #2      Responsibility: Giving Your Child The Capacity
               To Work

Chapter 9      Using Positives to Develop Work Habits
Chapter 10     When Positives Don't Work—The Principles of
               Punishment

Pillar #3      Creating A Healthy Self

Chapter 11     Self/Other Balance and Self-Esteem
Chapter 12     Building True Self-Esteem and Healthy Expression
               of Emotions

Pillar #4      Teaching Your Child To Be A Moral Person

Chapter 13  Morality and Kind Behavior: Inborn or Taught?
Chapter 14  How Morality Develops in Children and When There
                   are Lapses
Chapter 15  Religion and Santa Claus as They Relate to Morality

Pillar #5      Raising An Independent Child

Chapter 16  Concepts of Independence, Separation, and Some
                   Cultural Differences

# Pillar #1

## LOVE: RELATIONSHIPS

# Chapter 7

## Nurturing the Loving and Emotionally Well-Adjusted Child

### INTRODUCTION

In this chapter, we will discuss the nature of love, the phenomenon of attachment, and the development of healthy emotional expression. Parenting behavior that contributes to a child capable of healthy, loving relationships will be discussed here and in more detail in Section IV, Ages and Stages.

### WHAT IS LOVE?

Creating a loving child is your most important task. The ancient Greek, Sophocles, said "One word frees us of all the weight and pain of life: That word is 'love.'" Love is the extreme expression of positive emotion and takes many forms. Expressions of love are shown when a three-year-old child greets a parent, quiet love is shared by a long-married couple, and when caring for an ill friend or family member.

The ancient Greeks used three words to describe Love:

- Eros represents sexualized love (parental love, which isn't covered here).

- Philos depicts friendly love.
- Agape is love for all humankind.

You experience love for your child, and this love is the basis for developing loving relationships in your child. The Greeks didn't put a word for parental love in their list, but love of parents for their children is in a special category. It has been described as *"unconditional love."* Parents will lay down their life for their children and sacrifice their own present happiness for a child's future. Even when a child makes huge mistakes (e.g., committing a crime), parents will be loyal and supportive.

How does human love come about? How will your child reach that mature stage of sacrificial love? And while you answer that question, picture your child nurturing their own children—your grandchildren—in the same way you are nurturing them. The nature/nurture issue is involved. Nature appears to be on our side, as psychologists studying newborns found that they are human-oriented and will look more at a face-like image than a non-face image (1). At three months, infants will look more at faces than at similar patterns (2).

## ATTACHMENT AND LOVE

Given what seems to be an inborn preference for humans, what do parents do to enable a child to feel the connection, caring, compassion for another? Building a loving relationship starts at birth. Stages of relationship development are seen in early childhood when *Attachment* takes place. Let's look closer at that important phenomenon. The attachment felt in romantic love is akin to this early phenomenon. When you "fall in love," you resurrect the initial closeness with parenting figures. You get "attached." Use of that word is no accident. This phenomenon is an invisible connection between child and primary caretaker. No doubt you became attached to your infant shortly after their arrival. However, they will take longer to attach to you.

As stated above, the Greeks used the word "Philos" for friendly or brotherly love. Friendships are part of normal development, and of course you want your child to have friends. Recently, psychologists who use the theories of Piaget to understand child development have studied how children understand friendship. In doing so, they reveal the substance of what makes a "friend" a "friend." This interesting work will be discussed later in this chapter.

The final concept of the Greek *"Agape"* is a goal only for mature adulthood, not for childhood. The seeds for this healthy worldview are initiated in childhood. Refer to Chapters 13 through 15.

## Your Point of View on Love

It might be helpful to examine your own philosophy of human nature. I'll throw in three areas where people differ in their approach to humanity.

1. First, some writers—including Freud—have put greed, aggression, and selfishness at the center of human nature. Some religions base their definition of humanity on "original sin." Do you agree? You may recall the 1954 book *Lord of the Flies* (3), which is a fictional account of the misadventures of young boys stranded on a desert island. The story depicts how social ties break down and how aggression takes over to show the author's pessimism about the inner core of us all.

2. A recent book by a Dutch historian and thinker, Rutger Bregman, has questioned this premise. As suggested by its title, *Humankind: A Hopeful History* (4), he sees kindness at the core of human nature. He argues against theories (including religious) that humans are inherently "bad," and in a pinch they will turn aggressive and show their true

"human nature." Bregman based his premise on several observations of actual events in history, such as one when a group of young boys ACTUALLY were stranded on an island. Rather than turning into savages, they worked together and cooperated to survive. Bregman posits that there is a "kindness gene," which by virtue of natural selection is in all of us, and has helped humanity live to the present date. If a parent feels that children are inherently "bad" and need to be thrashed into civilization, they may parent differently from one who feels there is built-in goodness and kindness in every human. I suggest you read the book!

A second way people approach life is the "glass half-full/glass half-empty" issue. Pessimism or optimism can define how you view the world. Your point of view will influence that of your child.

3. And thirdly, sharing a generous spirit toward others can be a big influencer in Love. Giving another the "benefit of the doubt" is a positive attribute which can also be handed down to your child. Positive people generally are more successful in loving.

Which of these approaches fit your philosophical views on human nature?

## Ingredients in a Loving Relationship

How can you tell someone loves someone? A few essentials of what are to be considered healthy attributes of a loving relationship include:

- Spending Time
- Courteous Speech
- Attitude of Respect for the Other
- Affection in Words

- Affection in Body Language
- Actions which indicate one cares more for the Other than the Self
- Giving one another the benefit of the doubt
- Accurately respecting one another for who they are regardless of our assumptions about them.

Learning about others involves the use of assumptions, or stereotypes, which guide us in figuring out who the Other is. We have assumptions about every type of human based on gender, age, race, and lifestyle. Those assumptions, which will change over your lifetime, will have some truth but mostly will need some correcting. Children learn those assumptions from parenting persons. The child will be socially successful to the extent that those assumptions are flexible and will adjust to the realities of the outside world. Inversely, the degree to which assumptions are fixed, negative, and resistant to change, the child and eventual adult will be hampered. The most extreme and fixed assumptions approach paranoia. Can someone live their life without stereotyping? I really don't think so, but the flexibility and willingness to adjust one's stereotypes will affect your and your child's ability to connect with each other and other people.

In an adult couple, a healthy measure of the relationship is whether they "bring out the best in each other," and make each other "better persons." I will bring in the word *"respect"* here, as it is an underpinning of relationships at all ages. Respect for another is not only adjusting one's behavior to meet another's approval but would include "calling out" the partner on any unhelpful behavior. This feature of "respectful" and "constructive criticism" is paralleled in parenting by a parent correcting what is deemed inappropriate. So, in an honest and intimate relationship, loving doesn't mean always making the other person happy; it means standing up for the Self and correcting the partner/child even when conflict is uncomfortable. "Limit setting" for children falls into this category.

It is part of loving, and frequently parents confuse limit setting with LACK of loving. Parental love influences HOW limit setting is accomplished and will be covered in Chapter 8.

## THE PHENOMENON OF "ATTACHMENT"

Romantic love has its underpinnings in your relationship to your child. Attachment to another adult human is a hallmark of the development of Love; we know this term and use "attached" or "unattached" to describe the emotional/romantic status of adults. Psychologists use the term "Attachment" to describe a unique psychological phenomenon that takes place in infancy.

When your child was born, you felt a psychological connection to your child, but you may not have realized its importance. You are not the only one having those feelings—your child will develop those feelings for you! In the realm of adulthood, those feelings called "Attachment" can be defined as a "deep and enduring emotional bond between two people in which each seeks closeness and feels more secure when in the presence of the other," where the other is labeled an "attachment figure" (5). "Attachment is where the child uses the primary caregiver as a secure base from which to explore and when necessary, as a haven of safety and a source of comfort" (6). For babies, attachment is further explained as a "deep abiding confidence that the caregiver is available and responsive" (7). Erikson noted the "task" of infancy as "Trust vs. Mistrust." This deep abiding confidence that caretakers are responsive is Trust. An example of mistrust would be when a parent takes a long time to respond to their needs. An infant does need to develop a certain level of mistrust to fit in the real world.

When you read about infancy and attachment, you may come across the word "bonding." Is attachment the same as "bonding?" No, but unfortunately, professionals and others use the terms interchangeably and it gets confusing. The concept of bonding (8) was based on the concept that skin-to-skin contact during an early critical period was necessary for a close emotional relationship between parent and child. Picture a child being contentedly breast-fed by a smiling mother. Physical contact in very early infancy may be better seen as an opportune moment for the beginning of love, and a necessary experience for Attachment to occur (9). "Attachment" is the technical term and is a more intense phenomenon that evolves over the first year. Also, the concept of "Bonding" has not been a subject of research and hasn't predicted personality differences as outcomes.

---

**REFLECTION ON BEING IN LOVE**

Putting your child's capacity to love in context, let me review the hallmarks of "being in love," which is a desired experience for sure. By adolescence, the first feelings of being "in love" are usually felt. As mentioned before in this section, the word "attached" is used to describe two persons who make a "couple." In describing that relationship, words such as "completed me," "two make one," imply a major change in the emotional climate of two people. They are "in love." If the partners are apart, "missing" takes place. Also, if the relationship is in jeopardy or the partners (one or both) are contemplating ending the relationship, the feelings of loss, grief, anxiety, and emptiness are those we all (I think) can relate to. "This is the Love that makes the world go around," as they say.

---

## Baby Animals Get Attached

Psychologists have conducted studies of attachment in animal populations. Reviewing this information may give you some context about the phenomenon you observe in your infant. If you studied Psychology 101, you may recall learning about animal studies that showed ducklings waddling in a line following a human researcher. A group of European zoologists (ornithologists) observed the phenomenon in the 1930s (10). When ducklings hatched in an incubator saw a likely subject that moved (even a yellow circle or a duck decoy) during a critical period shortly after hatching, they "imprinted" on it; it became the attachment object. Those little ducklings saw the human as their "mother." Other young show the same behavior—staying close to their mothers. It is clear that survival of the species would seem to depend on this instinct.

The concept of attachment as an instinctual phenomenon and a product of evolutionary processes is relatively new in child development theory. Prior thought was that the close relationship between caregiver/parent and child was due to the fact that the child received food and warmth and came to see that person as positive. The infant paired food and warmth with love. That theory sounds reasonable, but a different topic of animal research shed more light on the issue of "motherly love." (Apologies to fathers.)

As we return to Psychology 101 in high school, you may recall Harry F. Harlow's studies with rhesus monkeys. How did he go about constructing the science of love/attachment? Harlow separated monkeys from their biological mothers and gave them two inanimate surrogate mothers. One mother was a simple construction of wire and wood, and the second was covered in foam rubber and soft terry cloth. In one experiment, the wired "mother" was equipped to dispense milk and the cloth "mother" was not. The infants spent time clinging to the cloth non-milk "mother" and only used the wired "mother" to feed. Harlow saw proof of attachment in a different experiment. The monkeys turned to the cloth "mother" for comfort when placed in stressful situations (a noise-making toy placed in the cage, nothing worse). Without the surrogate, the infant was paralyzed with fear, huddling in the corner, sucking its thumb. With the surrogate, the infant would explore and attack the toy! These experiments showed the effect of attachment in primates, and the need for soft touch to build that comfort zone (11).

Another of his studies with monkeys showed that those reared initially by humans for the first three weeks, then put in situations with other monkeys, showed preference for humans when they were stressed at two years.

What happens when there is no individual personal connection between animal infant and caregiver/parent? This line of study looks at "maternal deprivation." (Again, with apologies to fathers.) Animal infants can be reared in isolation and the aftereffects studied. Subjecting monkeys to various types of "motherlessness," Harlow found that the impact of deprivation could be reversed in monkeys only if it lasted less than ninety days (12), (13).

## Baby Humans Get Attached

What is the process of attachment in human infants? In the 1940s, John Bowlby, a British psychologist, worked with children with emotional problems. He noticed that they frequently had been deprived of parental affection or had disturbed or poor caretakers. He then came to believe that a primary caregiver served as a kind of "psychic organizer" to the child, who benefitted from a warm, intimate influence to develop successfully. He was writing in the mid-1940s through the 1980s and reported a sequence of psychological changes pertaining to human relationships.

The infant, prior to six weeks of age, has no particular connection to a specific caregiver. No distress is seen when everybody gets to hold the new baby! Then, as the infant develops an internal picture of faces, there will be smiles of recognition and preference for usual caregivers *(Indiscriminate Attachment)*. These are the smiles you've been waiting for! Gradually, there is more recognition and preference but by seven to nine months, a strong connection to one caregiver signals the onset of "stranger anxiety" *(Discriminate Attachment)*. Separation from the attachment figure becomes a big, big trauma. After ten-plus months, the infant will develop multiple attachments with other caregivers, and separation begins to be less traumatic. There will then be a hierarchy of attachment figures measured by who the child goes to first under stress.

Bowlby and his student Mary Ainsworth, in the 1970s, theorized which two benefits that Attachment offers the developing child. First, the child has a "secure base" in that they are confident that a parent will respond sensitively if needed. From that "base," they can explore their environment (i.e. play). Secondly, the infant has a "safe haven," where if distressed, they can find their parents and get comforted. As the infant matures over the first year, they make an image in their mind of these notions: e.g. If I am distressed, I can find X; if I find X, I will be comforted.

Human babies reared in institutional settings that may have deficient or multiple caregivers may not develop strong attachments. An experiment (14) was done where eight infants aged six months were given exclusive and 24/7 caregiving from one individual. The findings showed that the infants developed more social responsiveness than others who were cared for by numerous adults. Numerous studies from the 1940s showed the damaging effects on children when they were not given individualized attention (15). From his primate research, Harlow estimated that for human infants, six months of no possibility of attachment (i.e. multiple caregivers) would be the upper limit for reversal of emotional damage.

The idea of an optimal or suboptimal number of attachments has been a subject of study. Bowlby believed that an attachment was possible with only one main figure and problems could result from long separation(s) from the attachment figure. This knowledge began to have political implications as women began working out of the home. This research promoted changes in how children are treated when hospitalized for medical issues and allowed parents to stay with a child. Holmes (1993) discussed the research and concluded that there was a general consensus that a child can form attachments with several different adults and develop successfully. However, some form of attachment is necessary (16).

In the 1970s, an interesting lab situation was developed by Ainsworth to observe children twelve to eighteen months old when they were distressed and then comforted. It is called the "Strange Situation Test" (17) and consists of a twenty-minute procedure in a small room with a one-way mirror. Plenty of interesting toys are there for play. In several different phases, the child's behavior is observed with the mother and a second female adult who is the "Experimenter" (E), with only E, or the child alone with no adults.

The child's behavior is observed both when the mother returns to the room and comforts, and when just E comforts. Don't worry. If the child left alone was distressed, the mother returned immediately. The experiment has been criticized as stressing children; however, it simulates true situations when children are left alone safely for brief periods and for sleep while they are in the hands of an unfamiliar person like a new babysitter.

These experiments led to proposing three types of attachment (Benoit). Plus, a fourth type was identified later by Main and Solomon:

1. **Secure Attachment** is when the child greets and approaches the caregiver, maintains some physical contact, but will return to play. Benoit found this type to be 55% of the population.

2. **Insecure Avoidant** is when the child fails to greet or approach the caregiver, remains focused on play (23%).

3. **Insecure Resistant** results in a very distressed child by separation and cannot be soothed at reunion (8%).

4. **Disorganized-Insecure-**Inability to find a solution to distress and display contradictory behavior; their haven of safety is also a source of fear and distress.

A *securely attached* child will show separation anxiety (distress when mother leaves) and happiness when mother returns. They will be friendly with E only if mother is present; otherwise, E will be avoided.

The *avoidant* child will show no sign of distress when mother leaves and will show little interest when mother returns. The child is also okay alone with E.

A *resistant* child will be extremely distressed when the mother leaves and will resist contact with mother when she returns and will show fear and avoidance of E.

Other observations include the following:

- The resistant child cries more and explores less.
- For the avoidant child, the mother and stranger are able to comfort the child equally well.
- The disorganized-insecure situation is seen when parents are extremely unavailable and/or emotionally disturbed.

# Chapter 8

## Developing a Secure Attachment and Healthy Emotional Expression

### INTRODUCTION

The implication is that the degree of caregiver sensitivity and consistency can explain different attachment types. For instance, those who pick up their upset children consistently and can soothe effectively, contribute to a secure attachment. Sensitive caregivers are in tune with the infant. Are they stressed or calm? Are they engaged with the child or on their devices?

Behavior outcomes would seem to be the critical feature of research and the most important for parents. Marianne Wolff and Marinus Van Ijzendoom (1) found a weak connection between parental sensitivity and attachment types. More consistent and sensitive parents produced only slightly more children with secure attachments. There have been many such studies with similar results (Cassidy). So, no matter if you are a consistent and caring parent, your child may be insecurely attached.

However, style of behavior (temperament) may explain why some children attach in different ways. In Chapter 4, Easy and Difficult temperaments were described. Nathan Fox (2) found babies with the "Easy" temperament more likely to develop secure attachments. A child who has a "Slow to Warm Up" temperament would be more likely to be insecure-avoidant, and babies with a

"Difficult" temperament were more likely to have insecure-resistant attachment styles (3). So, if your child has other than an "Easy" temperament, you may have to work harder to create a more secure attachment.

Also, researchers Rudolph Schaffer and Peggy Emerson found differences among infants in their sociability (4). Some babies prefer cuddling more than others from early on even before much interaction had occurred to cause such differences. Those cuddlers would be expected to make more secure attachments.

## HOW IMPORTANT IS ATTACHMENT FOR FUTURE DEVELOPMENT?

Now we know that babies develop these all-important attachments and that there are different styles, but do these style differences say anything about future personality development? As parents, you can only do your best in being trustworthy and available. Your child's temperament is a huge factor. Is there any research that insecurely attached infants will develop problems? There is some evidence that attachment style does make a difference.

Depending on the style of attachment, research has found differences in school-age children's behavior. Children with secure attachments developed more secure peer relationships, engaged more in creative play, and showed essentially positive functioning. Infants with avoidant attachment styles were more likely to exhibit aggression. Children with resistant type attachment in infancy were more likely to exhibit withdrawn behavior (5). Children with disorganized type attachment were most insecure and exhibited problems in functioning. Does this mean attachment style is a given and depends on temperament only? No.

Over a thirty-five-year period, the Minnesota Longitudinal Study of Risk and Adaptation (MLSRA) (6) revealed that the quality of early parenting behavior affected later childhood, adolescence, and adulthood, even when behavior style (temperament) and social class were taken into account. MLSRA studies showed that children with a secure attachment history were more likely to be more independent and showed having the following attributes:

1. A greater sense of self-agency
2. Better emotional regulation
3. More positive opinion of themselves
4. Better coping under stress
5. In general, better social relationships in later years including romantic relationships.

So, your caring and consistent manner will have a positive effect on your child's development; temperament will be important, but will not be the sole determining factor.

## "ATTACHMENT PARENTING"

The term "attachment parenting" was coined by Bill and Martha Sears (7) to refer to a parenting approach that emphasizes nearness and sensitive responding to the needs of babies and children. Seven practices (all starting with b) are recommended: Birth bonding, breastfeeding, baby-wearing, bedding close to the baby, belief in baby's cry, balance, beware of baby trainers. (Note: the last "b" about "trainers" refers to those dispensing child-rearing advice, including this book.)

These practices of attachment parenting have *not* been scientifically linked to a *secure* attachment outcome. The emphasis on home birth, breastfeeding, and co-sleeping is sometimes not possible, and may not be recommended for health or safety reasons. And the practices, if not done in a warm, interactive way may fall flat. Breastfeeding can be mechanical and not interactive whereas bottle feeding can be interactive and fun. It's not the method of feeding but the quality of the interaction. Also, well-meaning parents can overdo the responsiveness believing they need to meet the child's every request. This style is exhausting! When allowed to "fuss" in generally warm and responsive settings, babies can begin to learn to manage stress.

Regarding super-closeness, there is a note of warning as that style may be related to an *anxious* style of parenting. Anxious parents can be overprotective or over-attached and *not* able to foster successful development. However, the warm and close relationships with caregivers recommended by Sears ARE related to secure attachment and are recommended in place of more distant, cold, or strict methods. You likely became attached to your child shortly after their birth but you can watch expectantly while your child develops that attachment during their first year.

## EMOTION

Part of a loving relationship is the ability to express one's feelings. Expressing emotions may be natural —or difficult—depending on your own family history. Many families—and cultures—discourage emotional expression, particularly in men. And some cultures encourage vocal communication with feeling. Verbally communicating emotional states becomes an opportunity to develop a closeness or emotional intimacy.

Pre-teens sharing their innermost secrets with a best friend, or romantic partners working out differences that impact their relationship are examples of emotional intimacy. The emotions we feel can be a rich source of our humanity, or they may be feared based on how we have been raised.

**Emotional Intelligence**, for lack of a better word, means the following:

1. Being aware of one's own emotions
2. Organizing and communicating that information helpfully and tactfully to another.

Having an emotional language begins in childhood. Annoyance, joy, disappointment, fury, frustration, sadness, pride, embarrassment, and a host of other words may describe one's emotions. "I'm upset!" "I'm so happy!" are ways these feelings are communicated. Some individuals may think they're expressing their feelings when they say, "I feel like you are being hateful." or "I feel like you are trying to make me mad." You can tell that the former "I-statements" are direct and informative, while the second are not so informative, nor as powerful as a statement of emotion. Any therapy that concerns multiple individuals will cover the benefit of "I-messages" over injurious "You-messages." You can turn to numerous resources to help you replace "You're so lazy" with "I'm worried you will not get that work done in time." These styles of communication affect Self-Development and will be covered in a following chapter.

Young children are enthusiastic to express how they feel and begin to label those feelings in the second or third year. When I was with a three-year-old in a therapy setting, I drew faces expressing the various emotions, and asked them to name and then talk about the common feelings: "happy, sad, scared, and angry" (and I added "nervous" as it seemed a feeling they knew fairly well). The children were delighted to share how they felt about the difficulties they were facing.

How the family picks up and shares these statements of emotion will determine if the child continues to be available to their emotions. In my experience teaching pediatrics residents—many from non-Western cultures—I found that many had difficulty sensing emotions from very everyday scenarios. For example: "This homework is impossible! I can't do it." The task was to identify the feeling in the statement. The resident might answer "the feeling is that the homework is too hard." That response does not express an emotion. The feeling involved in the "homework" expression is "frustration" or being "overwhelmed." Another example: "Why don't you look at me!" Their response might be that the child wants attention. That answer is not wrong, but misses the feeling, which is "left out" or "ignored."

Perhaps the phrase "emotional disturbance" will get your attention. Emotional health is the opposite of being emotionally disturbed. To be emotionally healthy (and not emotionally disturbed), emotions must be recognized and socialized properly. Advice to parents is to label emotions with words as you see your child feel them. As children learn to use those, they can explain them and thereby moderate or regulate them better. "I'm so mad at my sister!" ("I can see you're really frustrated when she takes your toys.") "I can't stand broccoli!" ("That taste really grosses you out.") "I love *Frozen*." ("That seems to be your favorite movie.") "I love the Cubs." ("You are right on track, Buster.) "I can't stand the Packers!" ("You are a true Bears fan.") (Unfortunately, my grandson, now age six, has decided to cheer for any team that's **not** the Bears or Cubs. This power trip is highly embarrassing, and hopefully it is just a phase.)

One sticking point about I-messages should be clarified. Parents become conflicted if their child states "I hate you!" That is a true "I-statement" but parents have a problem with its intensity. My recommendation is to reflect something like: "I get that you're super-angry with me and hate me, but I don't hate you. I still love you." The "hate" feeling goes away soon, like all emotions. Getting "heard" is the validation necessary for children to be able to call upon those emotions in a healthy way.

## PARENTING STYLES

Parenting style has evolved over the centuries and differs from culture to culture. The "old-fashioned" way of "children should be seen and not heard" was most probably in effect until the twentieth century. My own thinking about this is that survival-based economies, such as those in harsh climates or situations of subjugation, require the absolute obedience of their members. Training children to be obedient and not to question authority was needed. The strict roles of family members (and strict rules for such) were needed for maximum chance to live from season to season. I can only imagine cave families parenting their children (yes, they were parents). We survive to this day because our ancestors made it through. But times have changed, and access to resources and better standard of living now allow the personal freedom of expression in those countries which espouse democratic political systems. Parenting styles evolved to the present.

When considering your style of parenting, it may be helpful to think of your child as an employee in their future career—whatever it may be. While respect for their boss is necessary, being a creative part of a team is also necessary. That part requires the ability to contribute one's thoughts and ideas, and to collaborate with others. Even a self-employed person has to cater to their clients. A person with both healthy respect for authority who also has confidence that they have something to offer, would be optimum. Parenting styles will be critical to create such a combination.

In the 1960s, Diana Baumrind, a developmental psychologist at the University of California at Berkeley (8), mapped out types of parenting styles commonly seen in US middle-class families. Based on extensive observation she identified three styles which later came to four based on research by EE Maccoby and JA Martin (9). Two-dimensional framework, illustrated below, uses a vertical axis being the degree to which parents expect (or don't expect) age-appropriate behavior and the horizontal axis being the degree to which parents are accepting to their child's emotional needs (or not).

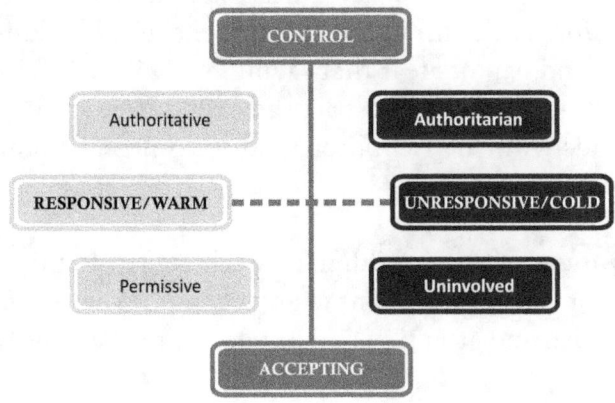

**Authoritative parents** have high expectations for children's behavior but put effort into maintaining a positive relationship with their child. Rules are set and explained to the children with open discussion of reasons for rules. Infractions are dealt with punishments that are thought out and related to the rule broken (see next chapter). Children may protest and try to negotiate infractions or press demands to a degree that does not constitute disrespect.

> **Outcome:** Children from families with this style tend to be well-adjusted, independent, socially skilled with peers, and not aggressive.

**Authoritarian parents** also have high expectations for mature behavior, but are less responsive to how the child feels. Rules are set and blind obedience is expected. Reasons for rules are "because I said so." Any protest is punishable; punishments may be harsh and less related to the infraction. They are more distant from their children, justifying it as "tough love."

> **Outcome:** Children from these families were found to be generally cooperative with authority, unhappy, less independent, insecure, exhibiting behavior problems, socially problematic with peers, and frequently angry and defiant.

**Permissive parents** set few rules and boundaries and are hesitant to enforce rule infractions or misbehavior. The kids run the household and parents fear that saying "no" will either harm their loving relationship or will restrict the child's "free spirit." They try to be friends with their children, and feel uncomfortable having authority.

> **Outcome:** These children may achieve less in the classroom, become highly resistant to any attempt to limit their behavior, demand attention and privileges, and become "entitled."

**Uninvolved parents** may be neglectful due to having mental illness or addiction problems. They don't spend much time with their children and expect them to raise themselves.

> **Outcome:** These children act impulsively and cannot regulate emotion well. They will have serious problems such as delinquency, addiction, and be vulnerable to self-harm including suicidal behavior in adolescence. Exceptions are possible when the child finds appropriately authoritative parenting from another source such as a grandparent or teacher.

Baumrind's styles have been studied since the 1960s and no psychological study has disproved the benefits of authoritative parenting, while many others have consistently shown its advantages. The assumption here is that BOTH parents espouse the same style. That is not necessarily the case, and the combination of two different philosophies by two different parents will require much creative discussion! One study found that teens were generally better off having at least one authoritative parent—even if the other parent was permissive or authoritarian (10).

Today, cultural differences exist among various countries regarding parenting style, and we will cover more of that in the chapter on the Self and in Appendix C about Independence. My pediatrics residents come to mind again; they came from various countries in Africa, South America, and Asia. When they shared their experiences with their families, they showed fearfulness when referencing father figures. In these Authoritarian families, "backtalk" was punishable. But as generations came, things seemed to change. One resident from South America said, "We were terrified of my grandfather; scared of my father; but I'm the nicest dad you could find."

# FRIENDSHIP

The capacity to love is nurtured in the family, as well as through relationships with peers. Think of your own adult friendships. Over the years, you have collected people who are positive resources in your life. You may call them all "friends" but you know that "friends" come in different varieties. You have friends who you share activities with, friends with whom you chat with in the market, and friends who you call when you are in distress. Starting friendships, keeping friendships, and sadly, losing friendships are necessary experiences for a well-balanced life, and you want your child to have such a collection of people.

Contact with others who are the same age, their peers, provides your child experiences with EQUALS. Parents and siblings do not provide the same issues and expectations as an unrelated peer. In the family, children are permanent members and cannot be rejected; but children can be rejected by peers if they do not meet expectations. So, your children are *motivated* to develop behaviors that maintain the friendship. The definition of a "peer" is someone of the same mental age (refer to Chapter 2 for definition) and generally the same chronological age. If the relationship is not "of equals," it will be skewed. Older children may be protective of a younger child, or an older child may dominate a younger one, but "friends" must be equals.

The progression of children's social relations goes through stages and will be described in more detail in Chapters 11 and 12, which deal with self development.

Briefly, infants and young toddlers watch each other, and learn from each other at play. As two-year-olds, they engage in "parallel play," playing alongside each other and occasionally sharing. At age four to five, there is a big shift, and they can engage in "cooperative play," where the children identify a play theme, assign roles, and use imagination like playing "house" where "I'll be Mommy; you be Daddy." Conflict is common. The social skills developed by putting forth "ideas," negotiating the "rules" or "roles," and handling conflict are skills that will be critical in future relationships. At age eight a child will identify good friends, and in preadolescence, around eleven, a "best-friendship" is formed.

You may recall reading about the Personality Theorist Harry S. Sullivan in Chapter 4 (11). He labeled the "best friend" a "chum." His emphasis on interpersonal relationships made a big point about how these relationships foreshadow the child's future close relationships in adulthood. He recognized friendship as the context in which mutual respect, cooperation, and interpersonal sensitivity may develop. The best friendship, or as Sullivan called "chumship," has qualities of intimacy, as personal issues, secrets, and fears are shared. Skills that will be used lifelong are acquired here.

Understanding how children *think* about friendship has been a subject of study recently. In interviews with children, researchers found two levels of understanding. The first Pre-Friendship Level is someone "who lives near you and goes to the same school." Friends are people "you play with" and who "act nice." Then thinking develops to Level 1 to "reciprocal relations, where friends are people who help each other." Level 2 is a continuous and stable relation based on mutual consent. "Friends help each other and you trust them" (12).

Ask your child how they know a child is a friend. What does the other child do that makes him a friend? What do you like about your friend? Parents are key to helping children negotiate the path to friendships by starting playdates with suitable children, coaching appropriate behavior, letting children work out their conflicts when at all possible, and affirming their social world will all be essential.

## SUMMARY OF PILLAR #1 (Chapters 7 and 8)

The capacity to love is an essential quality we want for our children. How love is experienced and expressed will depend on the type of interactions we provide for our children. Attachment is the instinctual phenomenon which is the foundation of close and intimate relationships. Some children are more prone to be attached than others due to their behavioral style. But warm and responsive parenting is critical in building a sense in the child that their world is to be trusted and will lead to more successful outcomes in the social world.

Emotional "intelligence" means knowing one's emotions and being able to communicate that information helpfully to another. It is the key ingredient in "intimacy." The family communication style will determine that of the child whether open and direct or more closed and indirect. Parenting style combines a dimension of love within the task of socializing behaviors. Since your goal is to raise a happy, healthy, kind, and responsible person, a love that is tempered with expectation will be essential. And lastly, love in the form of friendship is explored. Children's friendships evolve over these years, and as a result, both their behavior and their thinking grow in sophistication. Mutually loving friends are essential for a well-balanced life.

# PILLAR #2

## Responsibility: Giving Your Child The Capacity To Work

# Chapter 9

## Using Positives to Develop Work Habits

### INTRODUCTION

The previous two chapters covered Freud's first recommendation for a "good life," *zu lieben* (to love); Freud's second recommendation for a "good life" is *zu arbeiten (*to work*)*. The following two chapters will cover the best methods to teach a child how to develop that part of themselves.

### CONCEPTS AND BEHAVIORAL MANAGEMENT STRATEGIES

Producing an adult with a positive work ethic and a capacity for productive work is a major goal for parents. It means ultimate maturity and independence for your child! (Financial independence, too—hooray!) Along with the actual work, appropriate behavior is required such as showing up on time, behaving cooperatively with others, and respecting authority. Collectively, these behaviors are called WORK HABITS. All these behaviors are typically taught by parents in increments starting with early childhood. Without good work habits, the person with the best brain will not be a productive worker. Even those with limited intelligence or skills can be productive workers. Teaching appropriate behavior calls to mind three big concepts: *socialization, responsibility, and discipline.*

## SOCIALIZATION

The word "socialization" means to some, friendly chatting with others. But "socialization" in this psychological context refers to the teaching/training parents do to help your child behave in ways that are consistent with a successful life in their culture and successful behavior in the workplace. Socialization forms the following aspects of a person.

- Which style/dialect of language is used?
- Which polite manners are required?
- How much compliance to others' demands will be necessary?
- How timely will this individual perform productive work— i.e. meet deadlines?
- How will they express opinions?
- How well will they respect others?

All of these aspects, behaviors, and habits are requirements for living productively in the adult workplace and are your target behaviors.

## RESPONSIBILITY

Like socialization, "responsibility" is also a word that has multiple meanings. What would be your definition? When I taught pediatrics residents, I asked them to define "responsibility." Their first guess pointed toward what children took responsibility for when it came to their own behavior. While this aspect is admirable (and has to do with successful self-development), it is not the responsibility we are examining here. Here, the word is in the context of "duty." When we describe someone as "responsible," we are saying that they can be counted on to keep their commitments and perform assigned duties. Perhaps, that individual does not feel like doing such and such, but they will do it anyway because it is their duty.

Someone is counting on them to perform that task. Whether it's cleaning their room, getting ready for school, finishing home-work, putting their clean clothes in a drawer, or whatever, they are expected to perform it.

## DISCIPLINE

The word "discipline" (from the Latin word "to instruct") also has several meanings. When we speak of the "discipline of Psychology," we do refer to the instructional aspect. We are *teaching* them how to act successfully in our culture. However, in the everyday world, the word "discipline" evokes a meaning related to punishment. "He isn't disciplined enough" and as such, refers to a child who is out of control. And what about the word "self-discipline?" That meaning, "self-control", is the real goal of socialization and responsibility training. Let's agree that whatever the word, we want our children to act in ways and work in ways that make them successful!

## BEHAVIOR CHANGE

Now that we've viewed the "big picture," we'll get to the nitty-gritty of actually doing the tasks of changing your child's behavior. You probably know there are many programs available to parents to teach them how to deal with their child's behavior. While there cannot be studies of actual children getting one technique or the other (e.g. one set of children is rewarded, the other is not), there is an abundance of studies looking at the success of programs. Control groups can be used (one group has the program, the other one doesn't) to look at which technique best decreases children's disruptive behaviors.

In 2019, researchers analyzed 200 of those studies and found three techniques associated with better results on children's behav-ior. Parents have worried whether using incentives ("bribing" their children) to demonstrate good behavior is a good idea or not.

Parents cannot participate in any type of controlled study (where one group uses a particular strategy and the other does not) for obvious reasons. So, experimenters have had to look at the use of reward in the classroom to discern whether there are positive or negative effects by using incentives. You (or a favorite uncle) may have offered your child a reward for good grades. Is that wise? Studies of classroom rewards and achievement have shown positive results (better performance) and no down side to using rewards (1). It is generally understood that incentives do increase achievement (2). An article reviewing thirty years of research concluded that there is no detrimental effect with use of rewards in the classroom (3).

Again, since parents can't be forced to use or not use various techniques as would be necessary in a controlled study, we can use "intelligent conjecture" about it based on our personal observations from both of our own parents and from our own children. Plus, studies of parenting education programs can add something to our knowledge. That subject will be covered in a later section.

## Attitude Adjustment—Being the Boss

The word "discipline" may have caught your eye. You are now the "disciplinarian"—"the boss." This may be an entirely not-sought-after role for you, and one which you may have avoided. Your sweet infant is putting God knows what in their mouth. Your toddler is making their way to the hot stove. Your preschooler says, "You're stupid!" Your fourth grader stalls with homework. Your child needs guidance. If you've never had a take-charge role, you have one now. Going back to Chapter 6, you recall the demandingness axis in relation to parenting styles (Baumrind). Warmth on one axis. Demand on the other. We are in the process of creating a child who can love and who can work and behave appropriately. So how does the child get from A to Z in the realm of being able to work productively? I will set out principles here in this chapter; these concepts will be reviewed and refined and occasionally repeated in the Ages and Stages chapters.

## When Life Does the Training—Natural Consequences

Before you set out your own training strategies, be aware that there are life lessons your child can learn without your guidance. Letting your child experience them is a big help and saves you the trouble. For example, if a toddler plays rough with another, it is likely that they will get hit. Frequently, running fast or carelessly ends in a fall. If a child insists on wearing a pajama top to school, they will get feedback from their peers. Some parents teach "hot" by letting a child touch a hot object. This last example may have made you cringe. It seems needlessly painful, and letting "nature take its course" has its problems. If a child refuses to brush his/her teeth, they will decay. That natural consequence is just too harmful to allow. And it won't happen for a long time, so it can't be instructive. So, parents, you have to prepare to use teaching strategies that you devise. If you read other books, they may be called "artificial" consequences as opposed to "natural."

## Two Types of Training and Their Reasons

There is a wide range of behaviors to train your child, and it's helpful to map them out and understand the reasons and their importance. I like to categorize them into *two types:*

1. STOP the behaviors which feel to be "wrong" or maladaptive such as hitting others, destroying toys, and using disrespectful language.
2. START the behaviors which are desirable such as picking up toys, using good table manners, and treating others kindly. These can also be considered as the DOs and the DON'Ts.

I have found the following four categories of REASONS for these types of training are helpful. Keep these reasons in mind to explain them to your child as needed.

Four Reasons for Setting Rules & Training with Discipline

1. *Health* (eating a good diet, good sleep hygiene)
2. *Safety* (not running into the street; being home before dark)
3. *Responsibility training* (feeding the pet, doing homework, cleaning their room)
4. *Politeness practices or consideration of others* (not hitting others, saying yes ma'am, table manners, and not using certain words designated as out of bounds such as "shut up" or "f you").

## Using Incentives for Behavior Change—Reward and Punishment

Getting children to practice and manage self-control and to behave in appropriate ways has been a parental task since time immemorial. How best do children learn? Remember the rat lab in Psychology 101? Psychologists have studied learning in animals and have come up with principles of learning. Pavlov brought us classical conditioning; E.L. Thorndike and B.F. Skinner showed us that positive reinforcers (rewards) strengthen the probability of a behavior. Punishment is the use of an unpleasant experience meant to reduce the probability of a behavior. These uncomfortable experiences can range from verbal scoldings, administering physical pain (more on this controversial subject later), and removal or withholding of positive experience (4).

You can use these principles to mold behavior. But first things first, we must set goals. Helping children behave in the way you desire first requires your setting of goals. Some goals are obvious like safety and health and those you have in mind from your upbringing or parental education. Other behaviors may require some thought and a statement of the "rules." Positively stated "rules" help children understand what is expected! Rules are not bad; a rule is simply an expectation. Rules should be stated positively. For example, "no hitting" translates to "treat people kindly" and "no eating with your fingers" translates to "good table manners." And again, remember the four REASONS for rules stated just above.

Following is a summary of the tools you can use to change behavior. These tools will be reviewed and refined in Section IV, Ages and Stages. If you need more examples, there is much longer and more in-depth information in other books.

## Positive Consequences—Rewards

The easiest way to change behavior is by using rewards—and the easiest of them is praise.

## Praise

Praise is an art with certain important principles. **First, praise should be stated as specifically as possible.** Saying to a child "you are so nice" or "good job" is not wrong, but it does not give the child information as to what it was that was appreciated. For example, "I really appreciated it when you helped me put away groceries" or "when you gave Susie that toy, she really liked it." Or "I really am proud of the way you colored that picture, staying in the lines like that."

**Secondly, pay attention to the manner in which you praise.** Your body language should show excitement, moving close to the child will make the praise more meaningful. A heartfelt tone of voice also adds to the impact.

Children sometimes will squabble when away from parental supervision in an effort to engage the parent. This is called negative attention-getting. If a parent can "catch them while they're being good," this effort sometimes will prevent the (unnecessary) quarreling. Using praise liberally will give children a good incentive to behave in appropriate ways.

**Another helpful tip is to praise before you correct.** For example, if a child has picked up most of the toys but not all, praise the partial job first, then correct for the second. (If you are a manager of employees, you will know that positive feedback before negative is a good rule of thumb.)

**Avoid "left-handed" praise.** Sometimes frustrated parents give praise in a less than helpful manner. Perhaps your child hasn't cleaned their room for days, and does it under duress. How do you praise? Your praise might come out: "Well, I'm glad you cleaned your room...finally." It's sometimes difficult to bite the tongue. Note the part of the task that went well and say, "Your room looks great. I'm proud of you." Praise for the specific action without the "but" is most effective, and is most likely to lead to a repeat of the good performance.

Giving praise might seem easy to you, but some raised in homes where praise is sparingly if ever given have difficulty picking up the technique. When I worked at the county hospital which served many African-American families, I learned that the culture did not support giving praise. Even when I pointed out that the parent appreciated praise (which I gave them on the spot), they resisted. Reasons for not praising were several:

- "It wasn't the way I was raised and I turned out alright."
- "It will make my child think too much of themselves."
- "They need to do their chores because I do all the rest."

The answer to all these reasons is that praise works to improve the child's cooperation (which is the goal), and it does not "spoil" the child. If you have any of these resistances to giving praise, please think twice!

## Activity Rewards: First, Then System

"Grandma's Rule" is "first you work then you play." It is also called the "first, then system." "Eat your veggies and then you can have dessert." "Finish your homework, and then you can watch TV." (I'm not sure why grandmas get the credit for this—but maybe it is because it is old school and grandmas are old.)

People around the world since time immemorial have been using this strategy which is based on the Premack Principle of behavior (5). This principle states that making the opportunity to engage in a preferred or enjoyable behavior contingent on engaging in a non-preferred or disliked behavior, will act as an incentive for the (disliked) behavior. Historical examples from China, Turkey, France, and Italy are evident. Benjamin Franklin is recorded as using this type of behavior modification, as well as from the Buddha and other early Buddhists (6).

This manner of getting the "Do" work like chores and home-work done can be highly effective. It is the perfect incentive as the child has control of how much time is spent in "work," and will deprive themself of "fun" time depending on how quickly the work is done. A little quick thinking is helpful here. When your child requests an activity such as playtime, TV, time with friends, or favorite toy—check to see if chores are done. "You can do such and such when such and such is finished." In adult life, this structuring works to get your work done before you take a coffee break—and procrastination will be decreased. That is, if the adult has self-discipline!

## Token Reinforcers and Behavior Charts

Parents have found that using stickers, checks on a chart, or "points systems" that can translate to some material reward is a good incentive for both the Dos and the Don'ts. Structuring a behavior chart is a great way to produce results; the visual effect of your child seeing progress in plain sight makes the process more powerful. Prominent display on the refrigerator or child's room door is a frequent reminder of success (or not).

Here are some principles for chart-making:

1.  **The goals or "rules"** need to be identified; having a few for a younger child and no more than seven or so for older children is helpful.

2.  Once the rules are identified, they should be stated in *positive* **terms and listed on the chart.** For example: keep your room clean, get ready in the morning, pick up toys, and play "nicely" with others. One very good "rule" that covers all bases is "Listen to Parents," which comes in handy for those little events such as getting in the car to go shopping. (It actually means obey your parents, but in nicer language.)

3.  **"Take no for an answer"** also covers a multitude of incidents where the protests go on too long. Problem behaviors such as temper outbursts or grabbing another's toys can be targeted. Write these positively, too. "Be polite with others" or "get angry in the right way."

4.  **Describing the "rules."** For children who can read, the rules need to be in simple language, for example, "clean your room," or "come in on time." For pre-readers, pictures can be drawn of the desired behavior. Pictures from the internet can be used, but your own creativity helps here. Pictures of stick figure children playing and a "heart" shape drawn between the children gets the message across to "play nicely with others." For clean-up, a stick figure putting toys on a shelf gets the message across. The "rule" "take no for an answer" is tough to draw for pre-readers. I ended up drawing a picture of a bug and put a line through it for "No bugging." "Listen to parents" was a picture of an ear. As I said, creativity is needed. Exactness is not.

Daily or weekly charts can be generated, with goals listed, and space for feedback for each time period. Children can help choose the positive mark (smiley face, plus sign, stars) and the negative (sad face, zero). Each space is filled in every day. Busy parents may lapse in this important duty, and many a family therapy session will be spent trying to remember these things from the previous week. It's helpful to schedule a regular time perhaps right before or after dinner, when all parenting adults are present. Group attention to the week's progress is a powerful incentive. Kids don't like to review "bad" marks, and they love to see the "good" ones.

5. **"Bribes" vs. rewards.** Some parents are reluctant to reward children for good behavior or chores as they feel they are "bribing" their kids because they feel the kids should act out of an inner or "intrinsic" wish to meet expectations. There is a big difference between rewards and bribes and it is all in the TIMING. A bribe comes in the *middle* of the negative behavior, and the reward is determined *ahead* of time. Consider a situation where a child is acting up in a restaurant; the parents offer a deal; "If you can have good behavior for the rest of the meal, we'll get an ice cream on the way home." OR instead, *before* the event, the parents set up the deal; "Good behavior earns an ice cream." In the bribing situation, they are actually rewarding the "acting-up" because if the child behaved appropriately no "deal" would be forthcoming. Setting up the "deal" ahead of time gives the child the chance to self-control. A glance from a parent is usually enough to squelch any misbehavior. In both cases, ice cream is a treat, but setting up a plan when misbehavior is anticipated is a brilliant way to have, for example, a great dinner out.

6. **Allowance.** Another major way rewards are set up in advance is in giving money to your child on a regular basis—the

allowance. Children, once they know the value of money, may be given an allowance. Some British researchers looked into this issue. They found 91% of parents were in favor of starting some weekly-based system by six years old, with the amount increasing over time. Around 75% believed that children should be encouraged to save. Parents had consistent ideas and rules about allowance no matter if they were mothers or fathers or which social class they belonged to (7).

An allowance is the best opportunity for "financial socialization" or learning how to manage money. Children will observe parents' own habits and values toward money. The opportunity to do some financial education is not lost here. Children managing money will build their future money habits. Saving up for a choice purchase, making that purchase "using your own money," is a hallmark of growing maturity. When a child begs for a "loan," the appropriate answer is "no." Saving up and being patient are tasks that will pay off (no pun intended) in adulthood.

Another British study divided children ages six years to ten years of age into two groups. The first group would receive an allowance, and the second group would not receive an allowance. They gave children either $4 in cash or $4 in credit to purchase items in a store. Results were that the children who did NOT receive an allowance at home spent more money than the other kids. The children who received allowances spent less money overall (it didn't matter if it was cash or credit), which meant they knew how to manage their money better (8).

When a child likes money, you have a good incentive for building good work habits, if you make the amount dependent on how your child performs. When children understand the value of money, an allowance can be negotiated. Indeed, there are parallels here to the roles of labor and management in the workplace. There are many ways to set up the relationship between "workers" and "bosses."

- Some families believe chores are the way you pay for "room and board" or being a member of a family, and allowance is for learning the value of a dollar and how to save.

- Some parents equate the child as the "Labor" who by default, may feel underpaid and overworked by their parents who they consider "management" because they make the rules. While they may try to be "fair" (based on, hopefully, fair labor practices), the children may not agree.

- Others liken the allowance issue to their own responsibilities at work, seeing the allowance as a "salary." Adults get money when they work, and believe chores and behavior at home are the "work" expected for the child; thus the child receives a salary.

When children do not live up to expectations or if there is significant misbehavior, an allowance can be either docked or denied. This microcosm suits the goal of trying to build good work habits that will translate into the workplace.

Parents seem to be divided on whether a cash allowance should be based on successful work habits or given just because a person is a member of a family. As parents, you can determine which type of allowance you want.

---

**MOMENT OF CLARITY**

I recall a family therapy session where a young teenage girl begged her mother for money. She said, "You don't want me to be financially independent!" That was good for a chuckle as her mother and I emphasized that financial independence was indeed a goal for her.

---

How much allowance should you give? The amount of money and the types of chores will vary from family, economic class, and region. In 2012, an article in the *Wall Street Journal* reported survey results that showed 60% of children ages six to seventeen were paid $19/month for "usual chores" (doing dishes, taking care of pets, vacuuming, dusting, taking out the trash, and keeping their rooms clean) (9).

As children grow, they can learn to do a "side hustle" within the family. Large chores like shoveling snow, mowing the lawn, or household projects may be paid. The same article described results of a survey on "extra chores" and the amount of money paid. For example, 23% were assigned to mow the lawn for which they were paid $29/month. Again, these are "parent and child" or "labor and management" negotiation issues, and will change over time. Ten years later, $29 per month would not even cover a movie ticket, so inflation also is relevant. The principle here is that as the child grows, they get jobs that are more complex and have more responsibility. As such, their "salary" grows.

## Attention as a Reward

Parental attention is a reward in itself, and children will work hard to gain it. Attention can be used as a strategy (praise involves attention), but ignoring certain behaviors can reduce their frequency and hopefully eliminate them. Ignoring involves a simple type of "extinction," a technical term from the psychology of learning when the parent "discontinues rewarding a behavior that has previously been rewarded" (10).

All you do is keep silent and turn your back on your child and stay that way until the behavior stops. Some behaviors, such as temper tantrums, whining, and crying when nothing is physically wrong, deserve to be ignored. Other actions that involve danger or destruction should not be ignored. For example, a child hitting another, or a child using "potty language" in polite company needs to be handled.

Ignoring is a very active process for a parent and needs to be planned ahead of time. It takes nerves of steel to accomplish. Parents with strong selves and who can handle big challenges from kids have been known to crumple in such situations. Even if you say a little "no, not now," you have given attention. Be aware that the psychology of learning has shown that if a child persists in a behavior you are ignoring, and you cave in, the child has been rewarded for their persistence. This phenomenon is called "Partial Reinforcement" and strengthens the behavior intended to eliminate (11), (12). Gambling is built on this principle of intermittent reinforcement—you win just every so often.

# Chapter 10

## When Positives Don't Work—
## The Principles of Punishment

### INTRODUCTION

Yes, sometimes rewards don't work. And given my "old school" position, I feel that negative consequences are usually necessary to teach correct behavior. And, to repeat, when children aren't following the rules of health, safety, responsibility training, and polite behavior, a punishment strategy is necessary.

When your child engages in behavior that is unacceptable (God forbid), keep in mind that teaching self-control is the important concept here because you want your child to either *engage* in positive behaviors like doing homework or to *stop* provocative or harmful behaviors such as using foul language or coming in after dark. Whether it's called "discipline" or "punishment" is up for debate, but the whole idea is to get your child behaving in the desired way. I should note here that several authors of books on parenting discourage *any* punishment. "Punishment is defined as consequences that are unpleasant." Some people in this field stress the need to discuss the proper behavior with your child rather than impose negative consequences. (Maybe listening to your parents talk to you at length constitutes a form of punishment!) They feel that if the child fears punishment for their actions, they may focus more on the fear than the actual learning. To some parents, the idea of a child experiencing pain or displeasure is difficult.

However, I feel that punishments are necessary and instructive when teaching self-control. When I thought about the issue of imposing unpleasant consequences, I was struck by the fact that there were a number of issues that paralleled the justice system of our society. Number one—you are now a judge. Like the above situations where parallels are found between labor/management and work habits/salary, the principle operating here is the *penal system*. "Let the punishment fit the crime" is the big mantra, and involves parental judgment. The word "judge" is operative here. It is a big role, and as the parent, you'll need to set up "rules" for various types of unacceptable behaviors. For instance, the penal system, which we previously mentioned, determines if the behavior is a "crime" and if so, what is the sentence to be served. That's what judges do. Punishments vary as to their severity with a verbal reprimand for the smaller (misdemeanors), withdrawal of privileges for medium (felonies), and potential physical punishment for the major (capital offenses). Today's parent may set up a system of shapes or symbols that represent the action that begets certain reprimands; in the example below, the more sides or sharp ends of the shape, the higher the punishment.

- A heart means good behavior.
- A triangle means they are acting sharp, and they receive a warning.
- The square means time-out.
- The pentagon means grounding or loss of activities.
- The X symbol is when they break a safety rule, where I believe sometimes, a spanking amplifies the message. Some people will disagree, and I will share my full thoughts on physical engagement for discipline later in Appendix A.

The principal of punishment is that it inflicts some sort of discomfort. Whether physical or psychological, the child has to suffer to some degree. The displeasure (or anguish) exhibited by your child may be tough for you to tolerate, and your response brings out the "spine" of parenting and separates the "sheep from the goats." It tests the strength of the parent-self. You are not being cruel. You are being resolute. You are doing it "for their own good," and you are showing your children that you are to be listened to, they are to follow the rules, and respect the decisions you have made in their best interest.

Keep in mind that the temperament of your child can be a big factor. Some children with easy temperaments may be able to avoid experiencing things normally called "punishments" and will act in ways that parents like just because they prefer doing that. But then there's that other perfectly normal percentage who get in trouble, and then that percentage who are extra intense and require thoughtful and frequent "lessons" to behave appropriately.

## Verbal Interventions – Corrections, Reminders, & Warnings

The many strategies for teaching behavior involve interventions of different types. The opposite of praise is criticism. Calling a child's attention to an undesired behavior can run the gamut. Correction of a child should optimally be done away from the presence of other children because humiliation is counter-productive and should be avoided. If a child is misbehaving in the peer group, it is helpful to take the child to the side to discuss options.

The most common approach to children's behavior that you want to stop consists of verbal criticism such as "No!" "Stop bothering your brother!" "Use your table manners." "Get away from the street." These can certainly be effective but watch out to avoid intense and lengthy "scolding" which can either lower your child's opinion of themselves or bore them to death, and wear *you* out.

When goals are set, children will need reminders. The younger they are, the more they need.

- The "no" is a reminder for the "STOP behaviors."
- "It's time to…" is used for the START behaviors. "It's clean-up time." "It's time to start your homework." "Use your good manners at your friend's house."

It's a rule of thumb to give no more than *three* reminders—and a warning of the punishing consequence to come. This number reflects the "three strikes and you're out" premise, but it is not set in stone. It can be two, one, or even zero if behavior is reprehensible. Some parents prefer to count out a number that will lead to a punishment. "If you don't do it by the time I count to five, you'll get such and such."

*The importance of the warning is that the child has the opportunity to self-control.* And this is the point of all this strategy. Specifying the punishment to come, like, "You'll get a time out," "You won't go outside tomorrow," or "Your allowance will be docked," all requires quick thinking on your part. Specifying the number of the warnings is also helpful. "This is your second warning. If you do it again you'll get a time out."

Hollow threats such as "you'll be in trouble," or "you're getting on my nerves," and when you don't follow up on our warnings won't work. Children figure out quickly that you don't mean what you say; they will not respect you. If you think they're "not listening," you are the reason. Sometimes, a punishment cannot be figured out or administered at the time of the misbehavior. And you might be tempted to skip it as a result. However, if you can't think of something suitable at that time, it's acceptable to say that the punishment will be decided later. Then, there *must* be a later *and* a punishment. It helps to say when the punishment will be determined (e.g. when we get home) and hold yourself to it.

Avoiding humiliation was mentioned above but deserves a bit more attention. An important rule of thumb is to show some respect for the child if they are being reprimanded or punished. Depending on the age (beginning in preschool), peers and siblings *should not* be witnesses to your interventions. If others are looking on, humiliation becomes part of the process, and children will fight you tooth and nail in front of friends to prove they are not "weak." (There is only one instance of humiliation being used adaptively; you will learn about it in Chapter 21, part of the Preschool Age Section.)

## Punishment Strategies

## Withdrawal of Privileges

With situations where some privilege is being abused like rough or dangerous play at the playground, actions in the supermarket, or rude behavior with a playmate, the most reasonable punishment is to deny that activity. Children can be removed from the supermarket (even if you need to abandon a full cart of groceries), taken home from the playground, or have the friend leave when a punishable offense has been committed. For some children, a strategy is to deny them a favorite activity such as a toy, a TV show, or ultimately their favorite toy or technology device. The duration of the withdrawal depends on the degree of misbehavior (e.g. Susie goes home now because you were disrespectful to me versus no play dates for the rest of this week).

There are occasions when misbehavior is anticipated. Shopping, driving, and waiting are a few, and you can probably think of more. To allow your child to self-control, set up a warning and a reward ahead of time. "You know that if you act right at the store, we'll stay and shop, but if you don't, we'll leave." Bickering in the family car is another common challenge. Parents pull up and stop to figure out whether to keep going or return home. Usually because the parent is "in a rush," the temptation is to set up a "bribe," which is actually giving the child a reward for misbehaving. Remember, a bribe is rewarding bad behavior, and it's best to avoid bribes at all costs.

## Isolation or Time Outs

For younger children, removing a child from a situation where they are misbehaving and putting them somewhere to sit still for a period of time is called "time out" in the parent literature. Real "old school" was "sitting in the corner." You'll need to determine the length of isolation. Choice of a truly non-rewarding area is critical: a room with no toys, sitting on a couch wherever the child can't have fun, or in a designated "time-out" chair away from the ongoings of the family and/or household (and within earshot and eyesight). For older children, their room will do, maybe without a TV. The length of time depends on the infraction and the child's age. Rule of thumb is one minute for a child's age, when they are under five years old. Otherwise, for older children, you specify the sentence as an hour, an evening, or other time lengths suitable to the level of the infraction.

Now, what if your child refuses to go willingly to the isolation area? They may yell and scream, which does not help. You may have to keep the child in the situation by force. For young children, I found that being behind the seated child, folding their arms in front and holding hands will work. Truly out-of-control children will use their heads as weapons, so watch for that. Keeping an even tone and saying, "When you're quiet, time out will begin." And set the timer (again a minute for every year is an easy guideline). This effort may take an hour or even more for some children, but when they have figured out you mean business, it gets easier. The first attempt is the longest and most challenging.

If the child continues to refuse time out or isolation, you may need to resort to a physical punishment. The child can be warned that a slap on the arm will be forthcoming. More about physical punishment in the Ages and Stages sections and in Appendix A.

Once children are isolated, they have to be supervised somehow, lest they leave the time-out area. For older children sent to their room, you may have to sit outside the door to make sure they don't sneak out. If they leave the area, time out starts again. Once time out is over, a conversation about what led to the event and a session to share warmth, forgiveness, and praise is helpful to smooth things over. Best practice is to have the child explain what happened and why.

## Reparations for Property Damage

Rules of thumb for property damage are generally that the child cleans or restores property, or pays for restoration (e.g. new toy) out of their own funds. If there is no certain target that can be bought or if the price is out of the child's range, parents can foot the bill or the child can work for it doing special chores to supplement their savings and loss of revenue. The "punishment" should fit the misbehavior as much as possible. As the parent and "boss" addresses this, the child's obligation is fulfilled.

## Physical Punishment

Physical punishment is a controversial subject; it will be introduced here, but because it is so controversial, I have included Appendix A, where the subject will be discussed at length. But here is a thumb-nail description of the issue. Many parents choose to use any punishment in the book except this type. And they can. However, in my opinion, parents who choose to spank on rare occasions have, in my opinion, been unnecessarily vilified. If you ask a group of adults who had been spanked as a child, you will see most hands raised, and they will admit they were spanked for good reasons. They have not been ruined by the experience, and I think it gives the psychology of child-rearing a bad name when parents who choose physical punishment on occasion are classified as "child-abusers."

Physical punishment is not child abuse when delivered calmly and in a measured, considered way. But many questions have arisen about the effectiveness of this form of punishment once children are old enough to understand language well. Concerns have also been raised about the implicit message that problem solving by force is acceptable.

I will spell out my thinking here and it is related to "let the punishment fit the crime." There are a few but significant behaviors that rate as highly dangerous—capital crimes if you will—to your child. These behaviors include:

- Playing with fire
- Sex play beyond the age of six or so
- Stealing and lying
- Extreme forms of aggression to others (or animals) such as using boiling water or arranging for something to fall on them.
- Drug or alcohol use

Playing with fire is obvious; sex play with other children, even done out of normal curiosity, will backfire and get your child excluded from social gatherings. Stealing and perhaps lying is considered immoral and could be punished by the law. Shoplifting, which is common at five to seven years old, has its own punishment and will be dealt with in Section IV, Ages and Stages. Drug or alcohol use isn't healthy for any age and dangerous at a young age.

If a child forcefully refuses to be isolated (e.g. time out), they may be faced with a physical punishment. With appropriate warnings, and a very determined child, the introduction of a "big" punishment to facilitate the "lesser" punishment can be very helpful. Once your child knows you mean business, they will accept the isolation. However, there is the situation when a child prefers a spank than a lengthy isolation. In that case, you choose the one that will most effectively get the message across.

In your own childhood, you may recall getting a spanking that hopefully, you deserved. My own experience was with a group of school-age kids playing with fire in the garage, where a car was parked. My father came in, discovered us, and shouted, "What the hell are you kids doing?"—and we ran like hell. Later, in the home, he spanked my bare behind with a message about the dangers of fire play. Contrary to those that are dead set against them, spankings don't teach children to be aggressive, nor do they ruin a parent-child relationship. A deliberate and planned spanking—only when the "punishment fits the crime" and _done only when the parent is **not** angry_—can teach the important lesson when the behavior presents a danger to the child's welfare. However, parents can choose NOT to spank or physically punish. However, they need to be creative in finding a suitably powerful punishment.

The parent-child relationship can be negatively affected when parents over-spank as punishment or inflict severe pain (e.g. with a belt or switch) for small infractions such as making a mess, not following instructions, or not completing homework. When I counseled parents of African-American heritage who were raised "with the switch," my recommendation was that they save the big punishments for the big "crimes" mentioned above. They definitely understood. Under no circumstances given their own self-respect would they give up their traditional method of child-rearing entirely, but they could add some techniques to handle the "misdemeanors" as opposed to the "felonies."

Again, because this issue is sensitive and controversial, see Appendix A, Discussion of the Issue of Physical Punishment, for more information. My opinion is that, ideally, parents would resort to physical punishments rarely, if ever, but they should do so without feeling they are guilty of harming their child.

## Results of the Study on Parenting Techniques

At the beginning of this chapter, I mentioned that some child-rearing programs for parents were reviewed to see what techniques were the most effective in reducing disruptive behavior. Results showed the following three determinations:

1. Praise in particular.
2. Natural consequences had the strongest positive effects.

The use of what they called "non-violent" techniques of time-out, isolation, and ignoring were not as effective. Of course, children were put in groups, which does not allow seeing how individual children were affected. You will see what works and doesn't work with your child. Remember that the emphasis on positive reinforcement of good behavior should guide your decisions.

## SUMMARY OF PILLAR #2 (Chapters 9 & 10)

We've reviewed options to train your child to be a productive worker, one who has self-discipline and socially acceptable behavior. The temperament of your child and your parenting style(s) will determine the methods you use. Praise and things like allowance and privileges are great tools and have been shown to work by research. These tools may be sufficient for many children, but when they are not, then punishment strategies are needed. Letting the punishment fit the crime is a rule of thumb—children can tell what's fair and what's out of line! Your task is to be the authority, not the friend, and to be consistent and "judicious" in your decisions. So, in essence, if we use the penal system as our example, you are the judge, jury, sentencing judge, and warden, none of which you may have expected. Welcome to the world of parenting!

# Pillar #3

## CREATING A HEALTHY SELF

# Chapter 11

## Self/Other Balance and Self-Esteem

### INTRODUCTION

When parents view the future of their child, they see before them the task of developing a child with a "good personality" and a person happy with their sense of "Self." Frequent advice to a person is "Be Yourself!" "Be true to Yourself." A child's Self is the core of their personality. There are several aspects to this part of development which we will explore. So, what are components of a Self?

One of the shortest definitions of life might be "Life is Creation," and as a result of that creation, a Self will emerge. The newborn infant in your arms is a beginning, and their psychological Self will be their *masterpiece*, which will take a lifetime to finish. At six months old, babies are fascinated by their image in a mirror; by eighteen months, they identify "me!" For fun, you can put a colored spot on their nose to see if they see it and try to remove it (1), (2).

In this chapter, we will look at the following various realizations that contribute to a sense of Self and enable your child to learn there are others in the world. These factors include:

- Balances own needs and those of others.
- Self-esteem and what it does and doesn't mean.
- Factors that constitute a "resilient" Self.

- How a child's estimate of skills/abilities enters into self-development.
- Milestones in the development of the "Who am I" aspect of the Self.

Parents' actions in creating their child's sense of Self are without a doubt the most important factor in how your child will grow in this regard. Knowing about this process and how you influence your child may help you to organize your own thoughts and actions.

## UNDERSTANDING OTHERS

To be a social person, one must first differentiate oneself from the other, learn that there are different ways of being, and act accordingly. Try to imagine not considering another's point of view. Any interpersonal exchange involves the ability to consider another's point of view as distinct from yet related to one's own.

Starting from the beginning where there is no Self/Other, children must learn:

- Others exist apart from themselves.
- Others have needs and desires different from themselves.
- To figure out how to handle a relationship as a partner.

Over the years from infancy to school age (and beyond), your child will learn the whys and wherefores of understanding their behavior in relation to others.

One of Piaget's (3) major developmental concepts is the progression from (a lot of) Egocentrism to (Less) Egocentrism by the process of "Decentering." Young children naturally put themselves at the center of the universe, and for example, when asked about why the sun rises or sets, will answer, "So I can get up from bed (or go to bed)." Piaget noted that this type of egocentric belief gradually lessens from infancy throughout childhood, as children encounter the reality that their notions are not accurate and must be adjusted.

At preschool age, Piaget noted an increase in the ability to differentiate Self from Others. He measured non-egocentric judgment as to what extent a child could consider another's different view of a physical scene. The experiment, called the "Three Mountain Task" (remember, he was Swiss) consisted of a child on one side of a table and an experimenter (E) on the other. A card with different pictures of mountains on each side was shown to the child. The card was placed between them, and the child was asked what the E saw. Around the age of four and five, children improved in their ability to note that the E had a different view. In the 1960s, psychologists followed up the work of Piaget and furthered the study of how the child comes to know about the social world. The field became known as "Social Cognition," also named "Perspective Taking" or "Role Taking" (not to be confused with playing) (4), (5). Selman and others used visual stimuli like that used by Piaget. Their studies were instrumental in enlarging Piaget's notion of the general decline of egocentrism as they observed distinct—or stage—changes.

1. **Stage 0 – Egocentric/Undifferentiated (ages 3 to 6):** At this stage, the child believes, "Everyone sees and thinks what I see or think."

2. **Stage 1 – Subjective/Differentiated (ages 5 to 9):** This stage is where children are beginning to realize that other people can have a different point of view from their own.

3. **Stage 2 – Self-Reflective and Reciprocal (ages 7 to 12):** This stage is when children now realize not only that other people have their own perspectives, but also that they may be giving thought to the child's own perspective.

4. **Stage 3 – Third person and Mutual Role Taking (ages 10 to 15):** In adolescence, children can now "look down" on the relationship and simultaneously consider their own

and other people's points of view while recognizing that the other person can do the same (6).

How do children progress through the stages? In order to acknowledge or learn about a different point of view, the needs of the Self must be *suspended*—at least temporarily. One's own personal characteristics and preferences must be put aside in order to correctly infer the Other's point of view. The degree to which this can happen will determine whether the individual "gets it." The more emotions are involved, the more difficult the suspension of the Self becomes. Children are notoriously emotional, which makes the process more difficult, but if the Self can pull it off, there will be more understanding of Others.

My research for my doctoral dissertation explored the association of children's cognitive self-development with their social preferences in preschoolers aged four to five. First, I measured the children's ability to assess another's view of an object in a manner like Piaget's. The E sat across the table from the child, and a cube with different colored sides was on the table. The child either assumed the experimenter saw the same color as they did, or correctly inferred that the adult's view was another color. Thus, their ability to understand the different viewpoint of E was measured with the inverse, being egocentric thought. Then, to measure their social preferences, children were observed by raters in their free play sessions. Results showed that the *less* egocentric children were *more* child-focused, and vice-versa. Children who understood others more accurately preferred children's company as opposed to adult company.

As discussed in Chapters 5 and 6, the switch from adult-oriented to peer-oriented interest has been analyzed by Freud and Adler as resolution of the power-hungry Oedipal complex. This study revealed that children who have given up on "egocentrism" see the writing on the wall that they are not ruling the world, and shift to putting energy and focus on peer relations. My study shows the parallel growth of brain maturation and the social behavior of pre-schoolers. Freud rules! Piaget rules! (Of course, I thought this was ground-breaking! And it did get published in a reputable journal!) (7). A related study I did later, showed that children who increased in their ability to differentiate the Self from Other (role-taking, refer to the Theories chapter) tended to become more interested in children than adults in the nursery school (8).

## BALANCING "SELF" AND "OTHER(S)"

As growth progresses and children's personalities evolve, the Self learns more and more about Others because the needs of the Self are prone to conflict with those of the Other. "I want this; you want that!" Who prevails? The balance is critical to their personality. One hears of "givers" and "takers." One might conceptualize the issue as a normal curve, higher in the middle tapering to zero at either end with Self and Other at opposite ends. Most persons would fall under some sort of middle ground of balance of Self/Other, but at the far ends would be those that either put themselves first to an extreme or those that put others first to the extreme. The contrast could be labeled "Narcissists" and "Doormats."

While this area has not been a major subject for psychological research, a recent concept of "The Quiet Ego" has explored this Self/Other balance and tried to measure it. Coming from a place of "non-defensive strength," the quiet ego is a way of being that does not neglect the self but rather facilitates a balance of concerns for the Self and Others (9), (10). Optimally, your child will consider the needs of the Self and the Other equally. They will stand up for themself and get what they need while considering the rights of others. A balance is sought. The balance of your own personalities will be key to helping a child achieve it.

SOME INSIGHT ON HOW ROMANTIC RELATIONSHIPS GET STARTED

**A bit about adults.** In counseling adults in relationships, I frequently pointed out that strength of the Self vis-à-vis the other (the Self/Other balance) was a key component in establishing how the relationship will operate. Particularly in early stages of dating when "he" didn't call for a few days or "she" didn't return my call for a few days. The ability to hold firm and wait it out is necessary for things to go forward. This "waiting" is a test of the Self related to the Other. It is *not* a game. Self-respect and strength of conviction is involved here, with making sure one's own needs don't get overwhelmed by a desire to please the other (romantic interest). The romantic spark may happen with two matched selves. Optimally, a balanced Self can deal with an equally balanced partner when conflicts arise. Unbalanced relationships where one overpowers another are fraught with conflict and misery, and are of course unhealthy.

## Parents' Input

The growth and direction of Self/Other balance will determine to a great extent how your child functions as a social person. How and how fast it happens depends on the child and parent. What can parents do to enhance the process?

Now let's get back to that baby. When a child makes an erroneous assumption about another, it's the parents' task to add input to correct the situation. Verbal reminders to "consider others" occur everywhere and every day. "Johnny doesn't feel the same as you." "Mary wants to play something else." Along with this parental input and brain development, the sense of the Other grows.

Parents may on occasion criticize a child's self-orientation and call them "self-centered" or say they are "not caring about others." (Beware, the word "selfish" may unfortunately come up in face-offs.) As discussed above, depending on the age of the child, this quality is perfectly normal. Parents can introduce alternate viewpoints how the Other is feeling, but these exercises may fall upon deaf ears depending on the age of the child. What you say may be beyond their capacity of understanding. It won't hurt to try, but acceptance of your child's immature point of view is needed.

With this discussion, I hope you can see the value in developing a healthy balance of the Self with the Other. That balance continues developing throughout the life span, and is a major factor in adult experience—whose needs come first, mine or yours? You can note in your adult contacts where they are on that balance line: who is more self-oriented, more of a "narcissist," more other-oriented, or that of "doormat." Who asks about you and your life and listens, and who monopolizes the floor with tales about themselves and doesn't give you room to get a word in edgewise? Good relationships will have a sense of reciprocity—equal giving and taking. Your actions will help your child achieve this balance.

## Self-Esteem

Parents these days hear much about the benefits of high "self-esteem." The phrase may mean to many that a child "feels good about themself." You may see programs in schools that are geared to helping children achieve this sense of well-being, sometimes even in spite of the reality of the situation. This climate of "everybody is special" and "nobody is above or below anybody else" and "just trying is enough to be a winner" is wide-spread during this era. In reality of course, competition takes place, and children take a place in the wide range of skills/abilities/achievement. We will deal with some of the ramifications of the "Everybody is A Winner" culture later in this section, but first I would like to propose a way of defining self-esteem that takes a broader view of personality development.

## Self-Acceptance

The sense that one is generally on the right track and "doing ok" is a quality of the Self that is developed by parenting. Erikson describes the earliest task as being Trust vs. Lack of Trust with a balance sought. The child experiences the input from the environment from many sources but mainly from you. Sometimes you and the environment will push back and criticize, negate, or cause distress in your child. An environment which causes the least stress in the family will be optimum. However, it must be stated that a stress-free environment is not only humanly impossible, but it is not healthy. Children must have some stress and frustration in their lives so they can master the discomfort.

Harry Stack Sullivan was an American psychologist (recall his work from Chapter 5) who expanded on Freud's view that personality was developed by the interaction of impulses and the need to control them. Sullivan saw personality as developing through relationships. He emphasized the need for what he called a healthy "Self-system" which presupposes high self-esteem in a broad sense. The person with a healthy Self thinks highly not only of themself but also of others. Building a good opinion about oneself does not exalt the Self at the expense of Others.

What are the ingredients in a healthy "Self-System?" The healthy Self grows in an atmosphere *where acceptance of the child's behaviors outweighs rejection of the child's behaviors.* Parental anxiety and anger directed toward a child will induce the child to negate that urge/act that led to the behavior and push it to the back of awareness. And then it is not likely to become part of the Self. For example, if the expression of crying is scolded, the child will adjust the Self to ignore/deny/repress any such urge to cry. And then the Self is changed.

The degree of negativity in the social environment will determine to what extent that part of the Self is undeveloped. A "defense" develops when a "forbidden" natural emotion/impulse arises in consciousness. The more those natural needs are met with rejection, anger, or parental anxiety, the more likely those aspects of the Self will be shut down, and defensiveness will be developed. The following section will deal more about this issue of defensiveness.

In infancy, gentle and empathic treatment helps to reduce stress and/or pain as much as possible. When children cry, they will be soothed (or at least attempts will be made). Activities such as bathing, changing, and feeding can be made enjoyable and as stress-free as possible. When the child's wishes are determined to be outweighed by needs of health and safety, parents will set limits and the child will experience displeasure. For example, children can learn to self-soothe and sleep through the night without ill effects. They can adjust their behavior to parents' expectations. Their being upset does not ruin personality development. Being upset stops with time, and the child learns how to manage. The expectation here for optimal self-acceptance is that the *overall* experience of the infant be positive.

What about the child whose needs are not met with empathy in infancy? A child who is repeatedly frustrated, neglected, or treated harshly in infancy may not develop an accepting attitude toward themself. Rather they may shut down the Self's action to avoid the external experience of rejection or abandonment. The defense Freud noted as "denial" may have its underpinnings in infant psychology.

As the child grows to the toddler years, the exploratory Self is emerging, and the environment suddenly changes into one where there is danger. As the child is now mobile, a previously "yes-yes" environment can become a "no-no" environment. As you may guess, the more "no's" heard, the more self-development gets frustrated (Erikson sees the balance as Autonomy vs. Doubt, with more doubt from the "no-no's") (11). Childproofing a home is the first step to avoiding needless anxiety and "no's." With strategic gates, and protections, the home can develop into an atmosphere where the child can explore more freely and without raising parents' anxiety!

Also, a parent's calm manner in approaching missteps is also a crucial component of a child developing a sense of self-acceptance

(Sullivan). An anxious parent who overreacts to a child's behavior in fear or in anger will raise the same anxiety in the child who empathically responds to the parents' emotions. The part of the Self that evokes high anxiety can be shoved to the back burner of the Self! Again, the more a Self is accepted, other things being equal, the greater the child's confidence that they are "doing ok." Or the opposite. You can visualize a person coming from a restrictive environment constantly thinking they are going to be criticized.

A study in 2004 had children ages nine to twelve and their parents report their experiences of anxiety. There was substantial similarity between them on the variable of "acceptance versus rejection"—in other words, parents' anxiety was communicated to their child (12). Another study looked at the relationship between child-report, parent self-report, and partner-report of perceived parental rearing behaviors and resultant anxiety in children. The study showed a strong relationship between self-acceptance in adolescents and their view of their parents' attitude of acceptance (of them) (13).

Parents' general acceptance of the needs and wishes of the child will continue throughout childhood, with exceptions made when parents correct inappropriate behavior.

Conflicts between parents' and children's wishes occur periodically. For example, choice of extracurricular activities, such as sports or music, can be a major source of contention in childhood. How parents manage the decisions will add to the child's sense of Self. Children do not always get their way here, but parents can be needlessly heavy-handed. Here are some possible situations:

- There will be some "true" talents or interests that emerge from the child and may be in conflict with what caretakers think or wish.
- In later school-age years, the child may choose certain activities or directions which may not be supported by caretakers.

- And in teen and later years, some parents may push their children into areas they themselves choose (such as family businesses or the "family" traditional occupation). One hears about these conflicts which don't seem to end well. Where there is choice, and in later years career choice, the child's choice is best supported.

The point of this section has been that building the Self and a sense of self-acceptance comes from positive experiences from outside relationships. Now we turn to the experience of emotion and how it is integrated in the Self.

## THE EXPERIENCE OF EMOTION IN THE SELF

Emotions are a huge part of one's Self. Let's discuss them in general before we get into the details. Emotions run the gamut of too much to too little. You can see the process as a continuum with *modulation* in the middle and *outward expression* (externalizing) on one side and *inward expression* (internalizing) on the other.
Let's use aggression as an example.

- Hitting or biting the caregiver is the expression of uncontrolled anger.
- One step more controlled is throwing things AT the person.
- Next step could be throwing things NEAR the person.
- Next step could be name-calling or verbal abuse (typical of preschoolers e.g. "You're a doodoohead"). These are "You Messages" referred to in Chapters 21 and 22, and more to come in this chapter.
- Following is Modulated Anger, which is an "I-message" (again, refer to Chapters 21 and 22 and later in this section), which is a verbal expression with emotion: "I'm so mad."

- On the inward aggression side are pouting, withdrawing, shutting down, and self-injurious statements such as, "I'm so stupid" and "I hate myself!"
- Again, when anger turns inward, more extreme aggression toward the Self can be seen in self-injury like banging one's head and adolescents cutting themselves.
- The most serious internalizing emotion is suicide.

It's important to take action to train appropriate socialization of aggression attempts to get anger expressed in a healthy way.

**Modulation or moderation,** if you prefer, is the key here. To emphasize, emotions need to be present, acknowledged, and dealt with. However, they also need to be expressed in a manner that does not violate the social norm. Too much or too little emotional presence in a personality constitutes an "emotional disturbance."

In the past few decades there has been interest in the development of children's emotional expression, also recognized as "emotional competence" with Carolyn Saarni's work (14), (15).

In my psychology practice, when working with a child, exploration of five basic emotions was a core means of communication.

- Happiness
- Fear
- Anger
- Sadness
- Nervousness

---

*FUN TIP* FOR THE WHOLE FAMILY:

See the *Inside Out* movie for a wonderful depiction of these emotions.

---

Children can be very adept at spelling out their "feelings" and joyfully do so beginning around three years old. However, parents may not be so joyful about it and may profit from being more in tune with emotions. Parents will teach to fit the emotional expression to the family norm. Cultural norms are a factor; In the US, we often stereotype the British as having a "stiff upper lip," and we stereotype the Italians to wave their arms as they express themselves.

In the culture of the US middle class, parents sometimes have a way of dealing with emotions in children that discourages acceptance of them. "You don't really feel that way." "How can you be ___?" "Don't feel so ___." "You're making a big deal of that." On the other hand, when feelings are accepted by the parent, they will be internalized and integrated properly into the child's personality: "You must be sad." "I see you are getting frustrated."

Those emotions are more likely to be accepted by the child into their own personality. Emotions are "validated." All relationships benefit from this sort of "validation." Your communication about emotions is critical to your child's emotional health, and a published technique called *"Active Listening"* is available to help you get your child to talk about emotional issues and navigate the tricky situations where feelings are discussed. The technique encourages the open expression of emotions between parent and child. The trick is for the parent to first identify the emotion in question and say to the child, as mentioned above, something like, "It sounds like you're feeling (angry, frustrated, sad, discouraged)." This method will allow the child to make the connection and begin to use that word themselves, in the "I-message," which comes in the next section. Thomas Gordon (16) introduced this technique in the 1960s, and it has been available for parent education ever since.

## When Parents Express Emotions

We're dealing with healthy families in this book. But every person has their emotional breaking point when their own emotions come into play in the family. How emotions are expressed will be the example set for your child. And there is danger that angry expressions will damage a child's sense of Self. What about your own emotions, and how you express them to your children? In the previous chapter, we dealt with changing children's behavior. When they act "wrong," and you are upset, how do you communicate? Emotional "scenes" in the family—foul language, plates tossed—will model how to express anger. Be careful!

When you have a healthy sense of your own emotions, you can communicate your own negative feelings in a non-injurious way. Those of you who have been in parenting classes may recall exercises to communicate distress without causing damage or defensiveness in the one with whom you are communicating. The first rule of communication about a negative behavior is to *criticize the behavior and not the Self.* If the bed isn't made, that doesn't make your child "lazy" or "messy" or "careless."

---

**EXAMPLES OF I & YOU MESSAGES**

"I-Messages" (focus on the feeling and task, not blame the child)

- **I am happy to see you taking out the trash.**
- **I am upset that you haven't cleaned up your room yet.**

"You-Messages" (criticize the child's Self)

- **You are so lazy.**
- **Why don't you ever clean your room?**
- **Why aren't you doing your homework?**

---

A possible parental reaction to a pigsty room is "How can you be so messy?" This message will arouse negative feelings in the child, but you can deliver your message in a way that does not cause defensiveness, or imply the child has a character flaw. And at the same time you can communicate exactly what you mean. These are called *"I-messages"* versus *"You-messages"* for obvious reasons. Examples of "I-messages" are "I am happy to see you taking out the trash." "I am upset that you haven't cleaned up your room yet."

The first step for an "I-message" is to identify how you are feeling. When I gave parenting tips to beginning pediatricians, many of whom were from a different culture, they struggled to find the emotional language. So we practiced or role-played stating our emotions like angry, furious, disappointed, frustrated, sad, joyful, nervous, "scared to death," etc. Then they did exercises finding a suitable emotion to fit some scripts prepared for this task. And they learned quickly, even though they were learning in a second language.

In contrast, the "You-messages" that criticize the child's Self are harmful and also do not state clearly what you are unhappy about. "You are so sloppy. You never clean up your room." "You are really lazy." "Why don't you do your homework now?" It doesn't take much to see that the Self is attacked in these "You-messages." You can deduce that if the parent calls the child injurious "names," those names will stick and the child will label him/herself as such—"lazy," "dumb," "bad," etc. Building a positive sense of self requires effective communication of this kind.

When I searched for relevant research on these areas, I found little to nothing that would address the issue of "I" versus "You-messages." One study looked at how teens evaluated various kinds of "you" statements and found that accusatory "you" statements ("You're lazy!") were rated as more aversive than strong I-statements ("I'm upset that you didn't finish your assignment.") (17). Verbalized anger and accusatory "you" messages are cues for anger and antagonism among adolescents. These issues are so broad that they aren't suitable for research that would have to measure intangibles. There is a gap between clinicians and researchers for this reason: clinicians have to do their work without "scientific" evidence; researchers can't put their hands on the variables that would be helpful.

Described in a previous section but worth repeating is when a child says *"I hate you!"* to a parent. Parents divide as to whether this expression is disrespectful and deserving of a reprimand, or whether it is an "I-message" of extreme intensity and should be allowed. In my opinion, "I hate you" seems to be more respectful than its neighbor, verbal abuse, "You're a stupid parent." A helpful response to that hateful statement can be something like, "I certainly see you are angry, and you hate me right now, but I don't hate you, and I never will."

To review, emotional disturbance means just that: emotions are disturbed, and they are either too present or too absent for successful maneuvering in the world. Parents who teach balance of Self and Other, who avoid harmful and repeated injurious communication, who maintain a sense of positivity, and who allow respectful emotional expression will have the best chance of giving their child a healthy emotional life.

# Chapter 12

## Building True Self-Esteem and Healthy Expression of Emotions

### INTRODUCTION TO THE CONCEPT OF SELF ESTEEM

In my opinion, the chief aspect of personality that separates the sheep from the goats is the ability to acknowledge error. It's as simple as that. When a person errs, and apologizes for the mis-step, it requires personal courage. Nobody likes to be wrong; apologies take a big breath and willingness to "eat crow." We have all felt awful when we did something "wrong," but were able to bounce back to normal life after things were put right (and we were put in our place). I have adopted the term "resilient" to describe the process.

On the other hand, there are those who are always right, have the last word, and make excuses constantly for their mistakes. And they do not learn from their experience because it is always "someone else's fault." We all know someone who has to have the last word, never apologizes, blames others, and then continues to make the same mistake over and over again. This someone might continue to be late, forgets obligations, has an extra-marital affair, or any sort of thing. The inability to learn from experience comes with high defensive mechanisms like, "It's not my fault." And that individual will not allow in any information that does not agree with their own thoughts. We can infer that that individual is stuck at some developmental level and will not "grow" in maturity.

Parents are role models for how one deals with errors and will teach their children by example. Also, they will help a child learn to be responsible for their own behavior with encouragement to apologize or possibly force an apology when appropriate. (Note: forcing an apology when a child is too young to understand the mistake is of questionable value.) Highly defensive parents may also end up criticizing or blaming their children for their own mistakes. For example: "I dropped the vase because you were talking to me." A bit of theory may help you visualize this highly important process of owning up to one's own errors.

The term "self-esteem" in this context means the sense that the Self is able to admit error. Sullivan took the concept of defensiveness from Freud's explanation that anxiety is activated when the Self feels threatened. There is a continuum ranging from low to high defensiveness. A highly defensive person is someone who has difficulty seeing the error of their ways. Put simply, the more defensiveness in a personality, the lower their self-esteem, the less defensiveness, the higher their self-esteem. It's like a hydraulic system when fluid goes up one pipe and out of another, the proportion changes. We are all somewhere on that continuum. We all will show defensiveness at one time or another; the degree of our defensiveness is what's important. *Resilience* is the quality of adjusting these attributes, taking the "hit" of admitting fault, and then rebounding with a different sense of Self, which has learned the "error of one's ways."

However, one can go too far with this apology issue when those that take blame or fault for things that are actually NOT under their control but apologize needlessly. They exhibit a Self/Other imbalance. Poor judgment of knowing whose fault it is, is an emotional problem as well, and some healthy narcissism is required. It is necessary to stick up for oneself at times. The goal is for a REALISTIC judgment of the problematic situation, and some of them can be sticky. I hope you know someone you can trust to help with your own judgment. Your adult contacts will be helpful in this regard. Also, time which gives some emotional distance has an effect of making things clearer.

This concept of a "resilient Self" may be less familiar to many of you than the concept of a person "feeling good about themself," which is the more familiar definition. We will look at that next.


## YOU'RE OK—I'M TERRIFIC—SELF-ESTEEM

In the 1960s, a trend swept the nation to promote that children needed to have a positive opinion of themselves, and that parents and schools should provide it. The "Self-Esteem" movement was still going strong at the turn of the century and is still among us. Signs in the classroom might be "Applaud Yourself" no matter how little you work or how many tests you fail. Have you ever heard someone say or thought they might say, "We thank you for the praise which we are about to receive?" Self-esteem that is based on unreality tends to be unstable as well as feelings of superiority or grandiosity. Unfortunately, both are built on quicksand. As children grow up and socialize more, they realize people don't think they are as special as their parents and grandparents led them to believe. Reality rears its ugly head, their self-esteem bites the dust, and they may become angry.

In a 2003 study, titled "Isn't it Fun to Get the Respect That We're Going to Deserve?" researchers found that subjects who scored higher on narcissism were more aggressive when their work was criticized or after social rejection (1).

This unrealistic over-valuing of the Self is labeled "inflated self-esteem." It's such a problem that it's been mocked when the state of California established a "task force" on self-esteem. At worst, it's been identified as a trigger for hostility and aggression. Many child aggressors are from violent households or had mental illness, but one young man on trial for the murder of his mother and two students in Mississippi was evaluated by psychologists for the defense as "narcissistic."

A study published in 1998 evaluated children as to degree of inflated self-evaluation versus well-founded self-regard. All the students wrote an essay. The essays were then "graded," and the children were either praised or criticized from the children who were also in the study. Then, the children played a game of skill where one child was pitted against one he thought had either praised or criticized the essay. The "game" allowed the player to punish an opponent with loud noises. In other words, the child could decide to blast the other guy's eardrum. The findings were that the most narcissistic children were the most exceptionally aggressive in the wake of criticism. They went in for auditory torture three times more than people with normal self-regard (2).

Experimenters concluded that unjustified self-esteem needs constant propping up. When the real world fails to deliver, like when the narcissist gets rejected by a girlfriend or boyfriend or errs on the sports field, they may explode. The article concludes that praise for everything a child does may result in a child who cannot tolerate frustration. The idea that one can solve problems simply by telling children, "You're great" is seductive. The article concludes: "Giving kids something they can truly feel proud of is hard work for everyone."

Parents are to keep things real for their child(ren). They should praise and criticize appropriately (Chapters 9 and 10 review how specific praise is a powerful tool). In this chapter, praise is used as a means to develop realistic self-esteem. Every child has positives and skills that will add to their self-regard, and fake ones that don't really help. However, the real self-esteem is resilience. It is important for children to learn and can bounce back after mistakes.

## HOW YOUR CHILD'S SKILLS HELP DEFINE THE SELF

In the previous section, parent-child conflicts about which skills to develop were discussed. The Self has many components that include traits, preferences, and emotions; skills are a subset. Besides assisting academic skills, parents help their children develop in many other ways including sports, music, dancing, chess, and more. Starting with preschool age, and certainly in school age, opportunities such as piano lessons, sports practices, and essay contests are limitless. Each activity and skill contribute to a child's understanding of their self-worth (3).

It is beneficial that children know their capacity for certain activities. Their ability to understand what they are "good at," (their agency or self-efficacy) will influence what they will try and how hard they will try. If a child overestimates or underestimates their abilities, they may fail at the activity or may not try it at all, missing a potentially favorable experience. You have all tried to cajole your child into trying a new activity. Whether you succeed depends on your child's sense of capability and other factors such as willingness to risk. Once your child has some knowledge of their capacity, they will say "I can" or "I can't." If your child has fairly good judgment, there will be good outcomes and the reverse.

One tip for parents might come from some research which focused on "cognitive modeling" of parents as they appraise their own abilities. Researchers found that parents' thinking aloud in front of their children facilitated their children's own opinion accuracy. For example, "I think I can do this because I did such and such before." "Hmm, now this looks hard, but if I try, then maybe I can do it" (Bandura).

Starting with infancy, your child figures out when they do something, it produces results. A sense of "personal agency" develops: "I can make things happen." Newborns shake a rattle to produce sounds; they quickly learn how to influence others by their actions. When parents permit exploring and new experiences, they increase opportunities for the child to develop a sense of accomplishment.

Once language is developed, communication with the child can include urging children to try new things and also cautions against potentially harmful new experiences. Young children want to copy other children, particularly older children, which sometimes engenders some danger. Other times, it provides opportunities for real skill growth. Parents must provide realistic input to aid in their children's judgment and to provide for their safety.

Regarding safety, however, parents' degree of protectiveness, based on their judgment of a situation as potentially dangerous or failure-ridden, can certainly limit a child's opportunities. Hence, they may reduce the rate of their child's development or make the child needlessly fearful of situations. Good judgment is imperative here, and advice from other adults can help to reach a good balance of risk that will also allow for growth. A critical task for parents is to control their own anxiety, and at every step, understand that some risk is necessary.

Young children are fairly poor at appraising their abilities; that is part of their "power trip." For instance, preschoolers may insist they "beat" their parents at a game, when they did not. However, around the age of six, they realize that it is the performance of peers that is most informative (Bandura) (Flavell/Ross). Once the child is in school, self-efficacy is developed in a major way, as children are evaluated against their agemates. Schools may avoid practices such as grading, but skill acquisition will proceed at different rates for different children. Children have to learn to face displeasing realities about their abilities, which no amount of applause and self-congratulation will avoid. Remember, "We are so happy to get the praise which we are about to deserve."

Skills outside the classroom are optional, but academic skills are not. If your child experiences difficulty in any aspect of academics, schools and parents ideally work together to craft a realistic plan for success. Learning difficulties which are brain-based affect a large percentage of children (refer to Chapter 1 and Section IV, Ages and Stages for more information), and rather than being labeled "lazy" or "stupid" (which people unfortunately seem to do), they can be helped to understand their deficiency in the context of their strengths. In my work with children who had learning difficulties such as learning disabilities or deficits in intelligence, I counseled children on the skills and traits that they understood as successful such as sports or arts ability, and social positives such as kindness or being "fun." Understanding those skills in non-academic areas can help to offset any negative self-labels of their limitations.

Children can develop a positive sense of self-regard based on their WHOLE set of abilities, not just academic subjects. In my opinion, in high school, vocational education should be available widely and should be a well-respected choice.

As children progress through school age, they will appraise their abilities more and more. They begin forming an idea of the Self based on "metacognitive" means, which means they are able to look at a series of experiences as a whole. They will see themselves as "a gymnast" or "good at piano." And they will determine which area and how much effort they will expend to improve or whether they will change course. Parents are put in a difficult position in these skills decisions. If a child joins a team but faces frustration and wants to quit, parents must weigh the issue carefully and choose if it's more important to keep a commitment or acknowledge reality.

## SELF-CONCEPT – WHO AM I?

This chapter has so far focused on how the child develops a sense of Self based on acceptance, develops a sense of Self that is different from the Other, and creates a Self/Other balance. Further, we have covered how Self-Esteem and defensiveness figure in the Self-System, and how skills and abilities figure in Self-Creation. I saved the best for last. There is one more concept on the horizon that is critical in this Self category: the *"self-concept."* As discussed earlier, the development of the Self is a masterpiece which will take a lifetime to accomplish (4).

Again, "Who am I?" Sufficient brain/cognitive development is necessary for this process to occur (refer to the reflective Self noted in Chapters 1 and 6). As the brain develops, a child can differentiate themselves from others, see that others think differently, and learn that others are forming opinions of them. These processes are part of self-concept development.

As I have mentioned, the development of the Self is a lifetime task. You might even ask yourself on occasion, "Who Am I?" "How do I feel about myself?" The notion that we have opinions about ourselves is well-understood, and as parents the culmination of self-development in your child is likely to be a positive "self-concept." It may appear to be splitting hairs between a "Self" and a "Self-concept," but there is an important distinction. It is fairly easy to picture a child who has a healthy Self and loves themself. It is also possible to picture the opposite one who has an unhealthy Self yet loves themself: they are the narcissist. The self-concept, whether positive or negative, can be understood as critical to one's frame of mind and hence to one's general functioning. The healthy Self *knows* its strengths and its weaknesses, yet has an overall positive sense of itself. There are several personality theorists who have put self-concept at the center of their thinking, and I will delineate a few of their concepts.

In a book on personality theory, Hall and Lindzey (5) see "Self" as having two meanings: a person's attitudes and feelings about themself (self-concept) and a group of psychological processes which govern behavior of Self (6). Reflections on the nature of the reflective Self as mentioned in Chapters 1, 11, and 12, call it the Subjective Self, which is "What I am aware of in myself," and the Objective Self, which is "How others would describe me."

---

**MEANINGS OF SELF: Some Semantics**

**Self-Concept: A person's attitudes and feelings about himself**

**Self: A group of psychological processes which govern behavior**

---

Carl Rogers, noted theorist and therapist, (7) put the Self as central in his thinking about development. The entire personality is the individual's perception of themself. There exists a framework of interpersonal relationships in our inner world and our experience with others. The Self-concept develops as a result of interactions between the person and outer world. Once it is developed, it may accept or reject (by misinterpreting) perceptions in order to be consistent with the Self-concept. That is, an event may be perceived as either positive or negative depending on the frame of mind of the perceiver. There also is an "Ideal Self" which represents goals and aims, and motivates the individual to higher levels of functioning.

If a child develops a sense of themselves that is more on the positive side, they are better positioned to function positively in their endeavors. Conversely, if a more negative sense of Self is created, and doubts are present, that person may actually fail as a self-fulfilling prophecy.

Researcher Laura Berk sets forth milestones in how a child recognizes the Self (8).

## MILESTONES TO RECOGNIZE SELF

- **1 to 2 years:** A child can recognize their physical Self.

- **3 to 5 years:** The knowledge of the Self expands to what one likes and their typical emotions ("I have a dog." "I am a big brother.").

- **Preschoolers** cannot integrate two opposing characteristics such as nice/mean or happy/sad. They can think of just one thing at a time. "I am nice."

- **6 to 10 years:** The Self emphasizes personality traits and includes positive and negative attributes: "I like to read books." "I'm good at swimming." "I'm not good at soccer." "I'm nicer than my brother." Comparisons between the Self and others are seen.

- **11 years and older:** The Self-concept begins to include abstract descriptors that unify separate traits (e.g. "smart," "talented," and the like).

- With the onset of **pre-adolescence,** traits of positive virtues may be included such as "kind" and "fair" which will be combined into an organized system known as their personal identity, which will grow and develop over one's life.

- The notion that others have opinions about the Self ripens in adolescence sometimes to a ridiculous degree and becomes the most important issue in life!

This book will not cover adolescent years, but it should be mentioned that in adolescence the "True Self" begins to be developed. While younger children are not able to put themselves in other peoples' shoes and look at themselves from an outside perspective, adolescents do self-watching to a considerable extent. At this point, it might be called "self-consciousness" (9).

## SUMMARY OF PILLAR #3 (Chapters 11 & 12)

When you see your child developing, you might see physical accomplishments, increases in knowledge, or mastery of emotional issues, but do you see the Self? Knowing how this psychological phenomenon is developing may help you in parenting. Here are the key goals to encourage in your child(ren).

- Foster a Self/Other balance such that egocentrism is on the decline.
- Promote the ability to admit error and learn from experience.
- Build an emotional language.
- Build a Self-concept that is positive and free from negative labels.
- Foster Self-esteem that is realistic and not inflated.
- Help your child learn who they "are."

Knowing your child will be an adult who has and will continue to create a healthy Self will be your reward.

# Pillar #4

## TEACHING YOUR CHILD TO BE A MORAL PERSON

# Chapter 13

## Morality and Kind Behavior: Inborn or Taught?

### INTRODUCTION TO CONCEPTS OF MORALITY AND KINDNESS

Moral behavior belongs to a class of actions that "benefit the other." How do children learn to act in moral ways? Does it mean discerning right from wrong? Knowing which rules and norms of social behavior are important to follow? Does it mean faith in a religion? Over the years, children grow in their sense of which behaviors are "right," which are "wrong," and in their ability to censor their own behavior. Raising a moral child is tops on the list of desired attributes! Parents are keen to promote moral development and "right" acts.

Why is it important for parents to think about morality as you parent your children? The early years are a time in which various components of positive other-oriented behaviors emerge and develop. These components will form the foundation for children's moral and kind behavior. You may observe moments when your child demonstrates empathy and sympathy for another's plight or where you observe your child helping spontaneously. When you see this happen, register these moments as positive signs of moral development. If your child fails to demonstrate such, there may be cause for concern (1).

In addition to children learning what is on the parenting "good" list, a crucial sense of guilt or shame develops in young children. Children do not develop a conscience until ages six to seven. Psychological theories such as Freud's and Piaget's attempt to explain how this sense of *internal* standards evolves to allow a child to anticipate guilty consequences or experience regret for their own behavior which has slipped by the censoring mechanism. (This important issue will be covered in more detail later in this chapter and in Section IV, Ages and Stages.)

The topic of "morality" may be unfamiliar to most parents, so a bit of analysis will be presented at the outset. Then there will be a review of the important and interesting (in my opinion) points of how children develop standards of moral behavior. In the 1930s, Arnold Gesell, an American psychologist, and his team of researchers at the Yale Clinic of Child Development found that there are common moral behaviors based on particular ages. If parents see a moral lapse in their child, understanding these appropriate age-related morals will prevent them from worrying that their child might be a psychopath. It also helps knowing that only one percent of the population has this personality disorder (2).

Brain maturation and inborn characteristics are important. Also, various cultures have different "takes" on morality although there are some "universal truths." Psychology has studied what parent characteristics and actions tend to enhance moral development in children, and there has been some research on the role of religion in moral development.

Developing positive social behaviors such as *helping, giving, sharing, and rescuing* are also important goals for parents. This section will then differentiate the stronger "moral" imperatives from those positive social behaviors such as sharing, helping, and rescuing, which are categorized by psychologists as "prosocial." These behaviors will be labeled "kind." As parents wish their children to be kind, as well as moral, this chapter will also address psychological features of such, and parenting inputs that enhance such behaviors.

Morality can be explained as a set of *obligatory requirements for action to which everyone in a culture is supposed to adhere.* These moral directives and ethical norms must be preserved if our take on civilization is to survive. Right and wrong, virtue and sin, duty, discipline, punishment, justice, mercy, guilt, atonement, retribution, and salvation are all terms of morality. Compliance is mandatory for every person regardless of whether they want to accept them, and regardless of requirements of any other institutions such as law or etiquette. Another definition is given by Jonathan Haidt, an American social psychologist, (3) who defines moral systems as: "interlocking sets of values, practices, institutions, and evolved psychological mechanisms that work together to suppress or regulate selfishness and make social life possible." That's a bit wordy but, again, the focus is on the regulation of selfishness and the promotion of a social group. The assumption is that without moral restraint the world will go to the dogs (no insult meant for dogs).

We are dealing in broad concepts here, but it may be helpful to be more specific and list some areas that involve moral thinking. Elliot Turiel (4) divides morality into several forms: 1) harm versus care; 2) fairness and reciprocity; 3) group loyalty; 4) authority and respect; and 5) purity and sanctity.

You may have thought of religion as we discuss these values. Major religions do a good job in codifying actions that are considered "right" and "wrong." Judaism, Christianity, Islam, Buddhism, and Hinduism all prohibit behaviors such as harming, stealing, murder, and other "commandments." These codes may *not* be overridden by any non-moral requirement such as law or etiquette (5).

In addition, these religions share a code of "kind" conduct known as the "Golden Rule," which states that one should treat others in a manner in which one desires to be treated. Moral conduct and kindness differ in three ways.

- The first is that moral behavior is mainly made up of things you should NOT do whereas kind behaviors are actions.

- Secondly, kindness and consideration to others are important but do not have the gravity of "right" and "wrong." This "rule" *recommends* the positive social behaviors which we would love to see in our children. For example, helping others in need, sharing resources generously with others, or rescuing those in danger. Those behaviors are all desirable but not mandatory. You will not get in trouble with the law for failing to jump in a river to help a person or not stopping to help pick up groceries that have spilled on the sidewalk.
- Third, there is a big difference in how "bad" the behavior seems, and even preschoolers can tell the difference in "wrongness" between someone who has injured another or someone who has failed to help another child (Killen).

Despite how connected moral behavior and kind behavior may be, there is a difference between what is socially acceptable or non-acceptable and what is "wrong." How and why can this be clarified? What is the difference between a moral act and a conventional "kind" act? What difference does it make?

- Morality involves adjectives such as fair, unethical, wrong, and sinful. Examples are stealing, cheating, and seriously hurting others. Parents may react in horror if their child has stolen an item from a store or from them, has intentionally hurt another, has broken a promise, or has lied.
- Adjectives describing following social kindness norms would include inappropriate, inefficient, impractical, short-sighted, impolite; for example, not returning a greeting, not helping to pick up dropped items, or ignoring a hurt child.

Parents' reactions to these lapses of social convention would be less emotional; consequences would be less dire. When there is a transgression of a social convention, parents might supply reminders and a discussion of proper procedure. Also, if a child faces a situation where helpful behavior is expected like carrying some packages for a parent, and the child fails to help, parents may be disappointed, perhaps angry, but not horrified. When there is a transgression of a moral nature, a "negotiation" or argument is likely to ensue about who did what to whom. Children are likely to deny the act, or try to re-define it to appear innocent. Punishing consequences for behavior will be more serious.

"Why did she pinch Claire?" "Because Claire wouldn't let Susie play." versus "Why didn't Tom share his toy?" "Because it was still his turn." In your dealings with your child, you will naturally distinguish what is immoral versus what is a failure to conform to social norms of helpfulness. It is helpful for parents to distinguish between a moral breach and a failure to act in kind ways. Parents need to react seriously to the immoral, but not necessarily react in the same way to breaches of social convention or helping behavior.

A slightly different code is present for helpful or rescue behaviors, the absence of which may not be considered immoral but, if lacking, would be a breach of expected behavior. For example, if a child's friend has fallen, and the child does not act to help, that would be a lapse of the code of kindness.

In line with differentiating the seriousness of lapses, studies have found that children ages four to six have an intuitive moral competence in how they distinguish moral from social-conventional transgressions. For example, they can easily differentiate between the acts of throwing paint at another child versus not cleaning up their own mess (Smetana).

How do we learn to raise moral and kind children? You, of course, want your children to know right from wrong and to act in moral and kind ways. Religion took the first big step in defining what is right and wrong, but psychology only recently began looking at the how's and why's of behavior that benefits another.

## HOW DID PSYCHOLOGY GET INVOLVED?

Modern Psychology became involved in the study of morality in the 1960s by virtue of a very sad and tragic event. If you were alert and aware during this time, you may recall an incident where a young woman named Kitty Genovese in New York City was attacked on the street and loudly screamed for help. To the horror of the country, no one in the heavily populated neighborhood responded to her screams. It was then dubbed "the bystander effect," and later "Moral Psychology" emerged as a field of study. In a brief summary, the reason for the inaction was determined to be the assumption that someone else is more qualified to help; fear of embarrassment led onlookers to be inactive. When there was a clearly qualified person in sight, such as a medical professional, others deferred to that person who stepped in to help (6).

You may note that the rescue behavior does not exactly belong in the moral category as we defined above, but the only way psychologists can study morality, the difference between right and wrong, is through hypothetical questions which evoke reasoning from the subject. Moral events just aren't available for scientific study. However, kindness behaviors, including contrived rescue scenarios, have been areas of study since the 1960s.

The Genovese tragedy underlined an absence of action in a situation which required some risk to the helping individual. These types of acts like jumping into a river to rescue someone were labeled "altruism." This type of labeling muddies the water of morality and kindness even more. Let's clarify.

## CLARITY ON MORALITY, KINDNESS, & ALTRUISM

The term "morality" has many connotations, and when psychologists became involved, the terms used made things even more confusing. Kind behaviors became known as "prosocial" because those actions benefit others.

"Altruism" was then defined for when people risked their own safety or health to aid another with *no* anticipation of reward or reciprocal behavior. Examples of altruism would be: rescuing a drowning person, taking an injured stranger to a hospital; actions where you really stick your neck out to be a "Good Samaritan" (7).

As the field expanded, psychologists began studying various aspects of children's behavior intended to benefit another. These behaviors are subsumed under the term "kindness" in this book. (Parents cannot be expected to exhort their child to "be prosocial!" but rather "be kind!") Thus, we have "altruism," "kind behaviors," and "morality.")

## IS MORALITY INBORN OR TAUGHT? AND A BIT ABOUT RELIGION

Before we tackle the issue of inborn morality, the subject of religion needs to be addressed. Theologians and philosophers, as well as those who study culture, debate whether humanity is imbued with "evil" with aggressive and territory-seeking tendencies, or whether human nature is more characterized by "good" with kindness and behaviors that benefit the Other. (For a lengthy discussion, refer to the *Humankindness* book by Bregman cited in Chapter 7.) The old Greeks, Plato, Aristotle and their ilk, debated the subject of whether the human race is innately "good" or "evil." Major religions make this subject a key part of their beliefs.

- Christians believe innate evil came from the fall from grace of Adam and Eve.
- Judaism and Islam do not believe in innate evil.
- Buddhism/Hinduism believes evil is present, but changeable with reincarnation.

There remain two arguments on whether moral sense is inborn or whether all moral behavior is learned. If inborn, morality would then be brain-based or hard-wired, and would presuppose that people are "good." Learned morality presupposes the inborn tendency is "evil." If the latter is correct, parents have the task of building a moral and kind child. Therefore, whatever you show, model, coach, or exhort them about "right" behavior, your child will demonstrate the results. And if the child goes "wrong" you have failed in your duty. But is this the case?

It is interesting to note that as early as the late fourth century BCE, both Chinese and Greek philosophers wrote arguments in favor of an innate predisposition to morality. They claimed that all humans were predisposed to a sense of right and wrong, along with empathy, a sense of shame, respect for others/rules, and that underlying moral issues such as care/harm, fairness/cheating, loyalty/betrayal, authority/subversion, sanctity/degradation, and liberty/oppression are universal (Haidt). But commonalities in moral issues do not mean that they are brain-based, or hard-wired. Is there evidence to support the notion that the brain contains some inborn moral tendency?

## Animal Studies

The study of animals has shed some light on the issue. Are human brains the only ones capable of "morality?" Animal research has demonstrated that monkeys can judge a fair from unfair reward. Researchers gave monkeys better or worse rewards for lever pressing, and the monkey with the less tasty reward quickly became belligerent and viciously upset. They understood they were being treated unfairly. Even the monkey who was "over-rewarded" was aware of the difference, and acted in ways to indicate confusion or upset (8). This finding (check YouTube for a Ted Talk and video that is amazing) suggests that (at least) monkeys have a sense of fairness, and that it hasn't been taught.

## Brain Chemistry

Studying the brain's responses to moral situations, researchers have found chemicals that are related to generosity. For example, vasopressin has been found to be present in greater quantities in humans who act more kindly. Dopamine and oxytocin receptors have been found to be more plentiful in a group which behaved more positively to others (9).

In addition, there are studies of how the brain responds to moral questions. Researchers present subjects with a moral dilemma, and their brain activity is measured with a brain scan. Harbaugh and others found certain circuits in the brain activated after people engaged in charitable giving. Also, a certain area of the brain was found to be activated when persons were deciding about whether or not to help or be kind in a prosocial event (10).

## Infant Studies

There are findings in the study of infants that suggest that there may be some inborn tendencies to think morally and/or to act kindly. We have all observed "contagious" crying in infants, which is a behavior that has been interpreted as showing the beginnings of empathy. Experiments have found that infants will cry to others' cries but not to sounds similar in other respects. This behavior is not taught (11).

In more recent years, infant studies show some fascinating results. A series of experiments by Paul Bloom (12) where babies aged nine to twelve months old were shown short "plays" of puppets either being aggressive or helpful/kind to each other. Babies looked longer at the "nice" guys. Again, you have to admit there is no opportunity for teaching at this age. Also, J.K. Hamlin developed a series of puppet plays exhibiting one puppet helping another open a box and one of the puppets slamming the lid closed. Preferences were measured by visual tracking or reaching if they were old enough. Of 215 six-month-old infants shown the scenarios, 179 preferred to look at the helper (13).

By twelve months, you may have noticed that babies can be helpful communicators, pointing to a location of something for which another is searching. By fourteen-eighteen months, they will help pick up objects dropped by adults. Perhaps this behavior has been observed by children, and is not inborn, but perhaps it is (14).

We might conclude from this body of research that experience and socialization are not alone in guiding moral development and that inborn predispositions may guide our children on a moral path. These interesting studies provide parents with a notion that perhaps there is some factor possibly helping you in this direction.

## Necessary Components in Moral/Kind Behavior

Morality includes various dimensions. In addition to the cognitive ability to figure out that other people exist, emotions of empathy and sympathy are needed to develop the all-important *conscience* and the ability to feel guilt.

## Empathy and Sympathy

What happens when you witness a person in distress? Normally your adrenalin starts rushing and unless you are too shocked to think clearly, you will decide whether to act. The immediate impact of others' negative emotions like pain, shock, grief, or fear is a result of our sense of empathy, labeled a "moral emotion." You observe this effect in your children in situations when they see another in distress.

- *Empathy* seems to result when the individual feels the SAME as the one in distress.
- *Sympathy* results when there is some differentiation between the Self and the Other.

To what extent these emotions are inborn or learned is under question, but they remain as a factor in determining whether any behavior will result from thoughts. It is the *emotional* component that motivates the feeling of empathy or sympathy. However, it is not guaranteed that an individual will act accordingly.

Laboratory situations in social psychological experiences with children of various ages have presented the child with the sounds of a child's distress in an adjacent room. Preschoolers and older children typically react to another child's distress with both sympathy and attempts to help. Toddler-age children may be fearful in an unfamiliar situation and may lack resources to help another in an unknown distress. However, in real-life situations, even toddlers are observed to respond in ways to help others who are crying or distressed. As stated earlier, infants can feel distressed when they feel anxiety of others.

Clearly, empathy and sympathy are important contributors to moral behavior. However, the child's intellectual capacities are necessary. How children *think* about moral issues will be covered in the following section.

## Guilt

The all-important feeling of guilt and how it develops in ages 6-7 will be covered in the following chapter and in Chapter 25.

# Chapter 14

## How Morality Develops in Children and When There are Lapses

### INTRODUCTION

The previous chapter covered emotional aspects of morality; there is an intellectual component to being a moral person as well. How children *think* about a situation will determine whether and how they respond do it.

### HISTORY OF THE SUBJECT

Initially, in the 1930s, children's thinking about moral issues began to be studied. You are already familiar with the name of Piaget, who studied how children gained knowledge. Early in his career, he wrote the book, *The Moral Judgment of the Child* (1), where he described interviews with children who were presented with "moral problems." He presented "stories" of children who lied to test if his subjects could determine if the behavior was wrong. He found that children were aware of many different motives to lie. Some gave simple exaggerations due to fear, or told a lie due to desire for importance, or lied with intent to deceive in order to get candy or avoid punishment. Children evaluated the stories based on "naughtiness" (his word, or at least the translator's). Another example of a "moral issue" was his question, "Why shouldn't you cheat in a game?" Children were asked to determine which child was more at fault by virtue of rules, punishment, authority, equality, intention, and reciprocity. Another prompt for reasoning was asking a child what they thought about a parent giving the biggest piece of cake to the most obedient child. This activity was called "moral reasoning."

Piaget organized his findings into two stages, the sequence of which never varies, despite some children passing into them more rapidly or slowly than others. The first is children younger than seven or eight years old, **Preoperational morality** (heteronymous), where children guide their thoughts along "the rules."

- Justice is whatever authority commands.
- Rules are givens, external to the mind, inflexible and unchangeable.
- Wrongdoers will be punished.
- There is absolute right and absolute wrong.

The second stage, **Autonomous morality**, is seen around age ten.

- Since the child has had more peer interactions, they develop a sense of fairness where equality takes priority over authority in matters of distribution of goods or privilege.
- Rules and laws are created by people.
- Intentions should be considered.
- The child can deduce which punishment fits which crime, that is, fairness.

In the 1960s, partly as a response to the Genovese tragedy, American psychologist Lawrence Kohlberg expanded Piaget's thinking about how children think about moral issues (for both theorists, stages of thought are similar across cultures and imply a brain-based inborn pattern) (2). Kohlberg proposed there are three levels of moral development with each level split into two substages.

## Stage 1 – *Preconventional* – up to age 6 or 7 years

Concern for others is motivated by wanting to be liked by others.

- Substage #1 – Right and wrong are defined by what they get punished for.
- Substage #2 – Right and wrong are determined by doing what others want.

## Stage 2 – *Concrete Operations* – begins at 7 or 8 years old

By virtue of increased peer interest and interaction, the child develops a moral sense. Kohlberg called this stage "*Conventional Morality*" and found that most teens and adults function in this manner.

- Substage #1 – Child begins to accept social rules; authority is internalized but not questioned. The child behaves according to rules in order to get approval from others.
- Substage #2 – Child becomes aware of society's wider rules, so obeying is done to uphold the law.

## Stage 3 – *Post-Conventional* – begins in pre-teen years (ages 11-12)

Complex thinking about morality begins. Equality dominates and extenuating circumstances such as motivations, intentions, and mitigating circumstances are used in making moral judgments. The pre-teen begins to develop concepts of justice as a product of cooperation, reciprocity, and understanding the other's point of view. There is realization that laws exist for the good of the greatest number, but at times the law (a social contract) will work against the individual and may need to be broken to achieve moral rectitude. A small percentage (10-15%) of adults may develop into the substage of Universal Principles where one develops their own set of moral guidelines, which may or may not fit the law. Human rights, justice, and equality are paramount.

## Justice and Fairness

In addition to thinking about "right and wrong," some psychologists broke ground in studying how young children understand the concept of justice or fairness. In the previous section, we learned that animals can demonstrate an understanding of fairness in distribution of resources. Also, children as young as three or four seem to understand how to resolve competing claims between peers. American psychologist Robert Selman and psychology professor Diane Byrne (3) reported three stages of justice understanding:

- The child wants what they want and tries to get it.
- The child is obligated to recognize demands of others.
- The child identifies a resolution of how to define the rights and claims of both the Self and Others.

The fact that very young children seem to "know" the principle supports the presence of some inborn tendency. Of course, learning and experience will have played a part, too (4).

Is just thinking about morality and justice enough? Does just thinking about it lead to moral and just behavior? Or doesn't it? One might assume they are one and the same, but they are not. Knowing what is right and wrong is necessary but not sufficient for there to be moral action. In fact knowledge can contribute to some immoral consequences as below:

- One can be clever in understanding others and may be devious and "immoral" in using that information.

- One with good social understanding may manipulate an individual for their own (immoral) gain.
- Just because we know the principles of morality and think about them, does not mean that we act and behave accordingly.

Some studies have examined the reasoning skills of juveniles who have been on the other side of the law. Although their understanding of others' viewpoints is at the level expected for their age, their moral reasoning is lower than peers (5).

Thus, thinking about good and evil can be used for good or evil. No level of cognition or reasoning, no matter how advanced, bears an obligation to use it in the service of justice. A sense of obligation must be present to engage in moral acts. The obligation is the presence of conscience.

## Conscience

The development of a "conscience" is one of the more important landmarks in child development and a critical component of morality. It is a means by which one feels *guilty* and punishes oneself if one has violated an internal standard. This psychological mechanism is opposed to "shame," which is a bad feeling stemming from violating an external standard and being judged by others.

This complex process was analyzed by Freud and will be explained in detail in the Ages and Stages section. In brief, Freud theorizes that beginning at ages four to five years old, a child evaluates their place in the world. When they understand that they are not in a place of power, they "identify" with adult norms, and internalize them, accepting the values promoted by adults/parents as their own. Freud calls this process "identification." Freud theorized that as a child changes how they see their position in the world (lower than parents), they acquire their conscience.

Once the conscience is present, some religions begin to hold children responsible for their behavior, i.e. they are capable of "sin."

Some religions hold rites to commemorate the advance. Catholic Christianity and some interpretations of Islam mark seven years old as the age of moral responsibility. First Communion for Catholic children is at age seven. Muslim children in African countries have a ceremony called "writing on the hand" at age seven, which also signals the age at which they can be held responsible for their behavior (6).

Now that we have learned a bit about brain development, cultural aspects, and components of morality, let's take a look at the types of moral behaviors typically seen as children grow.

## THE PROGRESSION OF MORAL BEHAVIORS IN CHILDREN

So, your child's brain is maturing and they are able to think about what is right and what is wrong. How do we get from this thought to action? Can they talk the talk? And if so, will they walk the walk in terms of behavior? Which behaviors related to morality will you see, and when? (In Section IV, Ages and Stages, expectations by age are provided for what you may see in your child's moral development.)

I should re-emphasize that children have become smarter over the past century (yes, it has been almost 100 years) by acquiring more intellectual skills sooner; and as such, age standards from the 1930s may be woefully out of date (Flynn). But the sequence of learning those skills will be the same. Please use a grain of salt for the exact ages, but follow and apply more of the progression in "moral maturity."

## PSYCHOLOGICAL RESEARCH ON HOW THE FAMILY AFFECTS MORAL DEVELOPMENT

Psychologists have performed many experimental tests of what sorts of experiences lead a child to perform kind behaviors such as helping, generosity, and responding to distress of others. They have also examined which experiences produce higher levels of "moral reasoning" using Kohlberg's measures (Kohlberg). A Psychology "lab" provides children with the same experience where E (Experimenter) follows a set protocol and measures how the Subjects (S) differ on one variable such as donating, helping, or rescuing behavior. The Subject (S) is observed and the variable measured.

## The Role of a Nurturant, Warm Family Atmosphere

One major finding in many correlational studies (Mussen Berg, Carlo) is that a nurturant, warm relationship is positively associated with children's helping behaviors. Parental "control," which is the way parents set limits and discourage behavior that is undesirable, is also a factor. Both harsh and punitive ways of "control" as well as lack of setting limits do *not* tend to produce helpful children; rather child-rearing practices that some have called "authoritative" like setting limits with firm but not harsh input are related to kinder children (refer to Chapter 8). Parental practices of warmth and nurturance *without* effective limit setting (i.e. permissive) does *not* relate to increased helping behavior (Mussen, Henry, Eisenberg).

Measured by interview and self-report, parental values of sympathy, valuing kindness, honesty, helpfulness, and loyalty to the family corresponds to greater production of kind behavior in the lab.

## Parents as Role Models

Role modeling by adult family members is the chief way that moral behavior is taught to children. Do you talk the talk, or walk the walk? It goes without saying that when a family contributes as a whole to a voluntary effort, such as a food drive, or serving meals to the homeless, there is a tremendous impact on children. Also, parents need to be aware of how children view their own behavior by demonstrating honesty, keeping promises, not lying to children, differentiating when a lie is acceptable ("white lies"), and treating others fairly. If a family demonstrates or accepts immoral behaviors such as lying, breaking promises, or dishonesty, these factors would lead to children's lapses in moral behavior. This is common sense. Even so, it's still ok to tell your aunt you like the pajamas she gave you.

Acceptance of one's own faults/mistakes and the ability to apologize is also taught in the family by example. In my experience with family therapy, children with the problem of lying about misbehavior would be helped by parents showing them how to apologize and doing so in front of them. Some people can't apologize by virtue of their personality make-up, and this problem will be visited on their progeny.

Lab experiments have verified the importance of role modeling. Children seeing examples and hearing about the positive nature of kind behavior in the lab are encouraged to imitate the behavior. For example, children perform a problem-solving task which earns them money or candy. Then they hear the E speak about how important it is to donate or to contribute to the lives of children in need. Those hearing the statements donate/contribute more. Children observing a "stingy" model tend to donate less.

Helpfulness is also measured by whether a child helps an E who "drops" a box of paper clips. The friendliness of the E also affects the level of donating/helping. One set of experiments had children observe an E in a lab performing kind acts. Subsequent behaviors such as children's donations to "needy" children, writing cheery letters to hospitalized children, helping an E pick up "spilled" items, and sharing something with an E increases at least temporarily. Some experiments saw these behaviors last at least two weeks. The assumption here is that if the family communicates the same values, the children will respond by acting more helpfully (7).

These lab experiments focus on kindness behavior, but what about children's reasoning skills? Research found an important factor in how parents handle their children's moral "lapses." Higher levels of moral reasoning are related to the degree that parents "discuss" a moral infraction. Discussion may include various aspects: pointing out what was wrong about the behavior, consequences of their behavior on others including the parent, helping the child to confess to wrongdoing, coaching resistance to temptation, helping with an apology, making reparations. By taking the time to "teach" a lesson, parents are demonstrating their own commitment to moral values. This parenting strategy is role modeling at its best (Staub).

## Family Helping Behaviors

A factor that may help to understand cultural differences in positively oriented social behavior is the degree to which children are expected to perform certain tasks in the household. American anthropologists Beatrice Whiting and John M. Whiting found that children in cultures where they had major responsibilities in performing chores related to taking care of younger siblings were more helpful in the lab than children in cultures where there were fewer opportunities for such. In studies of Western cultures, older siblings, who most probably had opportunities to care for younger ones, showed more helping behavior when they heard sounds of distress (8).

Back to the Genovese tragedy, some lab situations set up "distress cries" from an adjoining room when the S is alone or with other children, and the S's reaction is measured. A variety of factors relate to responses: the age of the S, number of children present, whether one child has been singled out as responsible for the group, and information of rules of what behavior is permissible and appropriate. When children are deemed "responsible," and when they know that they are not breaking any rules by leaving the lab situation, rescue behavior increases. When they see an E also show concern for distress, rescue behavior also increases. Similar research with adults presented with a distress situation in their environment found similar findings, where the S was deemed responsible by either being alone or by specialized training such as medical.

Whether behavior observed in the lab showing influences of role modeling and instruction has bearing on real life behavior is a question. However, the connection between authoritative parenting techniques, strength of parental values, role modeling of positive other-oriented behaviors, and discussion of moral issues is not a lab one; it's in real life, and has implications for how parents teach their children about this issue.

## OTHER CHARACTERISTICS OF KIND CHILDREN

We have covered some family inputs that encourage a disposition to prosocial behavior such as role modeling, pertinent discussion of issues, parents' expectations, and early assignment of responsibility for others. Many issues remain to be examined including child participation in family decisions, restrictiveness of "rules," and the role of religion in the family. Generally speaking, prosocial behaviors increase significantly with age from four to thirteen. Gender may play a role with girls being more prosocial than boys in certain situations, and no differences in level of family social class.

There have been no clear-cut patterns found in lab studies that moral behavior is affected by family size. However, in naturalistic observations of various cultures, children who have no siblings and are the youngest children tend to seek more help and attention for themselves because of their egoistic behavior.

What about personality traits? Those children who are more active, stand up for themselves more readily, are more outgoing, and express anger more easily have tended to be more generous with donations and more willing to help someone in distress. The presence of the trait of anger/aggression is an interesting issue. One might surmise that children who rise easily to anger would be less likely to be helpful to others. However, at the older end of the age range, a "chip on the shoulder" or awareness of others' suffering might impel a person to be an activist or advocate for social causes. Anger *can* be put to good use.

In general, children who have qualities like those listed below are thought to be raised with good adjustment and are more likely to act in kind ways.

- Ability to delay gratification (considered to be an index of self-control/ego/strength)
- Resilient and can recover easily after a stressful situation
- Confident, self-assured, and satisfied with peer relationships
- Expressive and active

In sum, those children who act more helpful and generous tend to be emotionally better adjusted (Mussen & Eisenberg-Berg). Some studies have found that the presence of both guilt and shame in a child relates to more kind and moral behavior (9). But what happens when guilt and shame are not adequate to stop a moral transgression? At some point, parents will face such a lapse in a child's morality sooner or later.

## IDENTIFYING MORAL TRANSGRESSIONS

Handling a child's failure to clean his/her room is a walk in the park compared to handling moral lapses. With moral transgression comes some of the most difficult moments in parenting. What do parents do when their child has been caught doing something the child knows is wrong like stealing, sexual exploration/exploitation, deliberately hurting other persons, or destroying property? It is impossible to catalog all moral lapses, but you know it when you see it and you are likely to react strongly. Of course, age must be taken into consideration, as the child below five may not understand what "wrong" is.

To catalog the nature of immoral behavior, the Catholic religion has described seven "deadly" sins and their opposite seven virtues. Some of the sins are well-known, such as anger, lust, and jealousy, alongside their moral opposites are the virtues such as apologizing, making up for losses (reparations), and forgiveness and mercy for those who have wronged them.

| SINS | VIRTUES |
|------|---------|
| Pride | Humility |
| Greed | Generosity |
| Lust | Chastity |
| Anger | Patience |
| Gluttony | Temperance |
| Envy | Charity |
| Laziness | Diligence |

Similar to setting rules and punishment for misbehaving, the parent sets the same for committing moral infractions. But handling a moral lapse calls into play everything the parent has in their values and skills packet. Creativity, calmness, and fairness are important qualities to use in these situations.

Parents are faced with a decision as to how to handle a transgression by verbal reprimand, loss of privileges, physical punishment, or by means specifically tailored to the infraction. Helping children face their behavior is an important role for parents. Religion helps in some cases. Catholic children practice reconciliation with the priest after age seven. Jewish children learn to atone for wrongs each year on the day of Yom Kippur, in which the participant is expected to make amends with those people who they wronged and then ask for forgiveness from God. Other children will face humiliation when forced to apologize. None of it is easy no matter what the age.

## LAPSES IN KIND BEHAVIOR

Every family will have its own standards of what it means to be kind and polite. Parents may need to force the issue to share, in young children, when appropriate to "make" the child share, or praise a child's spontaneous kind behavior when they see it. Praising for kind acts induces more kind behavior. Children are more likely to feel "important" and such feeling motivates behavior.

When there is a failure to act in accordance with parental standards, research recommends that parents discuss the lapse, and use reasoning as to why it is important to be kind or moral. Principles of generosity, reciprocity, obligation, and reparation (making things right) are at play here.

- "Our family helps others when they need it; helping each other makes a good world."
- "You have many blessings, and it is important to 'give back' to those who don't have what you have."
- "We all help each other; when you need help, someone will help you."
- "When you don't act nicely, perhaps you won't get help. What goes around comes around."

## HANDLING BIG INFRACTIONS OF MORAL BEHAVIOR: HARMING OTHERS, SHOPLIFTING, AND SEX EXPLORATION

Moral transgressions are likely to happen in a child's life, and parents are put in a position to make an important decision about how to stop the child's behavior once and for all. First, hurting others and damage to property may not always fall under the immoral category, but there may be incidents where the degree of harm or destruction borders on the criminal. There is a wide range of types of intentional harm to others like hitting another person, arranging a piece of furniture to fall on another, and a range of serious property damage, including setting things on fire.

Small infractions are dealt with in usual punishment situations. However, intentionally harming another where major injury is intended or destroying significant property would be considered a moral lapse and would signal the possibility of emotional disturbance. Reparations for property damage follow the same guidelines for any such incident as mentioned in the chapter on punishment. Children must either pay for or perform some work to replace/repair the damaged item.

Secondly, stealing from stores or family members is such a common occurrence in five-and-a-half year-olds that Gesell and Francis mention it in the list of usual behaviors. Stealing is a "fun" behavior and must be stopped entirely. When I taught pediatrics residents from various parts of the world (Africa, India, South America, etc.), my students related incidents when they were caught stealing from stores and had to return the item to the shopkeeper and apologize. This technique seems to be universal in Western and non-Western cultures. It is the only time that I can think of when humiliation and embarrassment is used to deter future "crimes." It usually works! Suitable severe punishments, including physical, may also be needed to provide a deterrent.

In my experience as a family therapist, when a child stole, I became a moralizing agent using words such as "thief" and "crime" and "prison." Of course, I received the parents' permission to do so. These stern words coming from someone outside the family helped to deter future incidents.

Some parents may avoid punishing the shoplifter out of fear of their own embarrassment. "I don't want anyone to know that my child did something so wrong!" Or they may excuse it; "He's just a young child who doesn't know better." If a parent lacks the (moral) strength to confront this behavior, it may result in children who do not develop the self-control necessary for "good" behavior in this regard.

Third, children playing with others using genitals is common in early childhood but has moral implications when it is seen in children older than five or six years old. Curiosity about sexual "private" parts whether in the same or in the opposite sex is natural in children, and Gesell catalogs it as a normal developmental progression. Parents usually handle it carefully so as not to cast it as "horrible" and lead to hang-ups about sexuality. This sex-play activity is also "fun" as it satisfies normal curiosity, and touching can be pleasurable. But if it persists in later childhood, it would be considered immoral as it harms another, even if the other is consenting, as it crosses the respect boundary. Children requesting to see others' genitalia, touching, or offering candy or inducements to "see" others are loose cannons and are going down a very damaging path. Once the child is identified, they will quickly become the neighborhood "pariah" and shunned by others. When such behavior occurs, parents deliver stern warnings not to touch or show "private parts." Because it is "fun," it is necessary to implement a stern treatment, such as increased supervision of play, and strong punishment. Even physical punishment may be needed to provide the deterrent and to build an internal sense that such behavior is "wrong." (Appendix A will present more information about the issue of physical punishment). Professional help may be needed when children persist in this behavior especially if there is a pronounced difference in power between the two children, such as age or size.

## OTHER MORAL VALUES OF APOLOGY, MERCY, FORGIVENESS, AND USING FAIR JUDGMENT – REPARATIONS

We have covered the importance of the ability to admit error in Chapters 11 and 12. When a child intentionally hurts another physically or verbally or damages another's property, parents will frequently insist on an apology as part of the punishment. These behaviors may not fall into the moral category, but in my opinion, the apology is such an important part of development. The forced apology is a very important part where a child must at least look like they are taking responsibility for his/her own behavior. This "lesson-learning" part of parenting is essential for overall development. Parents will set the tone for apologizing by doing it themselves. Again, role modeling by parents is the best way a child learns that apologies are integral to moral life.

In terms of mercy and forgiveness, parents also will be role models of their values toward fellow humans, in the hope their children will emulate them. For example, when a child has had property damaged by another child, and the offending child apologizes, parents will prompt the child to accept the apology and forgive. As mentioned above, if the child has done the damage, an apology will not be enough, and parents will set appropriate "reparations."

# Chapter 15

## Religion and Santa Claus as They Relate to Morality

### INTRODUCTION

No discussion of morality would be complete without some mention of religion. This chapter will cover what psychologists have learned about how religion affects morality. The addition of information about Santa Claus is to give you parents some tips about a very common (annual) issue that is meant to enhance the holiday experience but that also may cause some concern.

### THE ROLE OF RELIGION IN TEACHING MORALITY

Religion is a controversial subject, but its role in influencing moral behavior and kind behavior should be noted. Families will choose if, what kind, and how much religion will be practiced in their family. Religion rarely gets noticed in psychological studies. Psychologists take a position of "neutrality" whereby no judgment is made on who defines issues of good or evil but rather pursue understanding of what leads to moral behavior. Parents, however, frequently choose to make religion a part of family life to various degrees.

Faith is different from religion. Faith is a belief, and religion is the way the belief is practiced. Morality is definitely associated with religious faith as the code of ethics and morality is written down in texts such as the Bible or the Koran. In Eastern religions, selflessness is a tenet of Taoist and Buddhist beliefs. As discussed earlier, most religions identify similar "wrong" behaviors (stealing, murder, greed, etc.) and many also command adherents to treat others as they would wish to be treated ("The Golden Rule"). So, kindness is also commanded! A question remains whether lapses of kindness would be considered sins, but this book is not about theology, so we won't consider it further.

You parents who espouse religion can refer to those moral codes as defined in religious texts to encourage and enforce appropriately moral behavior. And you have the advantage of a deity as the enforcer—God, Allah, Brahma—on your side. Also, moral transgressions are defined as "sin" or going against the deity, which is a stronger way of putting "wrong" behavior. As mentioned above, in many religions, Buddhism, Hinduism, Islam, Christianity, or Judaism, behavior has "eschatological" consequences. This fancy word means what you do can affect your life after death. Heaven and Hell are concepts which involve great reward or punishment depending on behavior; karma and reincarnation are after effects of living a "right" or "wrong" life. Good karma means the soul will come back in a "better" form of life (or worse, God forbid).

The extent to which faith/religion is a part of family life, including and especially child-rearing, is an important decision made by parents. Organized religion is a cornerstone of spiritual community and culture around the world. Many believe that religion fosters morality. But is faith in a deity necessary to being a moral person? Which religion or faith does one choose? If organized religion is chosen, how much participation in the religion is optimal for developing a moral sense in your child?

# RELIGION AND THE FAMILY

Families may define religion in many ways; there is a religion for every type of psychological make-up. Some religions define in-group and out-group as essential and shun participation with anyone who is not of their religious choosing. On the other hand, children may be raised by parents who define all persons as equal in dignity; thus, humanity transcends religious beliefs. And there is everything in between.

Emphasis on "sin" and "punishment" in a home would more than likely result in a less than warm and nurturant atmosphere; how does the family structure affect a child's tendency to be moral and kind? Parents make the decision as to what extent the family will follow a faith tradition, and your decision will be based on family tradition, personal beliefs, and the creed of the religious organization. Your children may or may not be included in the decision. Whatever the family belief system, participation or non-participation in religious life is an important decision. Once a path is chosen, then children's participation is decided whether to attend religious services, religious school, or religious instruction on weekends.

Should children be forced to attend religious events when they are not interested? One hears of anti-religious adults who as children "hated going" to church or synagogue or mosque. In some cases, children will want to attend, but in others there may be "push back." Children left to their own devices may not choose to participate in religious events, but parents' decision trumps all. One of my contacts "forced" her children to participate in the church for the main reason that she wanted them to know that in times of distress, the church and its clergy can be a source of comfort and help. I think that is a particularly good reason among others, as when life and death issues pop up, people turn to faith and religion.

It should be emphasized that formal religious training is not the same as the moral training that parents provide in life situations;

children can be moral citizens despite a lack of belief in religious dogma.

## WHAT RESEARCH TELLS US ABOUT MORALITY, KINDNESS, AND RELIGION

Family decisions about participation in formal religion are made on the basis of the belief that religion fosters morality, and that children will be "good people" as a result. But is this the case? Kind behaviors such as generosity, helpfulness, and rescue have been measured in the lab to see if they are associated with religion in the family. The most favored format to study religion and kindness in the lab is to examine children's donations to a child in need. Children "earn" some money from a task and then are given the option to give to a "needy" charity. Another design has been for the child to draw some pictures for a "child in the hospital." Measures are how many tokens or money is donated, or how many pictures are drawn. Religiousness (or religiosity, as some call it) is generally measured by parents filling out a questionnaire about their participation in religious events and their belief system.

There is a mixed body of research on this subject which may surprise you. The first study was published in 2008 by John P. Bartkowski, Ph.D. sociology professor (1), where researchers looked at religion and several dimensions of psychological development and social adjustment in early childhood. Many positive aspects of behavior were associated with the increased presence of religion in the household; however, when there was conflict between parents about religion, those effects were absent (2).

In 2015, research in a lab setting involving 1,000 children of varying religions ages five to twelve in six different countries, showed that families who stressed religious upbringing yielded children who were *less* generous. Children from the US, Canada, Jordan, Turkey, South Africa, and China were given the opportunity to share with others. Younger children were less likely to share than older; children from wealthier social classes shared more, but the tendency of religious households was that children shared *less*. Christian and Muslim children were studied separately, and findings held up in both religions. The more religion in the home, the less sharing went on. The authors proposed that on the continuum of "religiousness" where intolerance and harsh punishment for children were present in more "religious" families, kindness toward others (more in-group emphasis) would be compromised. And the opposite end of the religion continuum, which emphasized tolerance and understanding, would support kindness (3).

Further drama ensued regarding this study. In a rare instance, criticism of how the country of origin factored in their data analysis led the authors to re-analyze the data and retract the article in 2019. But the re-analysis did not affect the findings about more religion predicting less sharing.

In a study which looked at donation behavior in Jewish children in Israel, researchers divided second and fifth graders into religious and nonreligious groups. Religious children shared more, but *only* when the recipient was described as "needy" or as they termed "poor." Sensitivity to poverty was present by age six. Older children shared more (4). These researchers replicated this study with Christian Arab children in Israel and found the same results. When the "recipient" was described as "needy," the more religion present in the household was associated with more sharing behavior (5).

Bartkowski continued his work in this area (6). In a 2019 study, he used data from the same longitudinal study of third graders. Measures were 1) parents' religiousness; 2) children's psychological adjustment including interpersonal skills and problem behaviors; and 3) performance on standardized tests of academic skills. Households were divided into religious and nonreligious households. The more religion in this study, the *better* adjustment and social skills were shown by the children. However, in families which were very "religious," children tended to perform *lower* in academic areas, particularly in math and science.

The authors did not look at various denominations and stated: "Some religious groups may more effectively balance soft skill development and academic excellence than others." Regrettably, our data set does not inquire about denominational affiliation, so we cannot say if children from Catholic, Protestant, Mormon, Muslim, or other denominational backgrounds are especially likely to strike the delicate balance between social psychological development and academic excellence. Bartkowski commented that emphasizing moral codes tends to instill values of self-control and to aid in developing positive social relations.

I would like to emphasize that these studies do not recommend one type of religion over another; nor do they specify when religious effects become harmful to the development of kindness behavior. So, parents get to decide what "religion" means to you. Also, religion in the household does not automatically instill moral behavior. That you have to do as well.

The Christian religion has led to an issue where parents' willingness to suspend truth and reality is challenged. That issue to be covered next is Santa Claus!

## THE MORALITY OF BELIEF IN IMAGINARY CULTURAL ICONS LIKE SANTA

During childhood, there are several holidays and important events in life when parents commonly participate in something that is a tradition—lying to your children. Santa Claus, the Easter Bunny, and the Tooth Fairy are parts of the culture that are pervasive. Parents have an important decision to make: either commit to the myths or survive in a culture in which it is deeply ingrained. We'll look at this phenomenon through Santa as this myth is more discussed by psychologists. Opinions are divided on whether or not myths are a good idea.

As discussed previously, "white lies" are of course permitted in a child's life like telling Aunt Mary the hideous sweater is "lovely."

But Santa Claus may not fit in that category because the child knows the truth about the sweater. There can be concern by parents whether engaging in this myth does any harm. Do children who find out that their parents lied to them suffer emotional upset and distrust? Two of my contacts, including my editor, reported their children becoming aghast when they learned that their parents had "lied to them." No lasting issues were forthcoming, however.

Parents may differ in their belief that the Santa myth constitutes lying and will hurt their relationship with their children or whether helping children participate in a benign fantasy is a positive contribution to childhood joy and a good exercise of their imagination. We will look at that in a bit, but first, what have psychologists learned about the myth?

There is sparse, if any, research on the subject. Researching topics for this book has been an adventure, and in the case of the Santa Claus topic, it has been especially rewarding. I learned that one of my professors, Norman Prentice, who helped me with my dissertation, was an "expert" on Santa Claus research—and in fact about the only one. In a 1978 study, Professor Prentice reported that the Santa Claus belief starts between ages three and four with 85% of four-year-olds espousing belief. It remains strong between four- and eight-year-olds with 65% of six-year-olds believing, and declines after age seven with 25% of eight-year-olds believing (7). A more recent study in 2011 measured 83% of five-year-olds believing in Santa Claus, and found 8.4 years to be the average age when children disowned the myth (8).

It may have come to your mind, "What about Jewish or Muslim kids?" Santa Claus is only in the Christian tradition, and not everyone is Christian. Are those other-than-Christian parents spared the debate? In 1987, Prentice published "Santa Claus and the Tooth Fairy for the Jewish Child and Parent" (9). In it, he found that Jewish children believed significantly less in percentages in both figures than in studies which included Christian children, but some believed regardless of parental encouragement or family commitment to the Jewish religion.

But again, what about concerns when parents feel it is unethical or worry that children will feel they are not truthful in other areas? A few years later, Professor Prentice and his colleagues then tackled an issue precisely pertinent to parents' anxieties. They published a study where children who no longer believed in Santa Claus were interviewed to assess their reactions to discovering the truth. Parents also reported their attitude toward the Santa belief and what their child's reactions to the truth were as well as their own reactions to the child's discovery. Children generally discovered the truth on their own at age seven, and reported predominantly positive reactions on learning the truth. Parents, however, described themselves as predominantly "sad" (10).

One newspaper article from the *Washington Post* in 2016 summarized evidence and quoted psychology professor Jacqueline Wooley. "There is no evidence that belief and eventual disbelief in Santa affects parental trust in any significant way. Furthermore, not only do children have the tools to ferret out the truth, but engaging with the Santa story may give them a chance to exercise these abilities." In addition, there are various helpful writings by child "advisors" that can be found on the internet (11).

An added benefit is that children generally figure out the truth of the matter by themselves. As they see the multiple Santa's, and don't quite buy it that they are Santa's helpers, they begin to ask questions, which should start around age seven.

Some helpful hints to manage the transition from belief to disbelief are for parents to listen for questions. "Is Santa real?" Rather than answering the question, a parent might turn the question back to the child: "What makes you think so?" While continuing to protect the myth, parents can give "clues" that they are the ones impersonating Santa. For example, writing notes in one's handwriting or putting presents "from Santa" under the tree in full sight, may help a child figure it out.

Once children know the truth, they are "in on the secret," and that can give them a feeling of being "special." One way to help the transition is to encourage the now knowledgeable child to "be a Santa," and to give gifts to younger persons in the selfless and positive way that "Santa" does. The "Santa Spirit" of selfless giving and helping others is a true treasure in our culture, and one that parents can nurture (12).

## SUMMARY OF PILLAR #4
## (Chapters 13, 14, & 15)

As a wrap-up, let us consider morality in our world, and as mentioned previously in my remarks, "We are not raising kids, we're raising adults." Thanks again to my friend and fellow author, Barbara Yokum, for that insight. The world presents itself with many opportunities for positive change. When our children are older, they will have the capacity to look at chronic situations of unfortunate plight, and to comprehend the status of a group or class whether they be impoverished, outcast, oppressed, victimized, or handicapped. One might hope that all of us hope to leave the world a better place than when we found it! And we might wish to instill that value to our children. The liberal tradition of humanity is that by just being human, we are all of equal dignity and worth, and no matter where one is situated in society, the source of individual power is our power of moral choice.

Can you see your child as a moral agent, conducting moral actions for "the good?" Morality addresses social problems such as avoiding harm, benefiting others, avoiding physical violence, emotional hurt, exploitation, subjugation, unequal treatment, unfairness, social injustice, violating rights for some groups, prejudice, discrimination, peace, war, genocide, and enslavement. There is much good to be done.

Activists and advocates for human rights issues would be expected to have a strong sense of empathy and sympathy, and those that act on behalf of others are demonstrating the opposite of the egocentric person. You may hope that your children will espouse these beliefs and "make the world a better place."

Whether you or your child decides to be an activist or advocate is a matter of individual choice. It is not mandatory, but acting in a moral way is mandatory, and parents bear responsibility for raising a moral child.

# Pillar #5

## RAISING AN INDEPENDENT CHILD

# Chapter 16

## Concepts of Independence, Separation, and Some Cultural Differences

### INTRODUCTION

"Independence" is a simple word that has many meanings to parents. Is "dependence" its opposite? The notion of "independence" is that your child is successfully able to live apart from you. But what about the relationship between the two of you? What will the connection look like?

In the process of writing this book, I divided all parenting efforts into 5 "pillars" or important areas. We have covered Relationships, Responsibility, Healthy Self, Morality/Kindness, and now, Independence. In the writing process, whenever I told parents these areas in this order, and mentioned "Independence," they tended to nod vigorously. Independence seemed to be highly meaningful to them. Why? My suspicion is that parents have, in the back of their mind, the idea that their child will be financially self-sufficient and independent enough to live on their own. Hurray for the parents who'll no longer have major financial responsibilities here!

In my own life, when my son got a job and a girlfriend, he agreed to my request (rather, demand) that he move out of his old room in my home and get an apartment. End of story. I'm happy to say that he is now married eight years to his then girlfriend with three kids!

Earlier in this book, in the subject of allowance, I mentioned this episode in a family therapy session, but it fits here so I will repeat it. Present was a fifteen-year-old girl and her parent. The girl was fierce in her request for more allowance. When turned down she said, "You just don't want me to be financially independent." Her mother and I looked at each other, smiled, (stifled laughter, actually), and I said, "That is the true wish and goal of any parent!"

Independence + self-sufficiency = autonomy! These are desirable goals for your child. The road to independence begins with physical *Separation* as the infant/child has time apart from their parents. Gradually, the child spends time away from primary caretakers, in the care of others, and ultimately lives apart from family of origin and runs their own life. At the same time, as they become more independent, what will be the emotional connectedness between you and your child? Are the two goals mutually exclusive? Let's take a step back and look at how different cultures approach the issue.

"Western" cultures (Europe, Australia, N. America) look at independence in a different way from "non-Western" cultures (Asia, Africa, S. America). This chapter will look at the difference in importance of family closeness between cultures. Of course, you don't want your child to be independent AT THE EXPENSE of relationships between family members. But, at the same time, you want your child to ultimately be able to take care of themself. How "independent" do you want your child to be?

So, I want to bring up the subject of family closeness, also known as *"interdependence."* How often, and in what manner will you communicate with each other? Will your child consult you about important decisions? Will you eat together as a family? Will you have weekly family dinners as depicted in current TV programs like *Bluebloods* (1), which always ends in a Sunday family dinner where *everyone* was expected? Writing this chapter led me to review my own connections with my only son. Since I am an only child, and he is an only child, he is "family" (notwithstanding his own wonderful family). While we have a positive relationship, we don't communicate on a frequent basis. Having conversations and getting to know each other as adults takes some planning from busy lives. I intend to do this more often! He is an interesting guy and is raising great kids!

How many relatives will you include in your "family?" How will your children, as adults, act when YOU need their care in times of infirmity, hard times, etc.? To what extent will your cultural background determine your decisions? For example, if you are a fairly recent immigrant to the West, or adhere to your ethnic customs, your "closeness" traditions may be important to uphold. This chapter will provide information about how parents from various cultures manage the issue of independence. And you will have the opportunity to examine your own values and plan for your family connections. Appendix C provides more detailed information about this important topic.

## THE INITIAL SEPARATION: BIRTH AND EARLY INFANCY

The prelude to living independently is separation. The new infant is a separate being, and traveling from *in utero* to existence in the world requires "baby steps." New parents experience the fear that the survival of their child is in their hands, which it is. Not being in the same room together at the same time leads to anxiety for the child and the parent. Fortunately, it gets better over time!

No previous experience is like this in the whole world of *life and death*. New parents have heard horror stories of babies dying of SIDS, or other causes or afflictions. The little seven-or-so pound creature you bring home brings along with it a certain dimension of terror; at least for the first few days, weeks, and months. The first days are spent wondering if the infant is getting enough to eat, if they are still breathing when they're sleeping, and if a cough is a sign of illness. Moms and dads hover around the infant, install video communication to make sure a sleeping infant is still moving, and tend to worry until they become more comfortable with their new baby.

In providing guidance to new parents, I found it helpful to highlight this issue of terror over life and death and to normalize it. For parents to recognize that they are entirely in a different dimension of life is helpful. There is no relief in sight as this life is their responsibility for the rest of the parents' lives; heaven forbid there is a death. There is nothing worse for a parent. Being able to discuss the risks of the parenting role helps new parents to accept the new reality, which is that they are NO LONGER IN CONTROL of their world.

So a new parent has to adjust. Over time, you might not think much about losing "control" of your children until adolescence when the loss of control and influence is even more apparent—friends, driving privileges, dating, and that's just a few! At that point, parents will have as much, if not more, separation anxiety than when those teens were babies. Fortunately, you'll get to become more comfortable as the process of Separation starts at the beginning and gradually increases over their first thirty or so years. Now what about "Independence?"

## WHAT THE CHILD BRINGS TO THE EQUATION: MASTERY

From birth, children are on a quest for freedom from adult help. This is a part of independence professionals refer to as "agency." Babies try to spoon feed themselves, dress themselves, pour a glass of milk by themselves. "I can do it myself!" shouts the toddler when a parent comes to put a jacket on them. The craving for children to do things "by themselves" is a universal trait, and one that leads to them being self-sufficient gradually through life. The baby's inborn trait provides parents with a great opportunity to help the child gain skills. More details for this process will be found in Section IV, Ages and Stages. Of course, that desire to "do it myself" changes over the years, particularly in adolescence where having others do things for you like cooking dinner or cleaning your room is seen as quite desirable. (Ah, reality!)

As the child gains mastery over tasks such as feeding and dressing themself, getting desired toys, or walking across the street without holding hands, the child's Self is building a sense of accomplishment and competence. But the emotional task of mastering fear when parents are absent remains for a bit longer.

## SEPARATION MILESTONES

Once parents are convinced that their child is not in imminent danger of death, they can start the process of separation. Parental anxiety shows itself when other caretakers are involved. Leaving a child with a babysitter, whether relative or not, is a first goal-related task. Fears of safety and health come to the forefront. Your handling these situations gracefully and trusting the caregiver will help your child get over their own anxiety over leaving you!

Infants seem to prefer certain caretakers to others and reach for their favorite. Real "separation anxiety" begins around nine months and is related to the process of attachment (refer also to Chapter 8). This milestone is brain-based, and expected. Babies reach a stage Piaget and others called Object Permanence where they realize the parent exists even when they are not seen.

Major separations and for longer periods of time are when a child begins a group care situation. Teachers are very understanding when children protest a parent leaving. However, when parents return, children typically begin out-of-control behavior, and some teachers tend to assume the parent is too lenient. Psychologists see the situation differently. When children are in group care, they truly watch and control their behavior. For them, it is hard work. When the child is once again with the parent, they can relax their vigilance and "let it all hang out," venting all the pent-up frustration and "act up." It would be helpful if all teachers understood this phenomenon, as parents after a day of work don't need that "look" from a teacher.

Other separations will be play dates with other families, and then sleepovers at relatives' or friends' homes. Trusting that your child can handle themself is important, of course. Then, there is sleepover camp. These are all good experiences to help the child develop self-confidence and autonomy, both factors in "independence."

Parental anxiety is the factor that will sabotage all that. Overprotective parents will communicate their anxiety to their child who will likely internalize it (some strong-minded children may not). Recently a term has emerged for those parents who excessively interfere with their college-age children. "Helicoptering" parents, who insist on handling difficult situations for their "emerging adult," literally don't trust their child to manage themselves. Of course, we are talking about younger children in this book, but the pattern is clear. In a 2014 study of college students, researchers found that over-parenting, much different than parental involvement, was associated with lower feelings of self-efficacy as well as maladaptive responses in the workplace (2). A critical part of successful separations is managing one's own anxiety of being independent. We'll cover more details in handling separation in the upcoming Section IV, Ages and Stages.

## INDEPENDENCE: HOW WESTERN CULTURE DIFFERS FROM NON-WESTERN

We return to the issue of how connected you will be with your child as they become independent, and we will now look at how Western cultures (again, North America, Europe, and Australia), differ from *all* the others including India, China, the Arab world, South America, and Africa.

**WHY LOOK AT CULTURES?**

If you're wondering why this issue of cultural variation is empha-sized in this book, it's simply because I find it fascinating. I traveled around the world visiting most countries in Asia, except China. The Middle East has become a focus for me through my interest in the Israel/Palestine political issue. Anthropology and cross-cultural psychology have always fascinated me, although I haven't gotten into those fields really until now!

Anthropologists have separated the world's cultures into the Western cultures that emphasize *Individualism* and every other country that emphasizes *Group Identity* or *Collectivism* (3).

- *Individualism* means that a culture places emphasis on the individual as a bounded entity, separate from others with their own thoughts, feelings, strengths, and weaknesses.

- *Group Identity* places the emphasis on group membership; your family group is the major part of your identity and the center of your focus. For families in non-Western cultures, group membership, referred to as a family, clan, or tribe, is highly important, and individuals work hard to conform to expectations and keep the ties strong. "Respect" is a word I wish to insert here. It was noted by one of my friends of Arab ethnicity that family members (especially older ones) deserve respect. (Sounds good to me!)

"Westerners" in North America, Europe, and Australia empha-size the functioning of the individual apart from the family. A recent book by American anthropologist Joseph Patrick Henrich describes the Western culture as WEIRD, an acronym for Western, Educated, Industrialized, Rich, and Democratic (4). His fascinating ideas will come later to describe reasons for the cultural differences.

As you can tell, the Western area is much smaller than non-Western. A prominent Turkish anthropologist, Cigdem Kagitcibasi (5) uses the terms *"Majority World"* and *"Minority World"* to differentiate the vastly different perspectives of families about independence. Westerners such as those who live in the US, like I do, and perhaps you do, and those in North America, Australia, and Europe are in the Minority. Ironically, the vast majority of psychological research we will review has been done with US middle-class persons, and the important theorists in personality development are from either Europe or the US. Interest in how parents of other cultures raise their children is only recent.

You are probably familiar with the term *"Nuclear Family"* (and I don't mean the atomic kind) where parents and children constitute the members living together (Western) versus the *Extended Family* (all others) where multiple generations live together with lots of visits to uncles, aunts, etc., and lots of marriages within clan lines. Parents from ethnic groups who have recently immigrated to a Western culture face fitting into the dominant culture while preserving their family traditions. Since all European families began in tribes with the extended family or Group Identity Model, I found it interesting to learn how the system changed. Can you think of a reason Westerners are different? Spoiler alert! Henrich provides an answer in a coming section.

## YOUR CHILD'S DEVELOPMENT IN INDEPENDENCE: SOME CONCEPTS

But let us return to the issue at hand—your child's future in their current culture. Perhaps the best way to analyze this area is to break it down into competing concepts.

## Separate vs. Independent vs. Individualist

Are these concepts one and the same? If you are separate, does that mean you are independent? Does "separate" mean being able to function outside the family? Does separate mean having little to do with the family members? No parent would want their child to be indifferent to or lack connections with family members.

## Separate vs. Interdependent vs. Self–Decisions vs. Respect

Let's review the types of relations for clarity.

- **Separateness** is the sense that one is an individual apart from any family members.
- **Interdependence** is the connections and closeness one has with family members.
- Both nuclear and extended families would wish to establish caring relationships with **emotional dependence** within the family (family estrangements, God forbid, notwithstanding).
- But the idea of "Self" is somewhat different in a group loyalty family where what the "group" thinks can be more important than in an Individualist family.

To what extent will the family member "respect" the opinion of the family by considering their desires and ultimately conforming to their wishes? The degree of "respect" will determine whether:

1. Family wishes are taken into consideration but not necessarily catered to; or
2. The individual does what the "family" wants.

The extreme of this issue is in marriage when the family picks the spouse for their child. These ideas are incomprehensible to Westerners and some in the Majority culture, too.

## Independent vs. Dependent

- **Independence** may also mean the ability to accomplish things on one's own. An individual who can manage their own life issues without someone looking after them or helping them is "independent" in that definition. Initiative, leadership, resourcefulness, and self-discipline are traits that would be valuable to nurture for a child who will eventually enter the (US middle class) work force.

- **Dependence** would be the opposite—one who looks to others for direction.

## Components of Independence: Self-Determination Theory

A recent publication by Chinese researchers (6), incidentally members of Majority culture, described the "Self-Determination Theory" as healthy adaptation involving three components:

*Autonomy* – feeling that one has control in making one's own decisions.

*Competence* – feeling confident in one's abilities and achievement.

*Relatedness* – feeling that one is connected to others.

## Trying to Put it Together

Kagitcibasi offers the idea that interdependence can be divided into two aspects:

1. **Relational** (emotional)
2. **Collective** (or traditional group loyalty).

She summarizes that the long-range goal for socialization is becoming a competent member of a society and discards the notion that independence and connectedness are opposites and mutually exclusive. You don't have to have one at the expense of the other. She states that *both* values are equally valued but to different degrees in different family systems. Autonomy, competence, and relatedness are aspects that offer several variables involved in a successful separation of the Self from Others.

I hope this makes sense that there are multiple aspects in helping your child be "independent."

## HOW DID WESTERN CULTURE COME TO BE BECOME INDIVIDUALISTIC?

### Henrich's Analysis of WEIRD

Now we return to the Henrich book about WEIRDness. In review, in Western culture, children are raised to live on their own with options such as leaving home for college, living in an apartment with roommates, marrying someone they love, living separately from parents, or building a separate financial future for their own children. This structure is different from the rest of the world where Group Identity has more importance and the family functions as a supportive unit.

Henrich has some very interesting ideas about how these differences developed. He makes a believable case that the change in family structure derived from the Middle Ages, when missionaries from the Roman Catholic Church sent by Pope Gregory the Great in 497 CE came to the European tribes to convert them to Christianity. Tribes at that time were group-oriented "clans." To keep wealth in the family, there were traditions of arranging to marry a cousin of some distance (they had figured out first cousins were not good matches) or other relatives, living close to parents, and inheriting through the father's bloodlines (not father and mother). This is the cousin-marriage pattern. Do you know anyone who has married their cousin? Probably not. But one in ten marriages around the world are to cousins or other relatives, according to Henrich. Pope Gregory set new rules for marriage.

The rules of marriage for the Church were:

1. You were not to marry your cousin, not even a far-removed cousin.
2. Marriage ceremonies included the statement "I do" to signify voluntary consent to one's marriage.
3. The couple was to choose a residence apart from their parents.
4. They were to put their loyalty (and money) to the church, not to the clan.
5. Property was to be individually owned.
6. How one gave away wealth at death was an individual decision.

Henrich calls this the Marriage and Family Plan (MFP) where kinship ties were deliberately weakened. Apparently, the Church had acquired much influence over the society and would not sanction a marriage that did not conform to the MFP. The missionaries were apparently very successful as people followed the "Plan." This strategy resulted in powerful control of the newly converted Christians who faced losing access to church rites and privileges, like marriage, or funerals.

You may recall that the original Church split into Eastern (Orthodox) and Western (Catholic) wings; the MFP was *not* followed by the Eastern Church. Thus, the cultures of Eastern Europe and Russia maintained their family kinship ties. Henrich makes a point (with lots of statistics and maps) that the LONGER any cultural group was exposed to the MFP, the more "individualistic" the culture became.

Henrich further proposes, between about 400 and 1200 CE, the tribal connections were slowly dismantled. People formed new voluntary associations based on shared interests such as trade guilds or beliefs rather than on family relations. It was more *what* you knew than *who* you knew. These civic associations were the beginning of self-rule for cities, then nations. Leaders were elected on merit, not on their family position. He further asserts that analytical thinking developed and enabled individuals to process knowledge rationally, without worry that it would upset anyone (more about relational versus analytic thinking later). It is further argued that the lessening of intensive kinship ties *led* to the changes in culture.

Henrich notes that the average person (you?) probably thought Individualism came from the Industrial Revolution or economic prosperity or Protestants with their work ethic. But again, in his opinion, in Europe, the historical order was *reversed* in the middle of the first millennium with the loosening of kinship ties and growth of independent, professional associations. These MFP changes in family structure changed how people thought about themselves and their world. They saw themselves as independent agents within the family, as opposed to having to function in a hierarchical system (top down from the leader). The Enlightenment in the 1600s emphasized humans as having equal rights, leading to the downfall of authoritarian regimes (kings and nobility in some cases). Scientific progress, and geographic exploration proceeded from that time in the European region.

Naturally, there was a downside to all this change. As people's psychology shifted, and Individualism replaced Group Identity, there was the added stress of living on one's own, forging one's own way, and—with Protestantism—making your own peace with God. Henrich looked at suicide rates in areas where Protestantism was predominating and Catholics not. Suicide rates are stronger for those areas closest to the center of the German (Protestant) Reformation. The loneliness or stress of being on one's own may leave people feeling depressed, and even increase the chances of suicide (7), (8).

## SUMMARY OF PILLAR #5 (Chapter 16)

Beginning with birth, separation proceeds along the life path. As children build a separate identity, they build competence in doing things themselves, and a sense of individuality. At the same time as they build a sense of Self, children build emotional attachments to others. In the Western culture, a promotion of Individualism prevails. In contrast, other cultures stress Group Identity and family closeness.

This issue calls into question the give and take of cultures; one emphasizes family relatedness but may suffer in developing individual talents. Western culture emphasizes individual development and decision-making with a loss of family closeness. How parents manage "Independence" and "Interdependence" will depend on your own values.

Appendix C will give you a fuller picture of life in the Majority Culture—particularly in Arab (Palestinian) areas. Anthropological research is fascinating! Knowledge of cultural differences may help you to make decisions about your own family.

# SECTION IV

## Ages and Stages

**Infancy Age (0 to 15 Months)**

Chapter 17   Early Infancy – 0 to 3 Months
Chapter 18   Middle Infancy – 4 to 9 Months
Chapter 19   Late Infancy – 9 to 15 Months

**Toddler Age (15 Months to 3 Years)**

Chapter 20   Development in the Toddler Years – 15 Months to
            3 Years

**Preschool Age (3 to 6 Years)**

Chapter 21   Relationship Building and Teaching Adaptive
            Behavior
Chapter 22   Continuing Adaptive Behavior: Pillars of Self,
            Morality and Independence

**School Age (6 to 11 Years)**

Chapter 23  Education and Brain Growth, Including Learning
Disabilities & ADHD
Chapter 24  Physical Care, Relationships, and Communication/
Screen Time
Chapter 25  Elements of a Healthy Self & Moral Values
Chapter 26  Moving Toward Independence

# INFANCY AGE (0 TO 15 MONTHS)

# Chapter 17

## Early Infancy (0 to 3 Months)

### INTRODUCTION

When a baby is born, it is a tumultuous and wondrous event that changes so many things in the family. Parents, grandparents, and siblings are in awe of this tiny new creature coming to live with them. A new family member is celebrated! You are faced with a helpless creature needing food and comfort and letting you know, in no uncertain terms, if they are uncomfortable. Now, the activity of parenting and child development starts.

The arrival of an infant may stimulate adult conflict on how much to tend to a fussing baby. Responses range from "Let the baby cry it out" to "There's something wrong; I need to fix it" and everything in between. Parents' anxiety about what impact caregiving may have on personality development is evidence that parents are theorists! A helpful notion is that there is a range of parenting inputs that will lead to healthy development. Overly neglectful attention may spell problems, but babies tend to be resilient and seem to "make it" despite difficulties and obstacles. Some balance between tending a fussing baby and letting the baby be for a while is normal. Parents are only human and get exhausted; other caretakers if they're around can of course step in, which is one of the primary reasons why it's often said that "it takes a village to raise a child." Additionally, along the way, *"choice points"* are presented. At times, parents need to make decisions in their parenting strategies in order to best foster their child's development.

---

**IT TAKES A VILLAGE**

I was told an inspiring story about how a community addressed the arrival of an inconsolable foster infant addicted to a drug. A group of volunteers took turns for weeks holding the infant constantly, and I mean 24/7, until the drug was out of the nervous system and the baby was okay. In this case, "It takes a village" was true.

---

# FOR INFANCY: REVIEW OF PREVIOUS ISSUES OF BRAIN DEVELOPMENT AND THEORY

## Theory

As covered in a previous chapter, the theorists presented in this book see the infant stage in slightly different ways. Freud labels this stage "Oral" by virtue of the fact that everything goes in the mouth. My six-month-old grandson enjoyed his new cloth book by putting it in his mouth. I said, "He's reading his book; no, he's EATING his book!" Also, I recall chasing a crawling Gavin in the playground, trying to get those wood chips out of his hands before they went in his mouth. Exhausting!

Adler reported that "striving" is demonstrated in the effort infants exert in moving from one motor stage to the next like watching a baby try to roll over for the first time. It is impressive!

Sullivan and Erikson see the chief aspect of development as entering the social world. Sullivan noted how infants can experience anxiety through their caregivers, which starts the development of how the baby learns to manage it and in so doing, develops the "Self."

Erikson saw the trait of Trust/Mistrust established in infancy, and sees infancy as a time when a balance of these aspects is learned by the experience of gratification or frustration. Children have to mistrust sometimes because everything can't happen the way they want it to.

Piaget saw the infant as a bundle of senses and actions, with learning about their new world occurring at all times. Learning that objects exist, and the fact that they can light up or make noise changes the brain. Infants like interesting things and will work to make the experience last.

Whatever the theory, development takes place. Let's begin by reviewing the status of the brain, as that is what causes all of the excitement.

## Brain Maturation

Chapter 1 focused on the anatomy of the brain and will be reviewed here. The chapter described the neurons, synapses, and myelin sheath that speed the transmission of brain impulses to the body. Neuron growth takes place *in utero*, so when the baby is born, their brain contains billions of neurons. Myelinization begins at nine months gestation (birth). Grooves in the cerebral cortex, which increase the surface area needed for all the neurons, begin developing in the sixth month *in utero* and increases during that first year after birth. The brain triples in size during the first year, and ends at three-quarters weight of an adult brain.

Now recall the importance of synapses, the connections between neurons. Those neurons are useless without a connection to other neurons. Synapse creation starts with gestation and continues into the second year of life. That is why the cerebral cortex increases in thickness and weight. But wait! Those neurons with synaptic connections are still useless until they have some organization, which takes place with EXPERIENCE. Once those little eyes open up, and your child becomes aware of your world, the work begins.

This is not brain surgery (pun intended), of course. Parents know that each experience a baby has, matters, and that is why there will always be fuss and anxiety over parenting decisions.

Don't worry, your baby needs enough stimulation, but not too much. Mobiles, music, things that light up and rattle all contribute to brain development. They love to see images with strongly contrasting colors, especially black and white. When their eyes follow such a picture, and sustain a gaze toward it, you know they found something "interesting." However, there is such a thing as over-stimulation, and babies will retreat from it by turning away and averting their gaze. When handling infants, my approach is to expose them to "interesting," but not too exciting visual things, and hope a synaptic connection is made, which means something was learned. And, of course, talking to infants is stimulating even if they don't understand a word.

Brain development is measured by motor and language milestones that parents eagerly await such as rolling over, sitting up, creeping, crawling, and babbling. Your pediatrician will be checking for all the development milestones, too.

## Temperament

In the early weeks/months of infancy, your baby's emotional "style" or temperament will be evident. The way your baby moves from one state to another predicts their temperament. We covered the three types of style: Easy/Flexible (40%), Difficult/Feisty (10%), and Slow to Warm-up/Fearful (15%).

The challenge of a "difficult" temperament can put extreme stress on parents. That little creature will be intense and persistent in emotional responses, and they will cry a lot and be hard to console; they will be sensitive and perceptive to outside stimuli and irregular in sleep and feeding schedule. Patience and good teamwork will be necessary to weather this difficult period. There should be creative ways to get HELP with your difficult—let's call them "spirited" or "expressive"—infant. Parents who work together as a team have the greatest success and least amount of stress. The potential embarrassment of parents with such infants should NOT prevent them from getting help and getting extra caregivers to lighten the load. Even help from marriage counselors may be needed. People clucking in disapproval at extreme crying should be seen as utterly ignorant. Keep in mind that this temperament will be an asset in adulthood. This temperament is NOT caused by poor parenting! Persistent and passionate people have changed the world! When a baby is upset at the transitions (crying), it may signal an immature nervous system, and a temperament that is irritable, or in the medical/psychological parlance, "Difficult." Things may change very rapidly.

## PHYSICAL CARE—FEEDING AND SLEEPING

Your world will revolve around the feeding, sleeping, and elimination of this tiny being. Newborns struggle to coordinate all of their body functions including irregular breathing and body temperature. Their sensitivity to stimuli varies, and they are easily aroused. Gesell notes that babies are not full-born until four weeks! An important task is to pay attention to your baby's developing rhythms. Within two weeks, parents can usually differentiate cries, and work out routines for changing, feeding, cuddling, rocking, or just soldiering through babies that seem continually upset.

## Feeding

**A choice point for parents is whether to feed at the breast, to give breastmilk in a bottle, or to give formula.** There are physical and psychological issues here. Regarding the physical, there is no question that breastmilk meets unique nutritional needs of each infant and contains antibodies that protect infants from infection. No formula substitute is nutritionally equivalent. However, some psychological assumptions about feeding at the breast have been challenged. First, cognitive benefits such as intelligence have not been found in breastmilk fed babies. However, in premature or low birthweight babies, breastmilk may confer some cognitive advantages (1).

A major psychological issue is whether feeding at the breast enhances bonding. We reviewed in Chapter 8 the fact that attachment doesn't occur in the child until later in infancy, but bonding/attachment may occur in the mother. There have been few studies of this issue, and those showed inconsistent findings of breastfeeding and attachment.

Mothers are encouraged to breastfeed for its many advantages—food is always there, helpful antibodies are present in breastmilk, closeness is guaranteed. However, it is important to note that not all mothers have a wonderful bonding experience when they breastfeed. There can be pain, discomfort, and feelings of physical vulnerability. Other factors like the sacrifice of time and having anxiety about adapting their life to a schedule may actually interfere with the pleasant bonding and attachment experience of feeding. Fears of organization abound for mothers who work outside the home and pump breastmilk at intervals when meetings are not scheduled. Not all women will feel comfortable performing this most personal task outside the home. Certainly, they are to be congratulated, but if there is stress and anxiety and pain, which can be communicated to the infant, another approach should be considered. Empathy works both ways.

Feeding an infant, whether breast or bottle, is best when it is *an interactive experience*. This is an important time where tenderness, communication, and empathy are expressed through touch and sound. Bottle feeding or breastfeeding should never be impersonal like propping up a bottle or being on a device, but personal. You hold the baby; talk to the baby; look at the baby (not your phone, nor the TV). To get a break, it's also good for the baby to be fed by another parent or other adults. It is important to note that breastmilk production is stimulated by feeding or pumping milk. Stopping this activity and supplementing formula may curtail milk production, so a careful balance is needed.

In addition to deciding what the baby eats, which changes over time, parents will determine whether to feed at set intervals or whenever the baby seems hungry and fusses. These choices are described as **on-demand or cue-based feedings versus scheduled feedings.**

A well-respected advisor on child-rearing, and one who will be heavily quoted in this book, T. Berry Brazelton recommends following the infant's cries for feeding (cues), but then, to be sure to feed at least every four hours, which is six times a day! Babies can wait two to three hours between feedings. Current research favors on-demand feeding. A study compared thousands of schedule-fed versus on-demand fed English children born in the 1990s. They were followed until age fourteen. Results showed that on-demand fed children scored significantly higher on IQ and academic tests than those on a schedule (2). It should be noted that this study is a correspondence between the type of feeding and scores. It is not a controlled study, and it may be that certain types of parents choose the on-demand method, and some trait, possibly intelligence, is causing the group difference. A more recent controlled study, where two groups were fed with different methods, showed cue-based feedings of premature infants improved the babies' ability to take in more nourishment, and to leave the hospital earlier (3).

Initial feeding may include lots of spit-ups causing parents to become concerned that the baby isn't getting any calories at all! Handling air bubbles and burps will be a learned process. If your baby takes milk too fast, there will be air bubbles/burps, so you can learn the proper pace. At six weeks, weight gain should be a half-pound per week (4).

## Sleeping & Schedules

Your baby moves from sleep to wakefulness on a fairly but of course not entirely predictable schedule. The infant can shut out disturbing stimuli but needs quiet for sleep. Sleep patterns reflect the developing brain under three or four months. Before six weeks, the longest sleep period may be two to three hours. By six weeks, typical infants will sleep sixteen hours a day with the longest sleep period four to five hours. Neurological maturation, not hunger, causes this schedule. Hunger has little to do with how babies sleep (5).

In this stage of infancy, sleep deprivation is an issue all face. How do you manage your life when you sleep two hours at a time, and then get up? Some people are lucky enough to be able to fall asleep as soon as the baby does, but some are not. It's a tough six weeks, and longer for some.

Infants under three months old are not likely to be regular in schedules although some lucky parents have babies who are predictable at six to eight weeks. Infants will be awake and open to learning new experiences for *around two hours* at a time. More than this duration, the infant will become overtired and overstimulated, and will have more difficulty falling asleep.

**A choice point is how to put your child "down" for sleep.** Safety issues have led to recommendations for infants to sleep on their back. When the infant begins to roll, they can sleep in different positions. Some infants will prefer the stomach.

**Another choice point is where the infant sleeps.** Most families elect a bassinet or crib near the parents. Despite the potential danger of an adult rolling over and suffocating an infant, some parents have their child in their bed. It's called co-sleeping. This style may be rooted in the family's culture or something the family chooses. Some breastfeeding mothers who are sleep-deprived simply can't take the issue of getting up and feeding a crying infant. There are dangers involved in co-sleeping, and suffocating your baby is a tragedy. I suggest avoiding the danger; the grave risk isn't worth it. One suggestion to help with sleep deprivation is to have bottles available for the other parent to feed the baby. It's also nice for the non-feeding parent to bring the baby to the mother and return the baby to the crib afterwards.

# THE FIVE PILLARS OF DEVELOPMENT FOR THE 0-3 MONTH OLD CHILD

## 1. Building Loving Relationships

The moment the new infant is presented to their parents' arms, the relationship begins! The nature of the response of the parent/caregiver will set the tone of future relationships. Some anxiety is to be expected, but over-the-top stress will not be helpful. Postpartum depression may occur, and your medical professional needs to be involved so it can be handled.

During the first few months of life, the infant and caring adults get to know each other. The baby will begin to develop rhythms that parents will welcome. Inevitable periods of irritability, perhaps several hours at a stretch, will be frustrating to parents. This situation is often called "colic," which is a term that mis-represents the issue as it is *not* gastrointestinal. The problem is also NOT due to parenting issues (stress, bad milk, "colic"), but to a temporarily uninhibited nervous system causing excessive arousal (Weissbluth). Your baby will be able to feel your frustration, anxiety, or anger, which will only add to the situation. This is empathy in reverse, as mentioned above, when the baby reflects your emotions. Weissbluth cites the peak of fussy/wakefulness is around six weeks. Again, this is an immature nervous system that just goes haywire every so often.

A question about how soon and often you should pick up a baby has arisen since time immemorial. Should you tend to the baby at the first peep, or wait and let the baby fuss a bit? "Spoiling" a baby at this stage is not possible. There is no such thing going on in that brain. The baby is not trying to monopolize your attention. The baby fusses for various reasons—hunger, wet diaper, or just plain imbalance in the nervous system. Remember, all those systems are getting coordinated. But there is no reason not to tend to baby and see what's needed at this stage. My daughter-in-law is firm that any message from the baby means that something is needed. You cannot go wrong with this approach.

The smile at six weeks is a welcome milestone. Contrary to what people assume, this smile is not so much one of happiness or love or gas, but of recognition! The brain has formed an image of a familiar face and seeing that face evokes the smile. While connection and familiarity between infant and parent is important, attachment will not come into full force until later in infancy.

The loving relationship is expressed most when babies are crying and need to be soothed. Rocking, walking, driving them around in a car to get them to sleep, cooing, and singing are all efforts to put your baby in a good (or at least better) mood. This is YOUR empathy coming into play, and it will build empathy in your child. How parents keep their cool during this trying period is a test of their own personal capacities. Functioning despite sleep deprivation is a challenge every new parent endures. When the baby naps, parents nap. Phones should be off. There should be no disturbances when feeding or napping.

**A choice point is when to give care to another adult and to whom.** Keeping one's health and sanity means working as a team, getting HELP. Remember the Independence chapter: having extended family around is a blessing for those cultures where family is emphasized. Then there is no problem because someone else is always around.

2. **Teaching Adaptive Behavior** (not applicable in this stage)

3. **Building a Healthy Self**

As we learned in Chapter 11, a healthy Self is based on acceptance of behavior. Harsh handling, overstimulation, and stress on your baby will take their toll. Your baby expresses unhappy states—or sometimes a nervous system that is just immature. Your patience and "not taking it personally" are important. That is your own healthy Self at work.

4. **Morality**

Kindness has empathy at its basis. Your kindness will express itself in gracious, calm parenting despite the sleep deprivation, and handling the frustration at not being able to soothe a crying baby, and all the stresses you feel. The empathy you feel and transmit by touch to the baby is the foundation for their own empathy. The beginnings of moral behavior at early ages and its progression until school age was covered in Chapter 13.

## 5. Independence/Separation

In a nuclear family, the process of separation begins with introducing your infant to new caregivers and giving yourself a guilt-free break. Options abound and include parents, other family members, nannies, babysitters, group daycare, and the like. The family has to consider career needs and financial issues in determining caregivers, but at six weeks, group daycare generally can begin.

# Chapter 18

## Middle Infancy (4 to 9 Months)

### PHYSICAL CARE

### Feeding

The system that works best will continue; depending on the infant's weight gain, and the mother's wish to continue the breastfeeding, it will continue. Parents will be creative as to when, how, and if to introduce formula feedings and a bottle. There are pros and cons to both methods. For instance, there is no preparation nor clean-up with breastfeeding, and, with bottle feeding, mothers can take a break and let others help.

Foods other than milk can be introduced at four to five months, and parents will look for any allergies or rashes from them. Babies' swallowing mechanisms are not yet developed for solid foods, so pureed foods are necessary. Brazelton recommends holding babies at a thirty-degree angle or higher to help food get to the stomach and avoid spit ups. Children who are sitting up will do well in a highchair. Infants require feedings every three to four hours, with five per day on average. The typically healthy baby will double their birth weight by six months.

Teething begins around this time, and strategies for pain reduction are available for parents. It tears at the heartstrings when an infant is hurting and there is little you can do.

## Sleeping

Sleep and wake routines are one of those ubiquitous areas of parenting where, before becoming parents, it sounded simple. Then the baby arrives, and suddenly, a sleep schedule seems like "The Impossible Dream."

Beginning at around four months, per Brazelton, the infant will usually take three or four naps during the day and will develop a routine. By six months, they will take two naps per day. The importance of good uninterrupted sleep is emphasized by Weissbluth. Your baby will LEARN more when awake if they have good sleep. Typically, an infant will wake up at five or six a.m. for a feeding and/or a diaper change, and then return to sleep. Morning wakeful time will be about two hours, then their first nap, mid-morning, for a solid hour. Wakefulness in midday will be two to three hours. Then the second nap happens after lunch before three p.m. An hour nap will then produce two to three hours of wakefulness. There may be a third nap before bedtime if it doesn't interfere with early bedtime. There typically is a "fussy" period for one to two hours at the end of the day around dinnertime, which will persist for some time. Oftentimes, especially for parents with more than one child, this fussiness at dinnertime is known as the "witching hour." This behavior is normal and is the result of a nervous system trying to regulate itself. After such a period, sleep is generally deep and healthy (Weissbluth).

Babies can learn to sleep in longer periods from eight to twelve hours beginning at three to four months. **A choice point is whether to sleep-train your infant and when.** Weissbluth promotes a method of sleep training where sleep-deprived parents do not pick up a crying infant; rather they appear at the child's cribside, pat, talk a bit, but let the child cry. Most babies will cry for two hours before they resume sleep. The second day maybe a half-hour with the third day seeing only minimal crying. For infants who have sleep difficulty, try techniques such as warm water on tummy, heartbeat sounds, or white noise at low volume. For extreme criers, consider hiring a night caregiver to let the parents sleep.

Babies cycle between deep and light sleep several times a night as do adults, and in those periods of light sleep, they will thrash and move around. This is when they will find a thumb or pacifier and settle down. For safety reasons, blankets in bed prior to age one are discouraged, and "sleeping suits" provide cozy warmth.

Parents will be creative in developing a supportive bedtime ritual of singing, reading, etc. A pacifier and favorite toy will help. Weissbluth reassures parents that if they let the child cry themselves to sleep, they are not abandoning their baby, but rather letting them learn to self-soothe. This strategy can be difficult for many parents who feel they are harming their child; but babies are more resilient than they seem, and if parents can put up with a few nights of little sleep at this stage of infancy, parents' physical and mental health can be less affected.

Sleep deprivation is an issue all new parents face. To emphasize this point, I'll state it again. How are you to manage your life when you get two hours of sleep at a time, and then, get up? Maybe you can fall asleep as soon as your baby does, but maybe you'll lie there waiting for sleep to come. It can be a tough time for all members of the family. If you can get more sleep, the family will function better. Everyone needs their sleep!

Now that you and your baby are fine tuning your daily rhythms, we can look at psychological aspects.

# THE FIVE PSYCHOLOGICAL PILLARS FOR YOUR 4- TO 9-MONTH-OLD

### 1. Building Loving Relationships

Infants become much more social after four months, and parents become more confident. As the family re-organizes around feeding/sleeping schedules, life seems a bit more normal. Playtime is fun;

infants are fascinated by things around them, especially you. Things pretty much go along rather easily in the middle infancy stage.

Parents worry that they might "spoil" the child with too much attention, thus producing a self-centered person. Attention to an infant is not "spoiling," and let me define "spoiling" as the child never being told "no." There are no limits set at this age, hence no ability to "take no for an answer." That will come soon.

Problematic interactions may occur for the first time when solid foods are introduced, and the infant is less than interested. With solids being introduced, babies will smear the food, grab for the spoon, and do just about anything other than getting food into their mouth. This interaction can be so frustrating for parents and needs to be understood not so much as a rebellion but rather a curiosity-driven preference. The environment is so interesting to infants that they just have to participate. Maybe a toy will be enough to focus a child on feeding. There's nothing wrong with the food; it's just that the outside world is so cool.

Brazelton makes a great suggestion that when food is flung, parents wear a raincoat and go for it! Naturally, the important issue is to keep a calm and positive attitude and not to let frustration get the better of you. This energetic interaction can be the first of many!

At this age, communication begins with babbling. And babies love to play games. Playing peek-a-boo is now fun as children learn that there is a world out there that can disappear and reappear. Tickle games are another classic form of mutual entertainment. Those babies can laugh!

## 2. Teaching Adaptive Behavior

The sleep training discussed above can be considered adaptive behavior. Your baby has learned that nothing will be accomplished by crying, and that they can soothe themselves and get back to sleep.

It is easy for adults to control the baby during waking activities. They go where you want them to go. They are not doing much motor-wise except rolling and attempting to sit up. You need to be extra vigilant to watch for rolling babies on changing tables! When they are sitting up, they might pull to stand and will reach for any objects nearby. Some of those objects are inappropriate for playthings, so they are taken out of the baby's grasp. So, at this time, the "no's" may appear. Distracting an infant instead becomes a healthier way for parents to avoid saying so many "no's." Just find another toy/object and your child will go for it. Any upset will be soon gone with another interesting interaction.

As discussed above, there will be limits set at later times, but at this time "no's" are not really understood by a child; nor are they necessary. Babies this age can learn "no," but it's better to wait until there is more understanding of what you're trying to get across. Instead, when they are looking like they are going to do something where you might say "no," you can distract them with a ball or another toy they like.

## 3. Building a Healthy Self

The positive joyful interactions are setting the foundation for a Self that will be resilient. When an infant displays a difficult temperament, it is harder for parents to maintain that positivity. A parent's Self has to be realistic enough to know that they are not to blame for the sensitivity in their child, and not "take it personally." The parent does well to separate the infant's behavior from themselves. "My child has a nervous system that won't quit," and to look to the future when maturation will iron things out. You may recall a mention in a previous chapter of some infant studies where babies in this age group are shown short "plays" with "good guys" and "bad guys." Infants spent more time watching the "good guys." Again, the infant has no sense of right or wrong, but they somehow can sense kindness and caring.

## 4. Morality/Kindness

Loving care will be the basis for future learning of who others are and how to care for them. Infants take in the love with an empathic response. They feel what you feel. Same goes for stress/anxiety. This empathy has been labeled a "moral emotion." Again, the infant has no sense of right or wrong, but they somehow can sense kindness and caring.

## 5. Independence

Separation issues will be observed in mid-infancy. Infants can protest separations at four to five months as they know who is a "stranger" and who isn't. When caregivers help the family, infants will learn to deal with people other than parents and will start learning about separation. Typically, there is crying when parents leave, but babies adapt well to kind caregivers.

**A choice point will be if children are in group caregiving situations,** if parents haven't yet been forced into this option by work schedules and economic issues. Choice of setting will depend on the infant/caregiver ratio, and good facilities do fine with babies. Having other babies around is utterly fascinating to your infant.

# Chapter 19

## Late Infancy (9 to 15 Months)

### FEEDING AND SLEEPING

From nine to twelve months, you've got the sleep/feeding under control. Your baby is now well into finger foods and is mastering the cup and spoon. Brazelton recommends two ounces of protein and use of finger food. Cow's milk can replace formula at age one but not before, according to current recommendations. A minimal diet at age one would be sixteen ounces of milk or dairy equivalent. Fresh fruit and vegetables are needed along with a multi-vitamin if there is a battle royale about the veggies. Milk is always a go-to food if there are struggles around eating solids.

### MOTOR DEVELOPMENT

Regarding motor development, sitting morphed into crawling morphed into standing morphed into cruising around, and now your child may be walking. So now the guidance of appropriate behavior begins. Safety is an issue here, and you must make sure that the baby cannot pull objects or furniture down on themselves. Securing furniture, especially TVs, is recommended. Climbing is a favorite activity, and available shelves have risks. One suggestion is for you to get down to your baby's level and look around. You'll see better what is tempting. This childproofing will have consequences in building relationships, as we will shortly see.

Stimulating toys are loads of fun, and helpful for brain development. One suggestion (Eliot) to make exploration even more interesting is to rotate toys and place toys in different places, so your baby can "discover" them. Too many toys may overstimulate, so parents can provide an appropriate selection. Cognitively, babies at this stage are becoming aware of limited cause and effect—"when I push a button, the light comes on." This brain maturation will grow more sophisticated in figuring out what causes what each year.

Babies will generally sleep through the night particularly after they have mastered walking. Two naps a day are usual. Teething continues with molars coming in. One-word utterances are evidence of language development—"doggie," "Mama," and "no."

# THE FIVE PSYCHOLOGICAL PILLARS FOR YOUR 9- to 15-MONTH-OLD

## 1. Building Relationships—Attachment, Separation Anxiety, Stranger Anxiety

The psychological phenomenon of Attachment occurs at this stage. Certainly, caring relationships are developing every day; also, separations of parent and child have occurred. However, around seven to nine months, your infant's brain forms an image of a person that stays over time. This image is called "person permanence" or "object permanence" by some theorists. Prior to this growth, out of sight is out of mind. Now, the child KNOWS you are around even if they can't see you, and that you can go away for a time. The fact that the infant knows it is YOU, signals the onset of "stranger anxiety" at the same time. Separation now becomes a big trauma with prolonged crying and stressing out. Parental guilt rears its ugly head.

When parents have to leave, they have to leave, and eventually after experiencing several separations, the infant learns to accept care from multiple caregivers. Separation is then less traumatic, as the infant learns parents return. Weathering the storm of attachment, separation anxiety, and stranger anxiety will require patience and calm on your part, but also persistence. What may be seen as a regression where the child may seem like they are going backward in adjustment, is actually progress in brain maturation and psychological development. And the experience means that development of social relations will continue.

Language is emerging during this time. As mentioned above, one- to two-word utterances are usual, and parents and adults are instrumental in encouraging speech. "Tuning into" the baby's words reinforces them. If you use "baby talk" to get their attention, it doesn't hurt, but it may be time to step it up in terms of communication. Talking to babies is highly recommended, and current thought based on research recommends 21,000 words/day (1).

## 2. Structuring Adaptive Behavior

At this time, relationships will be affected by the need to apply limits. Safety is now an issue. There will be a new word entering the relationship; the word "No." The **choice point will be the balance between the behavior permitted and that which is discouraged/prevented.** Despite every effort to prevent danger, there will be a time when "no" comes. In the previous chapter about Self-Development, this phenomenon has been mentioned but it bears repeating. Parents "childproof" the environment not only for safety, but as a former colleague put it, to create a "Yes-Yes Environment" instead of a "No-No Environment" (thank you to the late Dr. Agnes Lattimer, pediatrician at Cook County Hospital). A child naturally wants to explore the environment, and lacking good sense, will invite danger. Creative childproofing using gates and drawer locks will allow for the least conflicts. Playpens are not used so much lately, but they are the best childproofing when an environment is a bit dicey or if childproofing is not possible. (My son and daughter-in-law bought a "Ball Pen" for infant Connor;

it is a little "tent" which contains lots of colorful plastic balls, and zips up to contain the child. Good idea.)

Referring back to family structure, authoritarian (no-no) parents will want to teach their child the meaning of "No." My child's paternal grandmother was of German ancestry, and while not wanting to stereotype, I think her decision to place valuable Japanese antiques at floor level was part of a cultural tradition to obey authority. In her home, cruising infants needed to understand "no" at an early age. We visiting mothers had to be extra vigilant and distract them due to their natural curiosity. Placing temptation at a child's eye level is definitely not recommended!

Even if you childproof, there are always the "forbidden" things, and infants will learn what those things are. For example, they may crawl up to and reach out to a TV and look back to see who is watching them. One incident with my son may illustrate the fact that infants around age one are understanding cause and effect—a really big step. He crawled up to an electric socket and pointed his finger toward it. My response was to say, "No!" He persisted, and I amped up the volume; "NO!" He persisted; I clapped my hands in front of him, shouted; he persisted, getting closer to the socket. I clapped my hands loudly and said, "NO!" He still didn't stop, so I slapped his arm once. He stopped and cried. And then he put his finger about four inches from the socket, kept it there, and looked right at me. This behavior was his way of illustrating that he got the message that this behavior would be punished, and that he would control his body in his own way. I got the message that he was protesting the whole notion of limits. But he understood! You may have figured out that the socket could have been covered in a childproofing effort as there are gadgets for that. In this case, it had been overlooked, and it could have been a plug that was the object of interest. Childproofing isn't always the answer, and teaching the "no" comes eventually.

Distraction from dangerous/forbidden activities works fine at this age, and "no's" can be kept to a minimum. But parents need to introduce limits into the loving relationship, which is the first challenge to YOUR definition of yourself as an authority.

### 3. Building a Self

Your child now has motor capability and can move at will. This starts the process of the Self-system for your child. Not that they have any idea who they are, but there is a willfulness that is now experienced. Your child wants to do what they want to do, and that sense of drive and motivation will characterize him/her for life. You may call this "spirit" and parents are usually careful not to squelch the spirit. Sometimes, parents feel they should not impose any limits so as not to "damage" the Self; however, the goal of creating a Self which is resilient makes it necessary to say the "no" word. Children can't get everything they want, or they will be unbalanced toward self-centeredness.

Reviewing a few words from Harry Stack Sullivan may add some clarity. If you will recall from the chapter on the Self, the Self-system is composed of those parts of the Self which are validated by others; the Self will *deny* the existence of those parts which meet with disapproval or punishment. The more denied, the more defensive and guarded the Self will become; the more behavior of the child is accepted, the more the child will accept themselves as a whole.

### 4. Morality & Kindness

As mentioned in the previous section, at around nine months, babies begin to understand the concept of "person permanence" that people when out of sight don't disappear from the face of the earth. Getting a notion that people exist when they're not immediately visible is a first step in understanding the more complicated Self/Other learning necessary for moral development. As their brain grasps this concept, they become more upset by separations. Differentiating the Self from the Other is proceeding and will be the basis for considering the needs of others.

## 5. Independence

That willfulness of desire seen at this age is also a beginning of independence. Wanting to walk instead of the stroller is continually negotiated. Doing it "myself" becomes a big issue, and children are proud of accomplishments. Parents are instrumental in providing opportunities for this and creativity comes in handy. You can use your judgment in toy or task choice to ensure success and pride in accomplishment.

Mealtime can continue to be a battle of wills, but wise parents battle only so long before returning to the bottle (baby bottle that is, not the one in the liquor cabinet). But the bottle can't be the long-term answer. This issue of getting sufficient nutrition in your baby can be a "hot button" when parents feel and are responsible. But self-feeding of course is a big step in independence.

# SUMMARY OF THE INFANCY STAGE
## (Chapters 17, 18, and 19)

From zero to fifteen months, a huge amount of development occurs—at a fast pace. Your baby who was a bundle in your arms is now struggling to get out of those arms and march around. Parents working as a team, surviving sleep deprivation are joyful participants in the "show" that their baby provides during this year. Rolling over, sitting up, smiling, babbling syllables, grasping objects, crawling, and now walking and running are welcome milestones. As infancy merges into toddlerhood, new challenges await!

# TODDLER AGE (15 MONTHS TO 3 YEARS)

# Chapter 20

## Development in the Toddler Years

## INTRODUCTION

A few months after that first birthday, your baby can be considered a "toddler." This time with increased mobility and dangers. Your child can drown in a standing bucket or burn themselves on a radiator. Supervision is required at all times. The brain is growing of course, with motor skills and language emerging with single words and two-word combinations if not short sentences. These are the times of running, throwing, ceaseless activity, and short attention span. There is no knowledge of the future. Teaching toileting habits is a huge task generally accomplished during this period.

## Review Of Developmental Theorists

*"Negativism"* is the name of the game. They don't call it the "Terrible Twos" (can also be Terrible Ones) for nothing!

- Freud saw "Anal" possessiveness as the predominant theme with hoarding, stinginess, and obsessive cleanliness coming out of issues at this stage.
- Piaget looked at continuing egocentrism as toddlers cannot see others' points of view.

- Sullivan stressed parent-child interactions as either validating or as removing parts of the Self.

- Erikson described this stage as building a balance of *Autonomy versus Shame or Doubt*. Again, both aspects are needed—hopefully more Autonomy than Doubt—as your child can't have their way all the time and will need to be corrected.

- But Adler comes into play in a big way with his emphasis on the "Will to Power." Get ready!

## Brain Maturation

Appropriate stimulation is still required for the brain to form those synapses. Toys, "screen time" in appropriate doses, trips to museums, and parks are important during this time. Again, however, overstimulation or "chaos" in the home will be counterproductive to brain development, since focus, exploring, and curiosity will occur only when there is emotional stability.

A big step in brain development is the onset of *cause-and-effect reasoning*—"if you do this, then that happens." Age two and a half is typical for parents to be able to "reason" in this way with a child about behaviors. Those behaviors become more intentional, and toddlers can be held a bit more responsible.

## Temperament

You will see differences in behavioral and emotional style by this age. Some toddlers will be more feisty and stubborn than others; some will be easy-going. The Difficult, Slow to Warm Up, and Easy types will be more easily definable. Be sure to note these are brain-based characteristics, and not indications of your parenting techniques.

## Feeding

Toddlers continue to feed themselves solids with their fingers. Insisting on doing it themselves, they are establishing the fact that THEY are in control (see Independence below). As they approach age three, they will show food preferences. It's difficult to determine if these are real or if negativism is just rearing its head. Breastfeeding may continue, or your child can be changed from a bottle. The bottle frequently becomes an emotional "crutch," and parents may elect a choice point **when to wean from the bottle.** A "sippy cup" can become a favored object.

Milk can be given in a bottle (or "sippy cup") at limited times (meals), at naptime, and at bedtime to aid with soothing. Pediatricians will warn you of the effects of milk if a baby sleeps with a bottle—rotting teeth! Water is preferred.

## Sleeping

Consistent sleep through the night and regular nap times are expected. By eighteen months through three years old, one nap in the afternoon is usual. Using a favored toy or blanket as a "crutch" can help getting to sleep. If night waking occurs (and sometimes will, especially after a stress), parents can use the Weissbluth technique (details in Chapter 17) to help the child learn to get back to sleep by themselves. Doing nothing to soothe a crying toddler is *not* doing nothing. Parents are teaching the child to self-soothe and to be somewhat independent at this stage of the game. In addition, it may come as a surprise but children this age are able to climb out of their cribs. There are solutions to this problem which you can research, but be sure to keep the child contained as there is nothing more dangerous than a toddler on the loose at night!

## Toilet Training

At some point, children give up diapers in their toddler years. Different cultures handle toileting in different ways, and the forced toilet training technique—making the child sit on the potty until something was produced—was in fashion up until a few decades ago.

Beginning at the earliest, eighteen months, when there is (barely) adequate musculature and communication, parents may begin teaching. European and parents from other cultures usually begin earlier than middle-class US parents of European background, who typically wait until the child is two or older (1).

Some parents must force the issue for the child to be accepted in daycare, and for some, the cost of diapers is a factor. To even have a chance, the child must be ready in three ways:

1. The child can physically hold and release their urine and feces.
2. They can pay attention to bowel/bladder status and can hold the two ideas in their mind—"I want to play, but I have to go potty."
3. They have to *want* to use the toilet.

Currently, times have changed, and Western child-rearing literature and current customs focus on letting the child take the lead and leaving the decision up to him/her—to a point. **Choice point: whether to be laid back or to set goals in toileting.** If the decision is left to the child, the battle over the toilet is avoided, and the child seeking the ability to make decisions builds a sense of competence. Plus, the "shame" of toileting accidents is avoided.

Toddlers have mixed feelings about using the toilet versus diapers. Sometimes, they are interested; sometimes not. When they make up their mind, the job is done. I have witnessed my own granddaughter navigate the situation. Approaching age three, she was happy in her diapers. She let people know she was "pooping" in a chosen space that was semi-private. Her parents did not interfere but gave her a deadline of her third birthday to give up the diapers. The moment of reckoning was avoided when, after having received a reminder about two months before she turned three, she announced she was "ready." And that was that.

I was not quite so lucky with my own child, *and I* had the company of my colleagues in the Child Psychology department of the hospital. The toilet learning process was taking too long for some of us parents. I introduced Matchbox cars as an incentive—and called it "Pooping for Prizes." It worked. A colleague had a less positive approach and humorously called it "Potty Chair or Electric Chair." Just kidding, of course. Other incentives such as smiley face stickers may be less expensive and just as effective. Praise is the important factor; toilet training should reward success, not punish lapses.

## THE FIVE PSYCHOLOGICAL PILLARS FOR YOUR 15-MONTH TO 3-YEAR-OLD

### 1. Relationship Building

Relating with other children, toddlers graduate from just watching each other play to "parallel play," playing alongside each other and occasionally sharing. By now, you and your former baby, now a toddler, are communicating, attached, and having so much fun (most times). The expression of love through warm interactions will continue to develop that all-important foundation for caring. The autonomy that your child craves will challenge this relationship; parents who haven't yet realized that they are not in control of their child will soon learn.

Avoiding moments of loud yelling and of harsh handling is all-important for keeping the relationship positive and not changing it into one of fear. Some childproofing of the home continues to avoid unnecessary "no's," although it will need to be modified as the child gains competence. Keep the warmth and love in the family going, despite the need for altering your child's behavior in that all-important task of socialization, and you will foster healthy personality development. If I haven't stressed it enough, love is the underpinning of everything!

2. **Teaching Adaptive Behaviors—Here We Go!**

Infants are generally "redirected" when they are doing something dangerous or unacceptable like hitting others or heading for the stove. There is little point in teaching babies "lessons." As they get to toddler age, and have language and cause-and-effect reasoning, you can start teaching. When you start teaching, you assume authority. This can be a big adjustment. You may have difficulty giving up your youthful expectation that your child will be your friend. If you are to be a parent, you have no choice. To review, there are two types of behaviors parents face when socializing their child:

1. Getting your child to do something (**start** behavior).
2. Getting your child to stop doing something (**stop** behavior).

Fortunately, there are many approaches to encourage and discourage both objectives.

A. **Verbal Coaching**

Now that language is present, your toddler can understand verbal coaching for either stop or start behaviors. You may luck out and have a child who will cooperate with a "Please stop hitting your brother" or "Time to pick up your toys" to please a parent. How you present your direction can have a big impact on whether the child cooperates. A harsh, loud tone and command will likely get a negative reaction. The most composed parents add a "please" to their commands and use respectful tones. However, even in the most nicely phrased commands, negativism can result (yes, it is the age) and further steps are usually required to make the most of the learning experience.

## B. Praise

Although praise can be seen as verbal coaching, it is particularly powerful and deserving of a section of its own. When your child does something desirable, admirable, or praiseworthy, it's time to dole out the kind words. "Effective Praise" in toddler-level language specifies the exact behavior that the child did. Vague words such as "that's a nice thing to do" aren't as powerful as "Good job finishing your dinner." Or perhaps your child was playing rough with another, got a verbal reminder, then stopped and played "nicely." Praise can be, "I'm glad to see you are playing nicely with Timmy." It is important to make it genuine praise and not criticism masked as praise such as, "I'm glad to see you are finally playing nicely with Timmy."

## C. Natural Consequences

All through life, there are *natural consequences which are events that just naturally happen* like when your child runs carelessly and they fall down. They touch a hot item, pain ensues. Some but not all of these natural consequences can be used to an advantage. However, it is sometimes too dangerous to let children learn by experiencing pain/stress. Toddlers are in constant motion and exploring everything. As such they will fall down, run into walls, maybe get hit back by another child, and press every button in sight. Safety is an issue here, and parental supervision is essential.

Consequences imposed by parents are part of the teaching process and are the next challenge of parenting.

## D. Imposing Unpleasant Negative Consequences

To review, teaching self-control is the important concept here. Whether it is called discipline or punishment is up for debate, but the whole idea is to get your child to behave in a desired way. Using praise and verbal coaching may work, but sometimes parents have to impose a negative situation to get the message across.

## 1. Isolation or the "Time Out"

When you are in a bind, and your toddler persists in a behavior that is either dangerous or undesirable that requires you to either start or stop a behavior, you have choices. Sometimes the situation calls for a particular consequence: for example, a child refusing to hold a hand crossing a street can be carried; or children fighting over a toy can have the toy placed elsewhere for a time.

When the situation does not have an obvious solution, a frequent choice is the "Time Out" option whereby the child sits in the corner or a designated chair. If your toddler can understand when you say something like, "If you (specify the behavior) again, this (specify the consequence) will happen," you have a new strategy to work with. This *"cause-and-effect"* reasoning is generally present at two and a half years old and sometimes earlier. Without it, you simply continue distracting from the undesired behavior as the child won't "get" the lesson.

## Steps for Initiating a Time Out

a. Note the behavior and judge that it is in need of changing.

b. Communicate clearly to your child what your child should do or not do. For example, your toddler should stop (being rough with the cat) or start (picking up a toy).

c. Remind a few more times—use your judgment and then give a warning of time out to come. The importance of warnings has been stressed in Chapter 9—it lets them control themselves.

d. If the child does not respond to your warning, they get a time out.

## How to Initiate a Time Out

a. Tell the child to go to time out (if this technique has been taught before) or to physically place the child in a time out area.

b. The spot should have been pre-selected to be a very boring spot where the parent can watch the child. No toys or fun things should be available.

c. A minute or two of quiet sitting is specified.

d. A popular rule of thumb is one minute for every year of life. Very young toddlers have little conception of time so parents must judge what will be effective.

e. A timer is very helpful because the child can hear the bell that signals the end. You can also use it to get them to quiet themselves.

f. When your child is quiet, set the timer.

## How to End the Time Out

1. When the timer dings, meet your child at the chair.

2. Ask qualifying questions to ensure they understand/remember why they had a time out.

   "Do you know why you were in time out?"

   "You are in time out because you (hit Johnny)."

   "You broke the no-hitting rule."

   "What would be a good thing to do now?" (hint, "apologize")

3. If no apology, "An apology would make sense." Hopefully, they will do it or you can coach them or force the issue if it seems correct.

4. If the child does apologize, deliver praise for understanding the rule and handling the situation in a positive way.

## How to Manage the Angry and Physical Child While Initiating a Time Out

A preview to new parents: there may be a battle royale if your child has never had this experience, is used to getting their own way, and/or is a feisty sort. You, the parent, must win. The battle is almost existential with you establishing your authority, and the toddler learning. If the child refuses to stay in the place of isolation, they must be held by your own strength in a chair. It's not too hard to handle a child this age, but if they kick or scream, it is a struggle. In the struggle, the child will try everything to escape, including head butts.

With refusing and angry children, my technique has been to sit them in a little chair, stand behind the chair, to cross their arms in front of them, hold their arms, and to watch out for head butts. In dire cases when the battle is raging on and on, you may warn of a physical slap on the arm or leg if they do not comply. If there is still no response, the slap may be given—once. You are bigger and stronger than your toddler, and the message is clear. Parents are in charge. Learning this basic move—the time out and how to maneuver it—is a sign that socialization is proceeding. Once it's learned, the going gets easier. Children understand "time out" and the fact that if they do not cooperate, the punishment is worse. By complying, they get a small punishment and avoid a harsher one.

When I was parenting toddlers (my son and two friends), they surprised me by running to the "time-out rug" when they were caught in some wrong act! All three of them! They were properly trained in the "lesser punishment."

Reflecting on how these issues parallel the justice system, the time out parallels jail time. Children in time out are in "mini-jail" and you are the warden (refer to Chapter 10).

2. **Grandma's Rule**

Once toddlers have language and can understand cause-and-effect reasoning, you can start to build good work habits with Grandma's

Rule: "First you work, then you play." This technique works only on behaviors that you want to START. You see a task to be done, and place a contingency on it. For toddlers, you can say, "Once you put on your shoes, we can go outside to the playground." "When you pick up your toys, we'll put on the TV show." Language has to be toddler-speak, of course.

3. **Physical Punishment**

Children of toddler age are only capable of doing a few things that truly endanger themselves or others, so painful punishments may be *infrequently or never used*. Possibly the biggest threat to safety is a toddler running away from you and into the street or going toward a menacing object such as a strange dog. The strategy of classical conditioning, pairing a painful stimulus with an action, may work to advantage when safety is concerned. When you can't scoop up the child to prevent the danger, pairing a slap and your shout may help. Otherwise, parents have to carry, strap in a stroller, or use a leash to control their child. Neither is a great way, but a toddler's safety is all-important.

---

RUNNING INTO THE STREET

A friend shared that her active toddler son was physically punished twice "within an inch of his life" to quote her (exaggerating, of course), for running away into the street. Then, the behavior was never seen again.

---

You may remember my relating an episode when my son wanted to touch the electrical socket. Because he wouldn't listen to "NO" in varying tones, I used a physical slap on the arm after all other means of preventing him from touching the socket had been tried. And it worked in that instance; he never tried it again. And if a time out battle is going on for an hour, a physical slap (preceded by a warning) might be needed. Physical strategies are to be used sparingly!

*Frequent* use of spankings or physical pain of any kind (pinching, whipping) to socialize children at this age and any age is to be avoided; frequent use not only takes away the impact of the action, but also will threaten the positive relationships. Some cultures use physical punishment frequently in socialization, even at toddler age; if there is a sufficient quantity of loving interaction, there can be a good outcome. Otherwise, the parent/child relationship becomes a fearful one, and the child will be eager to escape it. Refer to Appendix A for pros and cons.

At this toddler age, exploration of "private parts" is normal and soothing, and their actions can be redirected without making them feel ashamed or anxious. They may take things that do not belong to them, but at this age this behavior is normal and *not* considered "stealing." Before age three, they are not really capable of using matches or lighters but are fascinated with fire so need to be carefully supervised. More discussion of physical punishment will come in Chapters 21 and 22, and Appendix A where more potentially dangerous behaviors occur.

3. **Building a Healthy Self**

   a. **The Positive Self**

The struggle for autonomy in the toddler age is a big effort to build a "Self." Recalling Sullivan's ideas on the subject, when there is more acceptance than rejection, the positive Self can be built. The balance between acceptance and rejection of behaviors continues with the socialization process. As has been stated, the Yes-Yes environment is critical in preventing the inevitable "no's." Apart from childproofing, parents can take advantage of their clever and creative thinking to avoid potential battles. For example, if your child has a cherished and fragile toy, and a child visitor is coming, it might be wise to put that toy out of reach. Also, going over guidelines for expected behavior, for example at a store or in the car, and putting out the incentive (not bribe) for appropriate behavior is recommended. The more rejection and anxiety there is in the parent/child interaction, the more defensiveness will be built. Toilet learning is a big milestone here and avoiding harsh criticism/shame can go a long way toward building a positive Self.

Self-identity grows. Approaching their second birthday, children can recognize themselves in a mirror or photograph. They first establish their identity by their names. During these years before three, they are learning about themselves based on what other people say about them. If adults describe their child's traits as nice, bad, gentle, or rough, whether they are positive, negative, or neutral, these descriptions can become part of building their idea of their Self-image. Sometimes these "descriptions" can become limiting. For example, if a parent describes a child as "our shy child," the label may sink in—unintended to be sure. So, I recommend describing behaviors, as opposed to traits, so as not to over-define a child. "I see your kindness to Johnny by sharing the toy." "You can be so helpful when you pick up toys."

b. **Emotional Expression—Handling Emotions Including Tantrums & "Meltdowns"**

Building a healthy understanding and expression of emotion is necessary for a child's mental health. Emotional expression should be handled carefully without shaming or blaming. Toddlers will express feelings of happiness, sadness, fear, and anger in the blink of an eye. They hold nothing back. Handling these intense emotions is a task that is difficult for parents, and emotional "modulation" is part of the socialization process. There is no discussing these feelings. There is no deterrent or "punishment" or self-control. They just come out.

Anger, fear, and sadness are key emotions that will need to be socialized and modulated with the goal of acceptance being the key outcome. Punishment or shaming for these feelings can contribute to emotional disturbance. "You shouldn't be afraid of the dog. You're a big boy." Parents are prone to negating emotions with "You're not sad (scared)," "There's nothing to be sad (scared) about," and the like. Emotions are part of the child. Your acceptance and labeling of these feelings will give your child a vocabulary to express them. And accepting them will help your toddler integrate them into their Self, rather than separating them out as unwelcome. Accepting statements such as "You're really sad about this" or "That seems very scary to you" are recommended. With support and acceptance, the emotion will calm after a time. And with time (and brain maturation), emotions will become more manageable.

This age is typical for the temper tantrum or "meltdown." Parents all over the world have found certain helpful tips. Clever parents are strategic in decisions to take their toddler places (where aspects are too tempting) and to consider whether the child is tired or overstressed. If stressed, tiredness, and temptation are the current assessment, there is no outing. Toddlers can cleverly pick the places and times where you would be most likely to give in to their wants: when you are at the store, on the phone, or preparing dinner. That is their strategy! And they often win!

The tantrum may be about the specific situation or about pent-up frustrations saved up for this moment. And tantrums are saved for the people most intimate in the child's relationship. Aren't you lucky! The explosion is perfectly reasonable from the child's point of view.

Handling the tantrum requires quick thinking. Safety is the key issue, and the child should be removed to a place where they cannot injure themselves (or bother a bunch of strangers who would look sympathetically at you in the best of situations or judgmentally in the worst). Being on a floor is not a problem here. Maybe holding your child to prevent injury may be needed if the child is hurting themself. Parents usually wait for the tantrum to pass. When it does, a calm discussion is helpful, not to punish, but to help the child clarify what was upsetting. "You got mad because I would not let you buy the toy. I said you have toys at home. I know you wish you had that extra toy." Try to use words to say what you want; it works better than getting angry. Every tantrum can be a learning experience!

## 4. Morality/Kindness

To review, the first evidence of morality comes as infants experience feelings of joy or of anxiety or stress from the people around them. This feeling, discussed in the previous section, is a precursor of "Empathy," and has been labeled a "moral emotion." In the toddler age, defiance and demandingness come into the picture, but this behavior is not seen as immoral; just a natural part of the socialization of anger.

Knowing "Right from Wrong" is a long way off but Self/Other differentiation continues. At this toddler age, MINE stands out more than THINE. In the issue of *0 to 3 Journal* published in January 2019, Kathy Reschke quotes an anonymous author of "Toddler Property Laws: If I like it, it's mine. If it's in my hand, it's mine. If I can take it from you, it's mine. If I had it a little while ago, it's mine" (2).

Self-oriented behavior is not seen as immoral but as natural in a toddler. Sharing is not happening. But parents will begin to try to socialize their child to share and help. There will be acts of kindness and helping that are spontaneous and gratifying. How your toddler treats others—kindness behavior—is a focus for socialization. The Self/Other distinction is not very developed at this age, but parents should nevertheless try.

There are early precursors of guilt. Your toddler may know when they have done something which is against parental rules and may wish to atone for it. So, there is a sense of "wrongness" developing. Toddlers approaching age three years may experience discomfort when confronted with a mistake. In fact, it may result in an emotional outburst, and they may try to blame others or say it was an "accident."

## 5. Independence/Separation

Your toddler is now getting accustomed to multiple separations which will go along with increased independence, and will develop attachments with others, but never as strongly as with you! Negativism, the refusal to obey parental musts, is a precursor of eventual independence. However, it may not feel like it!

Western parents tend to be conscious of their child's mental state (refer back to Chapter 16 and to Appendix C on cultural research on independence). You are or will be seeing your child as an emerging person with a sense of Self and can guide them to a sense of competence. "See, you did it yourself!" Letting children proceed at their own pace helps to ensure success and builds confidence to be self-sufficient, as opposed to forcing the issue. This is not to say that there is anything wrong in urging or commanding children to act when they are capable of doing so, but there is a difference. Western parents seem to pay more attention to how the "Self" is doing in the interest of long-term confidence and adjustment.

---

**CHOICE POINT**

Group "school" experiences are now expected, and children may visit other families for "play dates" where parents are not present. Separations may be longer and may be forced due to parents' absences for illness or vacations.

---

## SUMMARY OF TODDLER STAGE (Chapter 20)

Getting from infancy to preschool necessitates going through the toddler years. The negativism and temper tantrums are a big challenge for any parent. Getting a schedule for eating, sleeping, and then toilet training are the physical nuts and bolts of this age. Beginning the "rules" of what to "do" and what "not to do" and coaching appropriate behavior with playmates is the task of socialization. But fostering a sense of autonomy and confidence despite all the opportunities to squelch the negativism is a tightrope that parents must walk. Keeping things positive and loving despite parents establishing authority can be a big, big challenge. They say it gets easier when children turn three! Now to preschool!

# PRESCHOOL AGE (3-6 YEARS)

# Chapter 21

## Relationship Building and Teaching Adaptive Behavior

## INTRODUCTION

You will see several changes as your child develops between three and six years old. At three years, your child typically will begin to experience group education suited to this age. There is lots of play and leeway in their schedule (hopefully). The beginning of the third year is characterized by a shift from the negativism of the second year to a rather cooperative attitude where your child wants to please you. Then, when your child gets closer to age five, things are likely to get rocky for a time. Then, things get back to reasonable. At six years old, your child will end kindergarten and begin first grade, when sitting at a desk for relatively long periods of time is the expectation. There is a very important psychological shift responsible for these changes, as you will see. It's a bit of a roller coaster.

## REVIEW OF DEVELOPMENTAL THEORISTS FOR PRESCHOOL AGE

In this age span, the differentiation between Self and Other progresses, egocentrism begins to be challenged by the real world, and leads to the big attitude changes of power-seeking, which Brazelton calls (with tongue-in-cheek) "early adolescence." Thus begins the roller coaster, with the child testing limits right and left.

Piaget and Freud came together to explain this phenomenon. A child's thinking about the world continues to be erratic. If a male child with two brothers is asked how many brothers are in the family, he will answer "two." If the same amount of water is poured from one vessel into another which is "taller" than the other, the child will assume there is "more" in the taller vessel. Nothing has been added to the water. This type of thinking that "it is whatever it looks like" is typical of the "Preoperational Stage" of Piaget (refer to Chapter 6). Freud's theory will come when we look at family relationships in a following section.

## BRAIN DEVELOPMENT

Brain maturation of course is responsible for these changes in thinking about the world. Despite the immaturity with the "looks like," your child will be able to hold two alternatives presented and choose between them at this stage. You can see the wheels turning! Parents will frequently enroll their child in a group setting such as preschool where brain development is challenged. Chapter 3 discusses how preschools differ and how they positively affect the brain. Your criterion for preschool choice should be whether it fosters a love of school and learning with free play, fun, reasonable "rules," and skips any over-challenging academic drills. Although children will benefit from reciting their ABCs, anything that is way above a child's head will create a negative experience. At this age, learning should foster joy and not frustration.

Language is going full speed ahead. Between the ages of three and five, Mussen notes that children are adding fifty new words to their spoken vocabulary each month. And they are speaking in longer sentences with multiple clauses. Grammar rules are internalized, and you can see them mastering grammar rules in mistakes they make (e.g. digged for dug).

Differences between children in intellectual maturation may be seen, with some delays and some advancements noted. Speech may lag behind other areas for example. The brain is likely to catch up with itself, so patience is needed, especially with speech. However, serious delays would warrant testing and proper interventions. Intelligence testing is more reliable at age four and older.

Although your child may have been counting and learning some letters in toddler years, the preschool years signal the beginning of systematic learning of alphabet letters and numbers. The letters and numbers are prominently displayed on the school walls, with the expectation that they will be learned; the preschool brain is ready to begin such learning. You may not realize how different those letters and numbers are from other types of learning. At this age, you can show your child how to do a task like tying shoes, and they will learn. But unlike hands-on tasks, letters and numbers *stand for something else*—the definition of symbols or abstraction. All written languages (and numbers) are symbolic. Most are phonetic where a letter stands for a sound; some like Chinese involve a pictogram, which stands for an idea. Making these connections in the brain is the beginning of "formal education," and it presents a different level of difficulty (more about that in Chapters 23 through 26). Exceptions will be those children whose brains are built differently.

## TEMPERAMENT

Activity level differentiates children at this age; some are excessively active ("hyper") and can be a handful. Particularly when they enter first grade and are expected to sit still for longer periods, teachers and parents will note problems in focus, impulsivity, and need for activity. This type of behavior could be early signs of Attention Deficit Hyperactivity Disorder (refer to Chapter 23 for extended information on diagnosis and treatment).

# FEEDING

Getting the proper nutrition in your child can be a struggle, although over the preschool years things get much better. Brazelton recommends minimally sixteen ounces of milk or milk products, two ounces of protein, some carbs, a few ounces of fruit, and a multivitamin to cover all the bases. Family dinners are socialization times, in both senses of the word. Conversation and manners can be encouraged to a point. Dinners should not become battles, and parents can determine their own strategies to keep mealtime peaceful. One strategy is that if the child leaves the table, their dinner is over, and they can't return. Snacks should be limited so children are not full by dinnertime.

---

**CHOICE POINT**

**Setting up family dinners will be a decision made by parents. Staying connected as a family is the goal here, in addition to teaching table manners, conversation, and sharing attention.**

---

# TOILET TRAINING

Your child has learned to use the toilet, but may have accidents on occasion, particularly if there is a new stress in the family. Diapers should be a relief, not a punishment. Night dryness is a goal; if your child can rouse themself when they need to use the toilet at night, this is major progress.

# SLEEPING

Your child should be able to sleep alone for eight to twelve hours. There are usually three periods of sleep per night consisting of light sleep and deep sleep. When your child wakes, their task is to get themselves back to sleep. Problems arise when children who have their own bed get into their parents' bed in the middle of the night as this habit can be hard to break. Unless there is a good reason (loud thunder, illness), children are discouraged from the parents' bed. "Co-sleeping" is a style some parents espouse, and certainly many cultures have this tradition, but this sleeping alone is training for Western independence. When the child tries to crawl in, parents take the child back to their own bed, gently soothe, and remind the child it is their task to get through the night by themselves. Incentives are frequently helpful. Refer back to Weissbluth (Chapters 16 and 17) for coaching.

# PSYCHOLOGICAL PILLARS FOR YOUR PRESCHOOLER

## 1. Relationship Building

Attachments and positive relationships continue to grow—both to intimates (you) and others caring for your child.

In the realm of your relationship with your child, even with the most secure attachment, and wonderful loving relationship, there is a *major shift* in relationships brewing. Freud described this shift as the "Oedipal complex" named after a Greek mythological figure who killed his father (he really didn't know that he was his father at the time, so it's not as bad as it sounds) and married his mother (again, unknowingly). Freudian theory states that as your child enters ages four or five, they have a growing realization that—alas—they are NOT the center of the universe!

This phenomenon corresponds to Piaget's observations that the decline in egocentrism is expected for this age. Now, back to Freud, your child sees parents as the "enemy" of sorts—because the child realizes YOU are in charge. How does your child respond? Some, with grace and acceptance, but many with a grab for POWER.

Freud first noted this transition, and Adler and his followers amended it to include not just the opposite-sex parent (father for boy, mother for girl) but BOTH parents. Or actually *anyone* with power. The child in the throes of this realization wants to continue to be in charge, and will make efforts to really make their wishes known. This is "tyrant" behavior, and the sudden onset of fierce aggression can really confuse parents. So, this apparent step backward is actually a combination of brain and emotional maturation. This is progress! And Freud meets Piaget!

The response to the "tyrannical" behavior should be firm and gentle limits, as parents practiced before. But the heat of "I hate you" or "you can't make me" can make the process more difficult. The desired end result will be, lo and behold, the child giving up on the parent struggle, and entering the competitive world of peers! At least they have a chance to out-power them! Previously in this book I referred to my dissertation, which showed more egocentric children preferring adult to peer contact, and vice versa. This finding is consistent with Freud's theory. Failure to adequately set limits on the "tyrant" will result in an adult who feels entitled, privileged, and narcissistic.

My personal experience with dealing with preschoolers who are "stuck" in the "tyrannical" part of this stage relates to the fairy tales that are popular with this age. Children fighting the scary creatures and winning is the major theme—"Jack kills the Giant in the Beanstalk," for example. Or in the story of the "Three Little Pigs," the wolf is outsmarted. This theme hearkens back to poor Oedipus killing his father even if unknowingly, and echoes in the hearts of children in the throes of the power battle.

The onset of certain fears and bad dreams is related to this psychological shift. Some children feel truly homicidal about their parents, and this scares them. This fear can show itself in nightmares where the child's angry feeling fuels the drama of big bad something scaring the heck out of the child. Get ready for middle of the night wake-ups and crawling into your bed!

When these children were in psychotherapy, necessary for those truly stuck, I had a special treatment for them. I role-played a "big bad ogre" who wanted to steal the "treasure" from the child, who was guarding it with a rubber knife. Children had to have a firm enough understanding of role play and that we were "acting," or they wouldn't benefit. During this time, I was calling the child "little," having "no power!" Be assured that the "insults" were not seen as such by the child but rather challenges which were refuted: "I'm not little!!" I coached the child to "kill" me using the knife to "chop off" my arms, legs, and ultimately my head; thus, the child was victorious! I "died" a "painful" death. Good acting is helpful for a child therapist, and the child was absolutely gleeful!

When I did this role play with my grandson, who at age four and a half was very bossy and into power, he said, "I want to do it ten more times." Then we did. Exactly ten more times, and then never thereafter. Somehow, playing out the wish to conquer the "big guys" somehow satisfies the child's true wishes. With time and consistency, the "field of battle" will change, and the child now preferring other children for relationships can engage in efforts to assert their "power" that the child can actually win. After the role play, I discussed fantasy versus reality with the child so they weren't misled to think they could "overpower" or cut people up in real life. A discussion ensued after the role play on what power the child actually has—I labeled it "kid power."

The point of this "battle" is that the child will eventually give up the battle with adults and reconcile themself to being a (subordinate) child. Freud theorized that as a result of the "battle," the child internalizes the values of the adults, and assumes the identity of the same-sex parent. From the battle emerges the "new" child, who gets a sense of power from the parent's nature, and who enters the peer group where a new identity is assumed.

Understanding and identifying your child's difficulty with the power difference between themself and you, the adult parent, can help in your handling of conflict. And using the word "power" can help to sympathize when they face rules they don't like. For example, "You'd love to have the power to make the rules. It stinks when you don't have the power." And using the word when giving your child realistic choices can help them realize the "power" they actually have. "Kid power" is the ability to choose between sets of clothes (your choice), friends, games/play, and food to a certain extent.

Also related to the power difference, children will use their wits to "trick" adults. They get so much pleasure out of besting you in this way. Putting the adult in an embarrassing spot will get peals of laughter. Parents, please don't discourage the tricking, but rather praise the child for their cleverness.

Here's an anecdote about how my grandson, age five and three-quarter, demonstrated his "power" via football. In a family of avid Chicago Bears fans, he decided to be a Green Bay Packers fan. Now any of you who know the rivalry between the two teams understand how annoying that choice was. Despite pressure from adults, he's sticking to it! What a stinker!

Playing board games becomes fun at this age. Preschoolers start out being sore losers and cheaters. Games at this age are based on luck, and they do not understand the difference between luck and skill. However, they mature into better game players and can compete with adults on games requiring skill not luck. Now, the fun begins!

---

**CHOICE POINT**

**When it comes to skill games, should you let them win or play your best, and they will consistently lose? In my opinion, letting them win is confusing as they would question your competence. Some of them play "memory" games better than adults at young ages, so they can win on their own. As they reach six years old, they might be able to beat you at Connect Four. In games based on luck, let the chips fall where they may.**

---

Another area of growth is in sibling relationships. The competition seen between sibs close in age is fierce. Who goes first? Who chooses the play? Whose is bigger, longer, better? Who does things better? Who IS better? You can be creative in negotiating systems where "fair" turn-taking is established. Younger children want to imitate the older and find it difficult to accept their limitations. Parents' interventions are helpful here, especially praise for peaceful interactions when you catch them while they are being "good." The times when they play successfully and peacefully are wonders to behold.

Part of relationship-building is friendship, which develops among age-mates. Those with secure attachments and positive senses of Self will develop more secure peer relationships. Friends will come and go and are based on how near they live to you and what their preferred activities are.

Regarding friends and play, preschoolers now engage in "cooperative play" where they collaborate to identify a theme, assign roles, and use imagination. For example, do you remember "playing house" where "I'll be Mommy. You be Daddy?" If you watch carefully, you can respect the tremendous sensitivity that is growing in how children determine who plays whom in the play, how one "actor" influences how others act, considers others' needs, anticipates a change, and adapts. If you think about it, the social skills needed for successful imaginative play are mind-boggling. This type of play is a tremendous boost to building skills needed for future social success.

## 2. Teaching Adaptive Behaviors

### Limit Testing in General

These preschool years start the coaching and training of following the "rules." In the preceding section, you learned about the power trip of the four- to five-year-old. This stage frequently results in outright refusal to follow rules. Be ready for some "smart talk" such as, "You can't make me;" "I'm the boss of myself" or "I won't do it." How to navigate?

Here is an anecdote on how my granddaughter, Payton, at age four tried to manipulate her mother. She was crying in a store because her mother wouldn't buy her what she wanted. She said, "I'll stop crying if you buy me the balloon." Do you think she got the balloon? No way.

## Tips on Communication to Get Your Point Across

Again, some behaviors must stop, like hitting your sister, and some behaviors must start, like picking up your toys. Becoming socialized implies understanding a clear hierarchy. Parents, not kids, make the rule whether the child likes it or not. And they usually don't like it. So, how to weather the storm? Some parents will try to soft-pedal the commands or avoid them altogether to avoid the battle. For example, when redirecting away from a "no," you can use a positive suggestion first: "Let's try gently petting the dog instead of pulling his tail."

Although it's understandable to be respectful of children, and not to come down too hard, it can be dangerous to be hesitant or unclear as your child is out to win. Regarding "rules" I choose to be straightforward. Rules are meant to be followed, and obeying the rule is the name of the game. Telling children to "listen" seems a bit softer than telling them to "obey." But "listen" can be misleading: "Of course, I can listen. I hear you." Obey is a different story. Rule is a rather neutral term.

Harshness in tone is unnecessary and generally results in refusal. Nobody likes to be told what to do! Think of how you respond to commands. Getting your child's full attention is necessary, so getting close, at eye level, and making sure your child is attentive to your words, helps to get the point across. So, having your child's eyes on you, phrasing a Stop or Start with a moderate tone, and using "Please" and "Thank you" are some good ways to get a command across.

---

**CHOICE POINT**

**To phrase a command or rule, get to eye level, use "please" and "thank you" in a respectful tone, and use clear language to be most effective.**

---

Most children this age will balk at commands by saying, "Why do I have to do so and so?" The question is really part of a strategy to change the "rule!" Really old-school parenting says, "Because I said so." More up-to-date responses include saying "it's a rule" and explain the reason behind the rule. Giving a reason is an opportunity to teach the child about the world and to promote a democratic family atmosphere that stimulates self-confidence of expression. In Chapter 9, I introduced the categories of rules: Safety (no crossing the street without an adult), Health (good food makes you strong), Responsibility Training (help the family out by doing some chores like setting the table), and Politeness (it's wrong to say shut up—or it's polite to say yes, ma'am). A short answer will suffice. In many cases, understanding the reason behind the rule is enough to get cooperation. If there is no reason behind the rule, it probably shouldn't be a rule. An example is when a parent objected to her child's frequent fooling with her hair. That didn't hurt anyone, and it was only the mother who was bothered. I counseled her to accept the behavior. However, if too many "whys" are asked, the child is getting into serious manipulative territory.

> **CHOICE POINT**
>
> **How to respond to a child's "Why do I have to?" Supplying reasons can aid in getting cooperation and in overall teaching. Keep it short, simple, and direct.**

## Choices

Giving choices can avoid some battles. I have observed my daughter-in-law be intentional when giving my grandkids choices when they have to do a "start" behavior. They get two choices for foods, for what to wear, and for other matters, which can really work to head off a confrontation. Also, children develop a source of agency or "power" ("kid power") in making that (limited) decision.

I'm not sure if she is following advice from the American Academy of Pediatrics or using her own good sense. The AAP suggests "helping children learn positive behaviors by providing children with opportunities to make choices whenever appropriate options exist." (1) Of course there is a downside here; when a child is faced with no choice, for example as a guest at a friend's house, they may just have to eat what is put in front of them.

## Effective Praise

Verbal coaching will be the main way your preschooler learns how to behave. You are a teacher. Your goal is to see that behavior again and again, and praise is a helpful tool.

"Effective Praise" in preschool-level language specifies the exact behavior that the child did. Children aged three to six will respond to specific praise of more sophisticated "Start" behaviors such as "I'm glad you were kind to so and so and helped them." Or "Good job putting away all your toys." Again, vague words such as "that's a nice thing to do" aren't as powerful as "good job eating your whole dinner." Praise for ending a Stop behavior is always a good idea. When your preschooler calms themself down after an upset, you might praise them with the words, "I can see you controlled your angry feelings. That makes me proud."

---

### CHOICE POINT

**Praise is so important that it is not so much whether you praise, but rather how much. As in the toddler age, when your child does something desirable, admirable, or praiseworthy, it is time to dole out the kind words.**

---

## Natural Consequences

As reviewed previously, all through life, there are *natural consequences—bad things that just naturally happen.* With more activity and choices expected from preschoolers and more refusals forth-coming, your child might benefit from "learning the hard way." Touching something hot is a sure way to learn, but also a sure way to get a burn. So, use your judgment. If they refuse to put on shoes, there will be no walk. Some but not all of these natural consequences can be used to advantage. However, it is sometimes too dangerous or unhealthy to let children learn by experiencing pain or stress. Not sleeping enough makes children tired and crabby and prone to ailments; not eating properly causes malnutrition. I recall hearing about one intervention using natural consequences when a child refused to get dressed and then wore pajamas to school. Peers took care of the situation; thereby considered a natural consequence.

Consequences imposed by parents are part of the teaching process and are the next challenge of parenting. Let's look at those difficult decisions.

## "Grandma's Rule"

"First you work, then you play" continues to be a helpful strategy for getting required Start behavior. A request for another game or activity can be made contingent on performance to clean up the current mess. Or, first you put pajamas on, then you can get your story. The child is in control of how long it takes to get their desired activity. If they aren't so crazy about the rewarding activity, this strategy won't work.

# Chapter 22

## Continuing Pillars of Adaptive Behavior, Self, Morality, and Independence

### CONTINUING WITH THE PILLAR OF ADAPTIVE BEHAVIOR

In the previous chapter, positive approaches to teaching behavior were covered. However, preschoolers who are not performing despite the use of praise or Grandma's rule, may need to suffer unpleasant consequences, that is, punishment. Behaviors to start for preschoolers will be some beginning tasks such as setting the table and picking up toys. Behaviors to stop are annoying or hurting others, destroying property, etc. Parents can give directives on what to do, but when a child balks or doesn't stop an activity, it's time to intervene.

### Warning and Losing Privileges

*Advance notice* of things to come, i.e. *warnings,* are not only fair to the child but effective in behavior change. Warnings allow the child to self-control before punishment is administered. Self-control is, to repeat, the goal of all your teachings. When some non-adaptive behavior is seen, the strategy is to first let the child know in detail what's going to happen if the behavior continues. Choosing the consequence can be tricky. Sometimes parents forget to think ahead and warn and shout out "You're going to your room!" And sometimes a consequence is chosen that is so extreme and unreasonable that it will never be carried out, like, "You're never going to have a friend over again!" And sometimes the consequence is so vague that it is ineffective: "You'll be in trouble!"

Once the misbehavior is specified and the warning is given, it is stated: "If you don't pick up the toys, you will not get to play with them for a day." Then here's what to do if the child doesn't start the behavior. In many cases for Start behaviors, common use is a limit of three directives—"three strikes, you're out." Some parents may prefer counting: "You'll lose your __ privilege when I count to five." These techniques are warnings which are extremely important in teaching behaviors; *they are not threats.*

Some Stop behaviors cannot get three warnings, as they must be stopped immediately. You do not get three chances to stop drawing on the wall. If the child does not stop immediately, you will need to physically interfere. A warning of a future punishment is in order. "If you do that again, you will lose your use of drawing for a whole day and get a time out. And now you have to clean the wall."

It goes without saying that you must follow through on a warning if it is not heeded. Here are some tips for choices of punishments. The mantra, "Let the punishment fit the crime" is appropriate here.

"Loss of privileges" is the general strategy for punishment. At this age, they are developing strong preferences for activities and things, and loss of the privilege of playing with these things or doing those things will be a good inducement for better behavior. Creative use of the "privilege" is necessary. If bedtime has been a challenge, an early bedtime the next day is the punishment. Another privilege is playing outside, and if a child does not play in allowed boundaries, the privilege is suspended. If there is fighting over a toy, the toy gets put away for a time. If there's excess bickering with a friend over, the friend can go home early, or not be invited for a time. The rule of thumb: if there is an activity being abused, that is the one removed. Parents call these activities "privileges," and indeed they are.

If there is no activity being mishandled, but the child is uncooperative or rude, depriving their favorite toy can be effective. Children at this time and age love their computer devices; loss of the iPad, in the case of my six-year-old grandson, and other special toys are effective consequences.

## Property Damage & Aggressive Behavior

For Stop behaviors, where property damage or aggressive behavior is in question, the principle of restitution or reparations comes into play. The child must make the situation "right." For example, if they have intentionally made a mess, they must clean it up. Or using crayons on inappropriate surfaces would result in helping with clean up and "no crayons" for a period of time. If they have hurt another, they should apologize in addition to a consequence such as a time-out.

---

**CHOICE POINT**

**How best to handle non-adaptive behaviors? Specify which rule is being broken or which privilege is in question. Warn the child in advance of the consequence and follow through with the punishment if necessary.**

**Note: Sometimes caregivers other than parents are at a disadvantage as they can be ignored by a resistant child, and they are not around to take away privileges. Warnings to give parents a "bad report" with ultimate loss of privileges can empower the caregiver. This strategy should be arranged in front of the child prior to parents leaving. However, caregivers should be permitted by parents to give time outs, get clean ups of messes, and in general enforce the "rules." When serious misbehavior occurs, an actual phone call to the parent (while to be avoided at all costs because you don't want to ruin parents' time) may be necessary.**

---

## Time Outs

Time outs as mentioned in the preceding section are still useful; instructions were given in Chapter 20. The same procedures for initiating a time out are to communicate what exactly is going wrong and to give warning about a time out. Choose an appropriate space ahead of time. Once they are in the designated space, set the timer. Keep your eye on the child for the duration. If they try to sneak out, the time out begins anew. After the time out, follow up with a discussion to re-emphasize the lesson.

Recently, I warned my grandson, then age five and three-quarter, that if he poked his sister "one more time," he would do a "time out." He did, and he did. He didn't annoy her again (that day at least). Hopefully, your child has learned to cooperate in the time-out procedure and will not need to be forced. However, it may happen that force is needed, much the same way as with the toddler. Your preschool child is bigger and stronger, and any struggle will be more difficult. But they are also more able to reason, so combining loss of privileges or increased minutes in time out if they do not cooperate may do the trick.

## Physical Punishment

As discussed in Chapter 10 and Appendix A, the use of physical punishment is controversial, and a few professional associations have published statements that counsel against using physical pain in any instance. However, I must disagree. Compared to toddlers, with the exception of those running in the street, preschoolers are more capable of doing a variety of things that truly endanger themselves and may require the severe punishment that is physical. And if a time out battle is going on unreasonably, a physical slap on the arm (preceded by a warning) might be needed to get the point across. These strategies are to be used sparingly and only when the parent remains calm. I know keeping calm seems hard in situations of danger, but if you are really angry and lashing out at the child, the teaching moment may be lost.

As discussed in Chapter 20, *frequent* use of spankings or physical pain of any kind (pinching, whipping) to socialize children at this age and any age is to be avoided. If parents rely overly on this technique, they risk turning a positive relationship into one of fear.

In this age group, you might see two very dangerous behaviors. Playing with fire is something preschoolers can do, and they are fascinated with fire. They can actually find lighters or matches and use them or find lit candles. Common sense says to store these out of reach of preschoolers, but in some cases, fire will be accessible. Interest in fire should be anticipated and the child should be forewarned of severe punishment (possibly physical).

Also, another issue is sex play. There is normal curiosity about genitals like playing "doctor" or "nurse," and this behavior should be tolerated in toddlers and young preschoolers but discouraged. Parental discussion about not touching "private parts" comes in here. Masturbation is also common because children discover that touching their genitals feels good. Helpful parents coach that this activity is "private." It is not wise to use words like "dirty" or "that hurts your ___" because that is untrue. Distraction to other activities usually does the trick.

In some cases, children this age may exploit or manipulate others to engage in sex play. "I'll give you candy if you show me your ____." When that behavior is apparent, severe measures are in order. If other parents get the message that this child is focusing on sex play, that child will become the neighborhood pariah. Clearly targeted physical or equally harsh punishment is needed to curb this behavior, which is again "fun." Loss of recess or playing with others would be a lost privilege.

Stealing or shoplifting is common in the five- to seven-year-old age group, and will be covered in the Morality section just below.

Although not as dangerous as the above behaviors, using "bad words" is also a punishable offense that can lead to ostracism in the neighborhood. You will have to choose which words are appropriate ways to "swear," and families will have interesting discussions about what is allowable. "Hell" and "damn" will generally wait until school age, when swearing becomes an art form. So what words can they use? Be forewarned, they will use the words *you* use, so beware lest you be accused of hypocrisy. Old-school strategies like washing a mouth out with soap, or in the Hispanic community a bit of hot sauce on the tongue, are still used. Maybe there's something different out there now, but usual praise and punishment will work to get a child on the "proper" path.

In Chapter 10 and Appendix A, I mentioned how punishment strategies mirror the penal system, the "capital crimes" deserve "capital punishment." The other lesser infractions can be considered felonies or misdemeanors, and handled with mini-jail or house arrest (time outs), penalties or fines (restitution), or deprivation of usual privileges (rather like jail).

## Using Behavior Charts

At this age, visual aids for good behavior begin to be helpful. Behavior charts displayed in prominent places are a very effective tool for children. Seeing it on paper is a nice supplement to verbal feedback whether positive or negative.

1. **Guidelines to Make Behavior Charts**

   - Not too many goals
   - Goals stated in a positive way
   - Reinforcements to be what will motivate the child (stickers, earning treats, earning outings)

2. **Typical Targeted Behaviors** for preschoolers are those that recur on a regular basis:

   - Play nicely with siblings (politeness)

- Play within set boundaries (safety)
- Pick up your toys (responsibility training)
- Use polite language (politeness)
- Eat your veggies (health)
- Get ready in the morning (responsibility)
- Calm bedtime (health)
- Take "No" for an answer—no excessive protest

3. **Specific Behaviors Targeted** might be:

- Sleeping alone in your bed
- Treating your sibling kindly (no teasing)
- Suck something other than your thumb or pacifier

4. **Avoid Negative Phrasing,** which is tempting to a parent to say, but avoid it.

- Don't crawl into our bed.
- Don't hit your sister.
- Don't suck your thumb.

In devising the chart, prior to the child's ability to read, you can draw pictures of the desired behavior. This took a bit of creativity on my part, but I managed to draw a stick figure of a child sleeping peacefully in bed; a child picking up toys; a child playing nicely with children (a heart in the picture is an easily understandable symbol); and speaking nicely (word "balloon" with a heart). The only time I used a negative was in "no bugging" because I couldn't think of a picture for "take no for an answer." I drew a picture of a bug with a slash in a circle through it (like on traffic signs). Nowadays, you can make a chart with clip-art from the internet.

# SELF DEVELOPMENT

In Chapter 11, we covered egocentrism, Self-esteem, blaming, Self/Other distinctions, and overprotection. A huge change in the Self occurs in the preschool age. As discussed in Chapter 21, the young preschooler experiences the realization that they are "powerless" in comparison with adults: "Who makes the rules is the boss." And hence the ensuing struggle for power. Your child gets a new Self out of the struggle, and by parents handling the battle with gentle firmness, the Self will emerge. "So what if I can't get what I want from my parents; kids are much more fun." At age six or seven, the preschooler will enter the world of children and the next stage.

Defensiveness and true self-esteem were also discussed in the previous chapter on the Self. Anger is socialized from the toddler's rageful wishes to physically injure others to blaming others or calling names. "He did it, not me!" "You are stinky!" This behavior is verbally abusive at older ages, but is normal at this age. Parents rightfully see name-calling behavior as maladaptive and work to change (socialize) it so that children communicate their feelings in socially appropriate ways.

**Defense mechanisms** against feelings of Self-inadequacy can be seen at this stage. Again, rather than taking responsibility for their own misbehavior, preschoolers are prone to blame others (projection). Other defense mechanisms that protect the Self against the anxiety that there is something amiss (again, Freud) can be seen: denial as when they say, "I didn't do it;" regression when they resort to sucking the thumb or other past habits; repression when they say, "I don't remember."

Again, defensiveness is the opposite of Self-Esteem, in Sullivan's manner of theorizing. Blaming and making excuses for misbehavior is common at this age. And this is the age where it is stopped in its tracks. "Blaming" and "name-calling" are punishable offenses, and children can be socialized into more adaptive behaviors by usual strategy of praise and punishment. Of course, if the family is one that blames and name-calls each other, these behaviors won't be stopped because they fit the family model. This is a dysfunctional family system to be sure (refer to Chapter 9 to review positive ways to communicate negative feelings).

At this preschool age, most parents will work to help the child to take responsibility for their own behavior and to avoid blaming others. Role modeling to show children how to acknowledge mistakes and offer apologies are the most effective teaching strategies.

---

**CHOICE POINT**

**When you have erred, it is an opportunity to show your child how it's done. Admit your errors and apologize when appropriate rather than demonstrating defensive behaviors.**

---

Children's Selves are growing as they learn more about what they are "good at" and "not so good at." This level of judgment of Self-competency comes into play in the new sports and physical activities that parents are likely to let their children try. Dance classes, T-ball, soccer, and swimming are all great outlets for an emerging Self. Only if they will try it! Parents will need to negotiate with each child what activities will be tried. Pushing a child toward what "Daddy" or "Mommy" did will likely backfire.

As for how preschool children understand their own Self, knowledge of the Self expands from knowledge of the physical Self to certain attributes: "I have a dog," or "I am a big brother." These competencies will add to the Self-Concept.

---

**CHOICE POINT**

**Choose activities that build competencies and not resentment. Know when to stick to or quit an activity.**

---

Being able to "do it myself" is a big plus in Self-development. Starting at age three, there is still a need for parental intervention in problem situations. As your child proceeds to six, you will find opportunities to let your child try something or handle it themself. This phase is where Self-development and independence intersect. Your trust in the child's Self to make decisions is also important. Overprotection or "hovering" is a dangerous way to act and will literally sabotage the child's feeling of confidence. Bailing out a child from a difficult situation requires good judgment on your part because sending the message that the child can't handle it will result in diminishing their sense of self-worth.

---

**CHOICE POINT**

**Judge when to let your child handle a situation or activity by themself and help only when need it.**

---

## MORALITY/KINDNESS

Kindness behavior is taught at this age. Sharing and helping are rewarded with praise. If a child fails to share or help, parental coaching is there. Empathy is observed in responding to hurt. Preschool age is still "pre-moral," as understanding the concept of "right and wrong" in a larger sense is still not available. (Spoiler alert: the resolution of the Oedipal conflict/beginning of the pre-operational stage makes the development of conscience possible. Not before. This phenomenon was covered in Chapters 5 and 21.)

Preschool children understand "rules" as givens and define "good" and "bad" according to the rules. Rules are to be followed; deviations from them are punished. "Good" children conform to the rules. A child will try to follow the rules to please adults and so as not to be punished. Prior to age seven, this system of thought prevails (Kohlberg). (Refer to Chapter 13 to refresh details of Kohlberg's analyses.)

## Stealing

As mentioned in the previous section, stealing or shoplifting can be a problem in this age group. It causes parents concern because it affects people outside the family. Children under the age of three take things because they don't understand this prohibition and what's "mine" is "mine." Children between the ages of three and seven understand that things belong to others and are taught to follow that rule.

Taking things from a store (shoplifting) or taking others' belongings is a phenomenon that begins around age five and a half. Gesell found it so common in his massive study that he included it in his list of usual behaviors. The property in question will frequently be from a store. Being pre-moral, they may not seem to get the importance of property rights or that stealing is against the law. Aware parents check children's pockets after a store visit.

To counteract this "fun" behavior (free candy), parents use a technique of punishment that is both unusual and universal. Recall back to when you might have performed such a nefarious act. What did your parents do? *They most likely made you return the item to the shopkeeper and apologize.* This technique is the ONLY one where humiliation is used to advantage. Other punishments are generally kept from other peers to avoid humiliation and embarrassment (Chapter 10). This mode of punishment is generally highly effective, but repeat incidents may earn physical punishment. The behavior must be stopped in its tracks. Stealing is such fun, but it is immoral as well as illegal!

A fascinating aspect of this punishment is that it is universal. As I wrote in the previous Morality section, in my classes with pediatrics residents from all over the world, they reported the SAME technique being used by their parents. No matter from India, Mexico, China, or Africa, children had the same tendency to steal and parents used the same "return and apologize" to deter them. Keep in mind that these residents were all highly educated and from middle- to upper-class families, so the punishment technique may not be totally universal across social classes. But it sure is in the middle class.

## Lying

Lying causes problems in the preschool-age group. Children at three begin to understand the difference between truth and fantasy. Make-believe play, fairy tales, and imaginary playmates are all enjoyed. But they grow to know what is fact and what is not. Preschool children may lie to avoid getting reprimands for failure to follow a rule. "I don't remember" can be a quiet lie, along with a psychological defense. You may hear "Yes, I cleaned up my toys" when they in fact did not. Also, they may lie to test adult rules and limits or to get their siblings in "trouble." Parents will confront children with lies versus truth and apply appropriate negative consequences, at the very least, a verbal reprimand.

There is much at stake in this area. When children lie, they cease to be trusted. Helping children understand what "trust" is and what a loss of trust means, is part of the teaching of morality. These are difficult concepts for a three-year-old, but as the preschool years continue, they are capable of knowing. A verbal reprimand to a lie will necessitate long conversations about trust, keeping promises, and telling the truth. Speaking of keeping promises, parents have to be good role models here!

## Cheating

Cheating at games is common in this age group. There are wonderful games available for this age, which generally involve luck, not skill. As children learn to play board games which have winners and losers, preschoolers want to win at any cost. They do not understand the difference between games of skill and games of luck, so they try to cheat. Adults may let them win at this age rather than endure big emotional scenes. My approach with playing a game is to play to win, but to stop the game if the child becomes upset when they are losing. And then do something else that is not competitive. This behavior is part of the Oedipal power struggle. The games, which are great at teaching turn-taking, might not be worth it until your child matures a bit emotionally. Then, they can be a good winner and not such a sore loser.

---

**CHOICE POINT**

**When it comes to whether you play to win or let your child win at a board game, depending on the child, it's a toss-up. A child's joy at "winning" is a plus, but for some, winning all the time might feed into a power trip. This issue is not a big one in the scheme of things.**

---

Children are now expected to perform some tasks, to cooperate with "rules," and not to hurt others or things intentionally. They will blame another when they have transgressed. Also, in terms of truth and honesty, they may exaggerate events and may have little distinction between fiction and fact. "Goodness" means conforming and cooperating. They understand "good and bad," but not "right and wrong."

---

**CHOICE POINT**

**Whether to enroll in some religious training or not. Obviously, family values are the key here. Whatever the religious system, and maybe there are two of them, parents have to coordinate carefully.**

---

Other values such as apologizing, atoning, forgiving, and show-ing mercy are taught within your family. The value of a forced apology ("say you're sorry") is questionable. Is your child really sorry? But that strategy is generally followed by parents who hope that it sinks in.

Parents are the ones that are going to teach by example these spiritual values that cross religious barriers. Apologizing for their mistakes ("I'm sorry I did/said that"), atoning ("I'll make it up to you"), and their own forgiveness help the most when it comes to teaching these important aspects of personhood.

## The "Santa" dilemma—are you going to participate in lying to your child?

To summarize from material presented in Chapter 15, an estimated 85% of American four-year-old children believe in the Santa Claus Christmas myth (1). This figure can apply to both Jewish and Christian children. Ages three- to four-year-olds are the prime time for this belief, and preschoolers do not have the mental wherewithal to figure out that Santa is not real. For those families participating, there may be a dilemma. A deliberate lie is told for the benefit of the child. The research in this area looked at possible ill effects.

Research goes both ways. Some papers argue that lying to children undermines their trust in adults; other studies show evidence that parental trust is not affected in any way. Most of the research (refer to Chapters 13 and 15) concluded that to believe in "Santa" is not a lapse of judgment, but a joyous ability for children this age to believe in a "good guy" who may help you in your socialization of moral behavior. No presents for those that misbehave!

---

**CHOICE POINT**

**Whether to indulge in the fantasy and when to let the child know the truth is of course a decision by the family. I personally can't imagine depriving a child in the Christian faith of this experience.**

---

Older sibs must be in on the illusion, which can make it a great family project. As the preschooler matures, the cat may be out of the bag—or not. Children older than seven will definitely figure out that Santa is not real. Parents choose their time; generally, when the child is starting to figure out that the guy in the shopping mall or on TV can't really fly in the sky and get down the chimney (if there even is one). In my years of conducting psychotherapy, this problem has never surfaced (Appendix B, Morality).

## INDEPENDENCE/SEPARATION

I discussed the issues of Individualism and Family Orientation in Chapter 16 and Appendix C. Since you are most probably a family who espouses Western cultural values, you will be training your child for ultimate independent functioning. In the preschool years, this goal of life away from you is a long way off.

The relation to your own family of origin (parents and siblings) will also be taught to your child. Parents will decide how often they consider their own parents in decisions, who is included in holiday and celebratory occasions, and who participates in a support network. Your child observes the type of independence/interdependence you wish for your (and ultimately their) family. One does not necessarily preclude the other; it's just where the emphasis lies.

Described below are several typical experiences in preschool years that lead to more separate/independent function.

## School

The biggest change in a preschooler's life is entry to the group care environment. Whether they go to daycare (even before age three), preschool, or mandatory kindergarten, this experience will be a game-changer. These experiences include being away from parents, functioning with other adults who are in charge, being with children who do not have to like you, and learning new rules of conduct with feedback coming from peers. Children in all cultures eventually get to school and have that inevitable separation experience.

Preschoolers may initially have difficulty separating from parents, particularly if they have not had much prior experience. And when they reunite with their parents, there is a tendency for them to "fall apart." Why is that? The most probable reason is the relaxation of and fatigue from your child's effort to follow the group. With all the time in group care, your child has adapted themself to the new environment; i.e. rules, story time, clean up time, snack time, nap time. This effort takes work! When "home" (you the parent) returns, the child can express all that pent-up emotion. Unenlightened caregivers may give you looks that essentially say in so many words, "They don't act that way with me." The falling apart (regression) is entirely normal.

A parent's job is to help your child navigate the school experience. You may get "bad reports" about your child's behavior. In a solid care situation, you will work with the teachers to correct behaviors. Some behaviors such as biting cannot be tolerated in group care, and parents must find help elsewhere. Your own resilient Self is needed to take complaints reasonably and respectfully. Complaints about teachers, rules, and children must be handled tactfully. The stakes will be higher in first grade and on.

## Back Talk

Preschoolers can be as "mouthy" as they get, especially in that tyrannical phase where they sense their loss of power and try to retain it. This issue will be discussed at length in the coming School Age section. Whether back talk is independence or just bad behavior is up for debate. But the child's independent Self is shown in their attempts to get rules to go their way. Parents will set the tone for the household with the freedom they give (or do not give) for your child's response to commands known as "the rules." The respect, or lack of, your child gives you should be what you wish your child will ultimately express to authorities in their world. It is also a forerunner of self-confidence. Your own self-respect is in play here; how *you* wish to be treated by others is your guideline. Is your child treating you with respect/disrespect? So, the extent to which "independence" is nurtured at this age is a function of your own comfort zone. Necessary guidelines for teaching include making your "rules," explaining why the rule is there, praising strides toward self-control and demonstrating respect, and enforcing the rules with punishments if necessary.

## Going with the Group

The negativity sometimes observed here can be your child's refusal to go along with the group, usually the family. "It's time to go to Aunt Sue's." "I don't want to see my cousins." Is this a wish to be independent of the family or an everyday expression of negativism? Occasions such as this may allow expression of the need for interdependence or the importance of the family versus the Self.

## Choices

Independent functioning entails making choices. There are many opportunities for preschoolers to assert their own preferences, but of course within limits. Parents give choices for dress, food, and timing of activities, for example, to the extent that they, and not the children, are running the household. Choices can prevent battles as well, as a choice doesn't seem so much like a command.

Developing independence can be accomplished when your child comes to you and says, "I'm bored." "What can I do?" "What should I do?" Let your child decide. One parent suggested offering "work" options such as folding washcloths or straightening shelves, which may suddenly promote some other "independent" ideas from your child. Great idea!

In the chapter on Self-development, extracurricular activities were discussed. Choices of "extracurricular" activities are made jointly by parents and children. The numerous opportunities for dance, sports, swimming, and art are lovely opportunities for children to discover their loves and talents. There are big differences in the three to seven age group, and children closer to five will be best candidates for "lessons." Parents must carefully assess the maturity of their child, as an unhappy group participant will present a problem for everyone.

As discussed in the previous section, struggles can ensue when parents have pre-paid for lessons and the children want to quit. Prior planning from observation and trial lessons may lessen this dilemma. Children this age aren't too good at "toughing it out" and again, a reluctant member of a class is a real problem. It's a parent's choice to throw in the towel or put up with an unhappy child (and teacher). Length of commitments to any activity are best kept short! But it is a good lesson to teach the child to honor his/her commitments.

---

**CHOICE POINT**

**Choose activities that build competencies and not resentment. Know when to stick to or quit an activity. One rule of thumb may be that when your child willingly gets up early, gets ready, and doesn't complain about the activity, they are showing clear indications of their interest. Perhaps it is the activity to nurture and continue.**

---

## Tasks & Chores

Children this age are able to perform tasks by themselves. As much as this process is part of teaching adaptive behaviors (on command), these behaviors enhance their sense of independence.

Preschool-age tasks that are usual include: dressing themselves, brushing teeth, helping to set the table, putting dirty laundry in the hamper, trying to wipe themselves after toileting, washing their face and hands, and the like. They may not do the task to your standards, but perfection is not so important as independence. Watching your child handle a small task, even brushing their teeth, helps consolidate the sense that your child will be doing these things on their own. And independent of you—eventually!

**CHOICE POINT**

**Choosing appropriate tasks that are challenging but not overwhelming your child's abilities is key to success.**

## SUMMARY OF PRESCHOOL AGE
## (Chapters 21 & 22)

Preschool age will take your child from the egocentric and negative toddler stage to the school-age child, ready to conform to rules of school and peers. These are very formative years, of course, when relationships advance in the peer group. Behavioral self-control increases such that going with the group is accepted. The ability to admit fault is growing, and your child can assert an independence that is a preview of the person to come. The next stage is marked by a sea-change in your child's ability to judge themself.

# SCHOOL AGE (6 TO 11 YEARS)

# Chapter 23

## Education and Brain Growth, Including Learning Disabilities and ADHD

## INTRODUCTION

The years between six and eleven years old will be considered here as "School Age." (Or "Middle Childhood," according to others.) Once your child enters this stage, there are some significant changes at first but then pretty much smooth sailing until adolescence. (You will need another book for that interesting stage.) In this chapter, we will cover brain development and the diagnosis of learning disabilities and ADHD, in addition to the usual "Personality Pillars" of Relationships, Behavior, Self-Development, Morality, and Independence. Spoiler Alert—morality will show a huge shift.

## Review Of Developmental Theorists

In Chapters 5, 21 and 22, we covered the Oedipal complex describing the struggles of a child sensing their loss of "power" to retain their sense that the world revolves around them.

Freud and Adler described their notion of how a child in this stage deals with this loss of the sense of power. The child ultimately gives up the fight and joins the peer group where at least they have a chance of exerting influence. In addition, a big change in *morality* occurs.

Freud postulates that changes in brain development correlate with the development of a *conscience*. This all-important part of humans is a huge takeaway from this age. More about the amazing age of seven later in this chapter.

Piaget sees substantial changes in the way children view the physical world such that he calls the new stage "*Concrete Operations.*" Children are no longer misled by their eyes to judge their physical environment. For example, a lump of clay divided into little balls does not gain mass. If water is poured into a thin, tall vessel, it does not become more water. Children now realize that if nothing is added or subtracted to volume, mass, or weight, the substance does not change. Before, in the "Preoperational Stage," their world was pretty much changeable and unpredictable.

Also, children now understand the notion of "class." If a child is shown four red cubes and seven yellow cubes and asked if there were more red cubes or more yellow cubes, they will now correctly answer "more yellow cubes." Sullivan calls this stage the "*Juvenile Stage*" where interpersonal relations increase in complexity.

Erikson sees this age as the psychosocial crisis of *Industry (competence) versus Inferiority*. As the child enters the competitive world of peers and acquires skills, they begin to feel industrious and confident about achieving goals. If their initiative is not encouraged or restricted, or criticized, the child will doubt their own abilities. Some failure is necessary to develop some "humility." A balance between competence and humility is the desired result.

## BRAIN DEVELOPMENT, FORMAL EDUCATION, AND LEARNING DISABILITIES

Most children have participated in structured group activities prior to entering first grade, but at age six to seven, there is a big change in your child's brain development; hence, there is a change in expectations. In every culture that educates children in groups at this age, children are expected to sit and focus for longer periods, to follow instructions from a teacher, and to learn math, reading, and writing skills. In Chapter 1, and the area of intelligence testing, I touched on the issue of learning disabilities where academic progress lags significantly behind general intelligence. This section will go into more detail as parents of school-age children frequently face learning difficulties of some kind.

Math, reading, and writing constitute *"Formal Education."* The preceding Preschool section described the beginnings of learning the alphabet and counting, but I will describe it again here. Formal education, like learning to read, differs from informal "hands-on" teaching, like learning to tie one's shoes or load the dishwasher. What is the difference? In my classes of pediatrics residents, I asked them how these areas were different. Can you figure it out? Even though many of the students dealt with different languages and different alphabet systems, very few figured out that language and math involve *symbols*, which are *arbitrary* squiggles and differ from language to language. Some stand for sounds, others for ideas. With *informal* learning of hands-on tasks or physical skills, there are no symbols involved. When symbols contain the information, the brain is challenged in an entirely different way.

## Learning Disabilities

With preschool and kindergarten education, your child may be getting prepared to deal with those symbols, if not reading already. At age six (seven at the latest) brain development is at the point where this skill can happen. Again, it is the same age all over the world. The speed of acquisition will however vary among children. Mental Age can now be estimated for most children as the grade level of their math or reading skills. Academic tests have norms for children's ages; the average first grader reads at the first-grade level and so on. Multiplication skills are taught in third grade, at a mental age level of eight. The normally developing child will have skills at or about their chronological age.

But sometimes, the acquisition of those symbolic skills will lag behind the general functioning of a child. Why is this? I'll walk you through an exercise for you to understand how complicated this process is, while it seems so easy. We'll start with the two inputs: visual and auditory (spoken). See a word on this page: Let's choose "Child." Say it out loud. What did your brain do to speak it? You saw the word, searched for an image in your brain, recognized the word which traveled to your mouth to say it. That is a *receptive visual* to *expressive language* transfer. So complicated, yet it seems effortless. Now, hear a word from someone else and write it down. Your brain recognized the spoken (auditory) word, searched your brain for the correct spelling of it, and then instructed your hand to write down the letters of that word. That is the *receptive auditory* to *visual expressive* modality. Inputs are auditory and visual with output modalities of receptive and expressive.

The exercise above necessitated a lot of brain cells working in harmony. But sometimes they don't work that way. In some children, areas of the brain fail to properly connect, and that part just doesn't work as well as the rest of the child's brain. Autopsies of brains of people with learning problems of this nature show different anatomical details. In these cases, the brain is simply built differently. And there is a genetic component in this type of problem. Frequently a deficiency in the reading area will be accompanied by talents/gifts in the artistic (visual-spatial) area.

Again, when a child's learning of math or reading (generally one or the other) lag below their general mental development (intelligence), the child no longer enjoys school or at least the problem area. A child may feel that they are a failure, and parents get worried. "Why isn't my child learning?" Labels of "lazy" or "dumb" or "bored" are frequently used as parents struggle to understand their child's problem. Teachers may be blamed. Tutors are hired. Obvious problems in the Self-Concept of the child ensue.

In the public school system, when the lag gets large, two years minimum for a diagnosis, the school will evaluate the child to see if a "Learning Disability" diagnosis is present. By virtue of testing and a teacher/parent conference, the child may be eligible for Special Education, and in so doing will have an Individual Education Plan (IEP), which is valid up through the age of twenty-one. Various interventions to help the child achieve will be put in place including supplemental tutoring or placement in a smaller classroom with a specialized teacher. Expectations for achievement (hence grades) will be modified to accommodate the child's realistic capacities.

"Learning differently" is a better way to describe the idea of learning disabilities, as a child with visual difficulties will end up learning through their ears—by the auditory channel (books on tape for example, or oral exams). And a child with auditory difficulties will end up learning through the visual channel (writing down lists). Compensating techniques to utilize the strong channel should be available in the school.

While this problem exists, the child's self-esteem is at stake.

The psychological toll to the child can be huge. Again, it is common for parents and others to think that their child is either "lazy" or "dumb." They see the child struggle with reading or math, yet excel in other areas, and still attribute these very negative qualities. The concept of the learning disability is difficult to understand. The child's Self-Concept suffers and needs help developing their strong abilities.

I counseled numerous families with this issue. These children are neither "lazy" nor "dumb." Their brain lacks the normal connections to make those complicated moves. To aid in understanding, I would draw a "brain picture" for the family. I divided the brain into six or seven different areas. I drew pictures of the numerous areas the child had mastered such as music, sports, other academic subjects, friendliness, as well as the problem area such as "reading." I shaded only the problem area so the family could see that most of the brain functions for the main areas just fine, with just that one problem area. The family needs to be a chief support to their child who is finding school really tough. This was one way to instill confidence in the child and the parent.

Regarding the future, some children outgrow their discrepancies and their brains somehow "catch up." Others will struggle life-long. (Tell Einstein about it—he had difficulty reading, as did many famous people.) And they will develop lives and careers which utilize their strong suit and avoid the weak one. For example, an auditory learner will develop skills in sales, customer service, or consulting. A visual learner may become a lawyer or researcher, and deal more with reading than team membership.

---

**CHOICE POINT**

**When a child struggles academically, parents and teachers need to become allies and:**

1. **Find help for the child through private tutoring**
2. **Ultimately give permission for an evaluation.**

**If the Learning Disability diagnosis applies to the child, the school district will devise a detailed plan for the student's education. From all of these evaluations will come a legal document that will follow your child to any public school in the US up to the age of twenty-one.**

---

## Temperament: Looking at Attention Deficit Hyperactivity Disorder (ADHD)

Attention Deficit Hyperactivity Disorder, characterized by high activity level or lack of self-control as a type of temperament, was mentioned in Chapter 4, with a history of its discovery as a medical diagnosis, its origin in the brain, its diagnosis, and its treatment. This section will repeat some of the material covered earlier but will add more detail. School age is a time when certain behaviors in the classroom are required. High activity level, impaired ability to focus, and impulsivity are the three hallmarks of this disorder, all of which can be distractors in the classroom. Some parents who have been able to manage a lively child in preschool or kindergarten find that the first-grade environment presents serious difficulty.

A second category of this disorder involves Inattention, without any Hyperactivity. These are the "spaced out" children, or those that seem to daydream. These children are also at risk in the classroom. One of the criteria to make the diagnosis, based on medical diagnostic guidelines (1), is that problems must be observed prior to age seven. If onset is later than that, it is due to some other problem. Why is age seven such an important benchmark? Age seven is when all children will have some first-grade experience, and it is that environment which challenges those with excess activity levels. Preschool and kindergarten may have been doable as there is a fair degree of movement allowed, but the behavior required in first grade is different. High activity level children will have difficulty sitting in their seats for the length of time required, and difficulty paying attention to 1) the teacher and 2) their "seatwork." They will also talk out of turn, blurting out answers without raising their hand. Parents of these children will hear negative comments from the teacher and possibly other parents. The child will hear: "You forgot to raise your hand." "Please be quiet." "Get back in your seat."

Mental health professionals also use another system of classification for diagnosis: *Diagnostic and Statistical Manual of Mental Disorders-V* (2). The age at which symptoms must be observed has been changed to *age twelve*. Why? During the decades that treatment has been available, many cases of adults who have not been successfully diagnosed or treated have come to light. For those individuals, who are trying to look back many years to identify a pattern of behavior, the age change allows for more accurate diagnosis. In my practice, I came across a number of young adults, clearly having experienced ADHD and its difficulties in school years but having navigated school (even college) successfully and landed a job. Then, they struggled with work requirements and deadlines on that job and faced firing. Accurate diagnosis and successful treatment with medication helped them to keep the job and continue their lives. They were upset to say the least that they had not taken care of this problem before, as they had expended so much wasted energy.

Since there is a continuum of activity level, three subcategories are available for the diagnosis: Mild, Moderate, and Severe. The child with the "Severe" or "Moderate" diagnosis benefits greatly from medication to enhance self-control. Many parents who are unfamiliar with the stimulant medications used are fearful of 1) whether the child will be "addicted" or 2) whether the child will turn into a "zombie." In the case of the former, children treated for ADHD are LESS likely to have drug problems in later life as they do not have a big problem that they need to avoid. And as far as the "zombie" issue, a child who is over-medicated may show symptoms of "overcontrol," which can be altered by lowering the dose of medication. The goal which parents seem to understand easily is an optimal activity level of "normal" for the child's age. This medication has been in use for over seventy years; the risk of serious side effects is extremely low. A parent can always discontinue the medication, but trying it is a must for the sake of the child.

A mental health professional such as a psychologist or social worker can aid in the diagnosis, but a primary medical provider or psychiatrist must write a prescription. Medication is prescribed according to 1) the level needed to control the symptoms; and 2) the time of efficacy to cover needed activities where concentration is needed, such as at school time and homework time. A period of time is needed to evaluate how symptoms are managed and for how long, so a few doctor visits are required to find the optimal plan. Children diagnosed with Moderate ADHD may or may not benefit from medication. In all cases, classroom modifications will be needed for the child's success; with mild ADHD, changes in the child's classroom experience will be all that is needed.

Children diagnosed with Inattention (Attention Deficit Disorder without Hyperactivity) can also be treated in the classroom and possibly with the same medication as for the highly active child. They are subject to the same negative experience as they are frequently reminded "keep your mind on your work" and are assumed to be uninterested.

With your mental health professional and the school as an ally, a conference and development of an education plan (Individual Education Plan or IEP) can be developed, which will include modifications of the classroom experience and possible medication. This plan usually does not entail placement in "Special Education," but may contain a list of "Accommodations" such as making a distraction-free desk available in the classroom, allowing permission to walk a bit (maybe to the wastebasket), or even work standing up! Dividing classwork into smaller chunks with breaks after each chunk, helping to get the work done, is an accommodation that translates to homework completion!

The sum total of these interventions should be that the child has a more positive experience and does not suffer the insults to Self-esteem. Parents now have to run interference for their child, who has been seen as a "problem child" and whose parents are seen as "problem parents," even by grandparents! In my work, I witnessed many miraculous changes in a child's life with successful treatment, usually medication-based changes. One boy, who was totally shunned by playmates due to his "rough" style, said, "I have friends now." He was actually my first patient who was prescribed medication. I became a believer for life, and helped many families find relief for their (impossibly) over-energetic child.

---

**CHOICE POINT**

**Professional help. Parents may recognize that these experiences stand in the way of building a successful sense of Self. The child is at risk in the classroom. Parents can consult their pediatrician and find a mental health professional who specializes in ADHD diagnosis and treatment. A successful treatment plan includes classroom modifications, counseling of the family, and often medication.**

---

# Chapter 24

## Physical Care, Relationships, Communication/Screen Time

### PHYSICAL CARE

### Feeding & Sleeping

By age six or seven, routines for bedtimes and meals will have been worked out. Brazelton and Gesell note that by age eight, children are likely to develop an increased appetite. Also, food preferences will change, and your child will possibly be a more adventurous eater. Mealtimes and schedules will vary by family, and let's just say keeping your child healthy can be accomplished in many creative ways. Bedtimes will get later. Earlier ages will have a 7:00 p.m. bedtime. At age eight, bedtime may be 8:30, and by age nine, bedtime will be around 9:00 p.m., with sleep needed averaging eight to ten hours.

# THE FIVE PSYCHOLOGICAL PILLARS FOR YOUR SCHOOL-AGED CHILD

## 1. Relationship Building

### Parents

Attachments to parents continue, with more secure attachments coming from parents with nurturing yet firm controls on behavior. Temperament also plays a role here, with "easy" children having little trouble, and "resistant" or "difficult" children requiring more parental inputs. Children in this age are generally cooperative and eager to please; they may request more "mature" jobs around the house.

Around age eight, children may start to discover that their parents aren't perfect and that they can make mistakes. They will compare their parents to other parents, but don't generally make a big deal about it. That comes later. Other relationships with adults come front and center, particularly with teachers.

### School

Your child will spend almost half his/her waking hours in school. And your relationship with your child will revolve around school. For more than a decade, the socializing agents at school will become your child's world. The teacher will be a substitute parent in the earlier years, helping with clothing, drippy noses, praising, coaching, and in general encouraging good behavior traits. What the teacher says becomes hugely important to your child at first. As school years progress, the teacher's role will progress from personal to more impersonal.

It is important that parents work with teachers to maximize your child's experience. A "team" approach to solve problems in school is desirable. Those parents who oppose any teacher who criticizes their child's behavior or performance are limiting their child's access to resources, opportunities, and ideas. Teachers provide constructive criticism, not attacks. Of course, there will be some teachers who treat children unfairly and who use poor techniques in the classroom. In those cases, parents may have to involve higher-ups to address the issue.

**PERSONAL NOTE**

I recall my mother observing my first-grade teacher use humiliation as a tactic to elicit compliant behavior in the classroom. The teacher pointed out to the class someone who wet their pants. My mother invited her to lunch at our home. She did not want me to be the target. (The invitation is definitely old school. Nobody does this nowadays.)

While you should not be afraid of confronting a teacher, do so judiciously. Teachers these days are leery of excessively interfering parents. It helps to see that teachers are human too. Teacher friends of mine remind me of the long hours outside the classroom preparing, grading, and the fact that summer vacation is really only eight weeks. Maybe you won't invite them for lunch, but your appreciation of your child's teacher will underline, to your child, the importance of his/her relationship to the teacher.

Relationships with children begin to focus on school achievement since middle-class parents view college or some post high-school education as fairly critical in maintaining class membership. A healthy home environment promotes academic progress. The home combining affection and realistic limits will be the optimum environment for learning. Children should not fear criticism or embarrassment; helpful parents correct mistakes with patience and understanding. Naturally, children can shut down the learning process when it is fraught with conflict. And then there is a big stress on your relationship.

Parents are needed by children for guidance and "help" with schoolwork. Participation in your child's schoolwork is like walking a tightrope. Not too much—not too little—the right balance. We all know of families that do the science project, give major input in papers, and the like. Teachers can tell the work is not that of the child. Your child's pride in accomplishment is at stake; and while they certainly need help at times, they know when parents have undermined their efforts. And your relationship may become strained as a result.

---

**CHOICE POINT**

**Set standards on expectations of when you will let your child go it alone, and when you or a tutor will provide assistance.**

---

Some children resist the learning process even if you are being patient and supportive, and parents sometimes choose to motivate their child in ways other than praise/reprimands. So the question is: Should classroom success be rewarded with material rewards? Or is it better to not reward and let success be its own reward? Will material rewards such as money or prizes take away the value of learning for its own sake? It probably doesn't matter much in the long run, as children who initially think the learning is for *you*, and resist it, will ultimately figure out that *they and not you* will benefit in high school, college, and job competition.

---

**CHOICE POINT**

**Although research has shown no detrimental effect on learning with the use of rewards (refer to Chapter 9), paying children for A's may send the wrong message about who is benefiting. Perseverance and hard work are traits that should be encouraged and rewarded. Your children may try to persuade you otherwise! Maybe a small outing of the child's choice can be the reward.**

---

## Friends

Peers will now play a huge and important role in socialization. Around age eight, your child will identify good friends, with friendships being more stable than in preschool years. As mentioned earlier in preadolescence, what Sullivan called "chumship" among friends will now emerge. This is the "best-friend" phenomenon where the children are confidants and trust their innermost secrets to their best friend.

Virtues of cooperation, loyalty, and sportsmanship will emerge from the peer group. Children gather in small groups, and form "clubs" with special interests and procedures.

The group can set up a lemonade stand, and children learn to handle money. Organized team games, informal games with their own "rules," and table games emerge. School becomes an opportunity to see friends.

With growing sophistication, your child may notice personality characteristics in their friends rather than just what they like to do. In handling peer conflict, the child in this stage differentiates between intentions and actions. A sense of fairness is present, and intentions are given more weight than actions. Studies cited in a previous chapter on "thinking" about friendship showed that children in school ages see friends as behaving reciprocally as in understanding "friends help each other and you trust them."

"Popularity" becomes an issue in the peer group. Social skills emerge with a developing prestige pecking order. How to enter a group, participate, and influence other children are skills that are needed. The degree of *Self/Other balance* generally determines how a child will cope. Those oriented more to themselves will become unpopular because they do not follow rules and want their way, and those that do not stand up for themselves will quickly become overruled and ignored by others. One rule of thumb I observed in my work was that if a child had an "idea," they could propose it: "Why don't we do such and such?!" If it were negated by the other child or group, they could try again: "C'mon—let's do such and such!" And if the idea were again negated, the child would compromise with others' "ideas." Group leadership is generally shared with confident and unafraid children assuming the role of leader.

At this age, genders separate for play. This phenomenon happens all over the world in both literate and pre-literate societies (Mussen). Boys will move in loosely organized groups, while girls may form smaller more intimate groups. There will still be interest in the opposite sex in the later years of this stage, with girls talking about boys, and boys teasing or showing off to girls.

You will recall in your own experience that the peer group can be like life in the jungle. Children can be cruel to their peers. You are needed to observe, coach, and find help if your child is not succeeding in their social world. "Play-date" situations can build a friendship and increase confidence in peer interactions. When conflicts arise or your child complains about another, rather than you running to resolve it, they should be coached to solve it themselves. Children running to parents or teachers for unnecessary help are targeted by the peer group as inadequate, and assume a place low on the totem pole. Again, judging when to interfere is like walking a tightrope.

Bullies are an ever-present problem in the peer group, and your child will no doubt be a target at some point. How your child responds and how you support the response can make a big difference in building a positive Self-concept. Schools try hard to handle the bully situation. A school social worker friend of mine described how children these days are coached starting in primary grades to handle a bully with "brave talk." The child in a loud and firm voice tells the bully to "Stop it!" or "Leave me alone!" or the like. The victimized child may be partnered with a more socially successful child in the classroom. Teachers are there to help serious cases and to get the bullying child necessary psychological help.

Hopefully, this training works. However, there are times outside the school when the child may need to be more forceful. Your child's confidence is critical in how they handle the situation. Some children are naturals and can give as good as they get, but

I saw children in therapy who did not stand up for themselves to bullies. My solution in addition to the "brave talk" comments, was to coach them to do what I called "equal payback." If they got a slight shove, they could return a slight shove, although they were not to escalate the situation. If they were called a name, they could return it with a similarly injurious name, but not make it worse. The "bully" generally comes back with more; this exchange could happen a couple of times, and then the child can get an adult's help. Schools do not support this approach and forbid any return of aggression. But when the victim does do "equal payback," and both will get punished, the victim's "street cred" will generally rise.

If parents elect the "equal payback" way, their support of their child's efforts here is necessary. Fearful or "good" kids fear that their returning aggression will get them in trouble with parents for attempting to solve the problem in this way. "But you're not supposed to hit or call people names," they argue. As stated above, schools will generally hold a line and forbid *any* return of aggression by a child but most teachers (and certainly parents) know the score. It's the law of the jungle.

I recall one incident from my own childhood when at about six years old, I hit my friend Elizabeth. She told my mother, and my mother told her to hit me back. I was surprised but took my "hit." Equal payback.

## 2. Teaching Adaptive Behaviors

Recall that we are teaching self-control and "discipline." By now, children should be used to doing chores around the home and showing responsible behavior. You can begin to "count on them" to do the right thing. They don't need explanations of "reasons." Reminders will still be necessary, but no more than three and fewer with age. When children do chores with NO reminders, you are really making progress! Job charts are still helpful, as chores change over the years. Children can move from setting the table to taking out trash, cleaning their room, vacuuming, loading a dishwasher, mowing the lawn, etc. Problem behaviors such as aggression to siblings or sassing their parents can be targets for behavior charts as well.

Good behavior needs to be rewarded with praise and with material rewards. Grandma's Rule or Activity Rewards of "first you work, then you play" is a big helper. "You can go outside as soon as you clean your room."

With jobs being assigned, parents now face the issue of allowance. Some parents feel that every member of their household deserves a sum of money no matter what. Others will pay an allowance contingent on the child meeting their responsibilities. In my opinion a child shirking their responsibilities or behaving poorly needs serious feedback. Loss of money is a real-world consequence of failure to perform (like you lose your job), and in my opinion, is a good choice. In addition, having an allowance contributes to the ability to manage money in the future. You can refer to Chapter 9 for a more detailed discussion and research.

---

**CHOICE POINT**

**Determine how your child will earn an allowance and how much you will give them. There are many advantages to your child managing their own money earned for good performance. The amount is negotiable. Here "Labor and Management" must figure it out.**

---

With age, new limits on behavior are needed not only in the home but outside. What streets to cross, where to go, and what time to be home are new "rules" that will change over the school years. Parents working together and frequently with parents of your child's friends have the best success when they determine safety issues. Punishments are generally loss of privileges that were abused—such as not being able to use the bike—or with "grounding," loss of activities outside the home. Loss of "screen time" can be an effective consequence.

Like time out for the preschool child, confining a child this age to their room or some boring place is a frequent punishment for poor performance (comparing it to the penal system, it is "mini-jail"). The mantra of "let the punishment fit the crime" continues to be the guide.

The super-dangers of "fun stuff" may continue—fire, sex exploration, stealing—but are less likely at this age unless there is a real psychological problem. Physical punishment for such behaviors is rarely needed or used, but you may recall my school-age experience with the peer group playing with fire in my garage. I got a spanking. More than one incident of the problem behavior would warrant assessment by a mental health professional.

Before we go to the next section, here is a strategy to get through the potential negativism of all those "no's" which a school-age child may hear. One of my esteemed contacts came across a very clever article which pertained to school-age children. Based on the premise that kids hear "no" frequently, the author proposes letting children plan a "yes" day, where they make decisions about what to do. This strategy seems to be a good one to have kids look forward to a day when they do the planning, and maybe better tolerating those no's. In the article, the author describes one "yes" plan as having the family play kickball, eat ice cream for breakfast, ride bikes, stay up late, and watch movies in a fort (1).

# Chapter 25

## Elements of a Healthy Self & Moral Values

We will continue the discussion of School-Age children and the Pillars of Personality Development. Here is Pillar #3.

### 3. Building a Healthy Self

#### Self-Concept

Self-development grows significantly in this age. Brain maturation and experience at this age allow a child in this stage to consider themselves as separate from others, and to acknowledge others' viewpoints as different from their own. Your child knows about their friends' characteristics and is also learning about themselves. In addition, the Self becomes more an object of knowledge defined as personality traits and positive and negative attributes such as "I like football," "I'm good at reading," or "I get scared of spiders." As your child approaches eleven (preadolescence), Self-definition may include more wide-ranging descriptors such as "fair," "helpful," or "not so brave." In the later years of this stage, your child will be able to reflect not only on their own thoughts but may anticipate another's different view. Ultimately, in adolescence, they can review the nature of a friendship in a third-person perspective.

A definition of a Self grows with different experiences. For example, if your child attends Boy or Girl Scouts, or goes to religion classes, they will integrate this knowledge into the Self. By age ten, your child generally will be less interested in evaluating their Self and accept who they are. Vague and frequently changed ideas of career and future family may become part of their plan.

Previously, the subject of Self-esteem as the absence of defensiveness was discussed. At this age, defensiveness will continue to be seen in how your child responds to negative experiences. Starting at seven or so, a sense of shame and guilt will be exhibited. But the tendency to blame others and make excuses for failure to meet standards continues to be present. "I didn't mean to do it." "It was an accident." "It's his fault!" However, although the first impulse may be to blame others, there is an increasing ability to take responsibility for acts and accept consequences. Your teaching and role modeling pays off when your child can admit a mistake, apologize, and say, "I'll never do that again." You are seeing a healthy Self in action. Congratulations. Caution: some children are prone to blame themselves even when they are not at fault. Extremes of this behavior may be signs of depression and would warrant professional help.

Over these years, your child more easily can admit to negative qualities and wish they were different. "I can get very mad." And to self-criticize, "How can I be so dopey?" Defensiveness may increase in the years approaching preadolescence around age eleven. Belief that they are being picked on by parents can be an issue as the power issue of adolescence begins to emerge.

In Chapters 11 and 12, the family's role in developing a healthy Self was described. As in years before school age, parents contribute (or fail to contribute) to a positive Self-concept by their language in correcting poor behavioral choices. Families differ in their style of communication contributing to positive or negative Self-Concepts. Toddlers and preschoolers may be subjected to injurious criticisms of the child's self. However, with older children the stakes seem to be higher, as parents' anxiety heightens, and criticism may be harsher. It is tempting for the parent to criticize the child's Self with negative labels: "Why are you so lazy?" or "You are so dirty."

These, you may recall, are known as "you" messages. Language which criticizes the problem behavior and not the Self is less likely to affect a child's Self-concept negatively, and "I-statements" such as "I'm upset that you haven't cleaned your room," or "I'm worried that your homework won't get done and you'll get a poor grade" are better ways to let your child know they are not meeting your standards. Many helpful aids to communicate effectively with children are available in books or online.

By the age of ten or eleven, your child's own individuality and personality are clearly apparent, along with their emerging Self. Remember, Self-development is a life-long process!

## Emotional Expression

A child in this stage will show emotional outbursts and impatience, but these will be less frequent with the years. Emotions will progress from fears of "monsters under the bed" and continue with fears of dark spaces like basements. In terms of anger, your child may storm off to their room and slam the door. There may be less crying and more shouting; however, a child will use whatever has worked to get their way.

Communication of angry feelings is a topic of socialization. While preschoolers call names and use language such as "You're stupid," or "You're a poo-poo face," families which use healthy communication will correct such disrespectful language. Unfortunately, some families will continue in this dysfunctional vein. Difficulty with the words "I hate you" was discussed in Chapters 11 and 12. Some parents have some difficulty deciding whether that statement deserves correction. Technically that is an "I-statement," albeit strong, it is not calling you a name. If a parent has the presence of mind NOT to overreact and can say, "I'm sorry you feel that way; I don't hate you," that can disarm your child. Over these school years, your child can learn to say, "I'm so mad at you!" or "This rule stinks" to express their anger.

> **CHOICE POINT**
>
> **Decide whether a statement like "I hate you" is disrespectful and needs correction. In my opinion, the child is modulating anger just enough to get their point across without disrespect.**

Here are some additional communication tips for dealing with your school-age child and in all relationships, for that matter. Your child may use dramatic expressions such as "This always happens to me," "I never get to do what I want," "You always treat him better," and "You never listen to me." These "always" and "never" statements are characteristic of younger children at this age, but like the "I" and "You" statements, they can characterize family style of communication. Many families in therapy have benefitted from changing these rather attacking phrases into ones that reflect reality. "Never" becomes "rarely" and "always" becomes "frequently." The communication becomes more effective and not just seen as an attack which gets a defensive retort, "No, I don't always do that." The degree to which emotional communication is healthy/unhealthy will depend on your own communication style. When the chips are down and you are upset, what do YOU say?

Another communication tip is to avoid the word "why" unless you are truly interested in the reason. "Why did you do that?" is usually not a question that deserves an answer, and merely states, "I don't like what you did." "Why don't you do such and such" is another "why" question that states, "I would like you to do such and such." "What" is a better substitute if you really want to know the reason. "What was the reason you did such and such?" It is easy to be less offensive in criticism by avoiding "why."

### 4. Morality

In this fourth Pillar, a big change in ages six to seven results in the acquisition of a "conscience" (Freud's superego). While toddlers want what they want, and preschoolers try to obey rules to be "good," and to earn parental praise, the child at this age will have *internalized standards of behavior*. Those standards are such that when your child does not live up to them, they will feel "guilt." Guilt is the way we punish ourselves for our transgressions. As the school years progress, your child's standards for his or her own behavior will change.

Conscience development requires brain maturation as the child needs to understand the concept of future time. But it is not just a function of cognitive maturation. When the concepts of good/bad are replaced by right/wrong, a child joins the human race in a manner of speaking. You may recall that the age of seven is, for the Catholic church, the age of First Communion, which signals that the child can now be held accountable for their behavior and thought. The Muslim religion, in some parts of Africa, has the ceremony of "drawing on the hand" at age seven, signaling much the same notion.

How you handle moral issues will impact how your child develops and whether religion plays a role. Also, whether your family's religious beliefs include the notion of "sin," "heaven," or "hell" will affect how your child's conscience develops. A reasonable conscience in parents will help avoid crippling guilt that some children experience.

Along with guilt, concepts of forgiveness and mercy are also in play. When situations arise, and you discuss these issues with your child, they have the opportunity to be fully human in a moral sense. Again, the role religion and faith play in your family will set the tone. But even atheists adhere to humanitarian and ethical guidelines, which are all part of this process.

> **CHOICE POINT**
>
> **Whether or how to engage your child in organized religious experience and/or instruction is a consideration. Involvement in a church, mosque, or temple can be a positive socialization opportunity. Parents can get support and help for tricky moral issues as needed.**

In the peer group, by the age of seven or eight, equality, justice, and fairness take priority over authority in matters of distribution of privilege or goods. "It's my turn—you're not being fair." By the age of nine to twelve, most children can judge unfair treatment (punishment should fit the crime) and will let you know in no uncertain terms! Also, children learn to define the rights and claims of themselves and others, and concepts of justice go from adherence to "rules" to a sense of fair play. In play situations, there can be exceptions to strict rules depending on the situation; school-age children can change "rules" if there is mutual agreement.

As children approach eleven, the preteens, moral thinking becomes more complex, with concepts of justice such as cooperation, reciprocity, and taking into consideration motivations, extenuating circumstances, and intentions in making moral determinations.

By virtue of the conscience, children should be able to be more truthful in general but there are important differences to be made. "White lies" such as "I love those pajamas, Aunt Susie" are allowed. Most lies are to avoid trouble. "Yes, I cleaned my room." They can be handled without too much worry. Some lies use exaggeration and bragging to make the child feel more important to others. Those are not good, and signal self-esteem problems. But lies to hurt others: "Susie just did that to me," when she didn't, are dangerous, and need serious correction.

There is another moral issue that is learned at this stage, that of "guilt by association." When your child participates in an inappropriate activity, even marginally, they are guilty. I recall an incident in my childhood when my friend had the idea to put a bag of dog poop on an elderly (who was crabby) neighbor's door. The woman saw us and called our parents. When I told my mother that "It was Elizabeth's idea," she held firm, "You were there." I was marched to visit the neighbor and apologized. Like shoplifting, this punishment involved humiliation, but it worked.

Studies of family structure and morality were discussed in Chapters 13 and 14. If you will recall, children of stricter parents conformed more rigidly to regulations while those from less strict families made more flexible moral judgments on the basis of respect for property, obedience to teachers, and truthfulness.

I have included kind behavior along with moral behavior in the topic of Morality. Helping, giving of resources, and coming to the aid of another in distress are all behaviors that parents wish to cultivate. Again, how you conduct yourself will affect how your children display these behaviors. Many parents enlist the entire family in charitable enterprises such as serving food for needy folks or collecting money for a charity. Also, many schools mandate community service to foster these traits in their students.

---

**CHOICE POINT**

**You can teach your child kindness by involving the family in charitable activities. Role modeling is the chief manner to instill this value.**

---

The research cited in the previous chapter on Morality noted increased helpfulness/generosity in children of those cultures where older children have responsibility for younger siblings and have important roles in the upkeep of the home. This information may be helpful in understanding that shared family jobs may help your child acquire a sense of obligation to others. When your child bellyaches that the chores are "unfair," this information may help parents to hold the line.

**CHOICE POINT**

Assign chores including care of younger siblings within reason to teach values of helpfulness and cooperation.

# Chapter 26

## Moving Toward Independence

### 5. The Pillar of Independence/Separation

#### School

The physical separation that comes with these years at school fosters your child's sense of independent decision-making and self-sufficiency. Let's start with independence from you. Close to half of a child's waking hours are spent at school in the company of peers and other adults. Both a sense of individuality and a sense of mastery come with separation and the freedom to make decisions on their own.

#### Supervision

When they are not in school, the degree of parental supervision will change from keeping an eye on them at home, to playing unsupervised with others in their room, to playing outside the home, and to going to the park and other places with their friends without you. You will make these "loosening" changes depending on how responsible your child is and how confident you are and the safety of the surroundings. You are reviewing supervisory requirements all along; typically, however, after age eight would be a time that children can be loosely supervised or unsupervised given their cognitive maturation.

The peer group is a source of both independence and mastery. When children have NO adult present, they are able to develop skills within that group that present good practice opportunities for independence in the future. For school-age boys and girls, living in a neighborhood where children play outside, meeting up near someone's front porch, and deciding as a "group" what to do or where to go is a usual occurrence. Girls will meet up and possibly make changes in location, but boys certainly will want to move as a pack. But when they do meet up, the issue of independence from parents begins.

Let me emphasize that there is nothing like a group of kids *with no adult present* to enhance social development; they figure out what to do as a group. It is, hands down, the best setting for social skills growth.

For many children, their friends live far enough away that meeting up has to be initiated by parents. "Play dates" start in toddler and preschool ages and continue in school age. Getting kids together so they can negotiate their activities independently from you is work, but worth it. Neighborhood children are a big plus, of course.

Children this age (usually boys) often move as a pack. When they get together, they decide where to go. Your child is part of this group and will want to travel around the neighborhood with the others and not be restricted. They will beg for restrictions to be lifted. And when they do, this "freedom" has to be negotiated, as parents are used to knowing exactly where their children are at all times. The issue of independence is when parents expect calls from their children; some parents want to be called *whenever* the group moves to a different place—"checking in." Cell phones have made this process easier. However, this arrangement may NOT meet criteria for a self-respecting child of eight or older. Some compromise may be needed. My solution when a family sought therapeutic help and the child resented having to "call in" has been to discuss *why* a parent needs that type of contact. The need to contact generally boils down to getting in touch with a child in the event of a family emergency: "Dad has been taken to the hospital," or "Aunt Susie just died." The odds of a family emergency like that are quite low. Before the advent of cell phones, a negotiated solution was for the child to move within a circumscribed area, Joe's house, the park, the convenience store. Now, the agreement is that the child answers the phone when called and keeps it charged.

The age at which a child should have a cell phone will be covered in detail in the next section. If the child in question does not have a cell phone, my recommendation is to have the child stay in pre-defined areas, rather than using others' cell phones to call in about any change of location.

Where your child goes and how they get there becomes another issue for negotiation. At early school age, starting with forbidding crossing busy streets, and riding a bike in a circumscribed area, parents will set boundaries. As they age, children will want more freedom to go farther. In cities, they will want to take public transportation. These outings without adults are great opportunities for children to gain confidence. Generally, due to safety concerns and to make the experience more fun, children will travel in pairs or more. In urban areas, encounters with mentally ill or homeless people on the street or on public transportation are common. Single children ages nine or ten may take a short bus ride to school if a parent deems it necessary and safe. Teaching your child to travel independently is a great opportunity to get them on the road to self-sufficiency.

When children are on their own, deadlines for coming home are needed. Dinnertime or when the street lights come on may work. When deadlines are missed, "grounding" is the penalty.

---

**CHOICE POINT**

**Choosing boundaries for movement, deadlines, and communication needs to maximize independence within a safe framework.**

---

## Screen Time, the Internet, and Cell Phones

Parents of school-age children struggle with decisions over use of "screen time" including TV, personal tablet computers, and cell phones. It's not so much "if" but "when," and peer pressure is intense. Pew Surveys in 2020 report that 80% of children ages five to eleven use tablet computers. Those under age five, 48% interact with a tablet and 89% watch videos on YouTube. Further, 65% own a tablet computer before eleven years old (1).

Computers are wonderful tools and when used properly are a great asset. Their use has been a factor now for some time, and it is necessary to have computer skills in today's world. Even pre-schoolers are getting used to "devices" and computers. Advantages are that there is great information available for youngsters. Also, they learn to type!

Kids love computers and want to use them to excess. Parents worry as to how much "screen time" is too much. Here's some information on what parents think about screen use. Pew Surveys report in 2020 (prior to COVID) that 71% of parents are concerned their children under twelve spend too much time on screens, but 84% are confident in their ability to know how much is appropriate.

How much do they actually use? Common Sense Media, a nonprofit organization, reports that US children younger than eight use screen media an average of about two and one-third hours per day (2). Eight- to twelve-year-olds are on screens for four and three-quarters hours, and thirteen- to eighteen-year-olds are on for an average of about seven and a half hours per day.

In school-age years, children are on the internet, and parents typically limit "screen time" and install supervisory software to prevent the temptation for children to go to sites that would be inappropriate or even dangerous. As interest in sex grows, pornography sites beckon. These are sensible restrictions that this otherwise-wonderful tool requires.

The overuse of computers to play games, and even to visit with friends (on social media) can be a problem. Speaking of social media, there is another big issue: competing over posting one's "successes" and the harmful discussions of others.

## Dangers of Too Much Social Media

1. Less reliance on face-to-face contact
2. Less exercise hence overweight
3. Addiction to screens
4. Exposure to inappropriate nudity, violence
5. Cyberbullying
6. Missing out on real-life activities and relationships

There are plenty of apps you can use to control exposure (3). The vast majority of parents limit "screen time," and "digital grounding" is common practice for a disciplinary tactic.

The American Academy of Pediatrics (4) recommends one hour per day maximum screen time for children two to five years old. Only three percent of parents surveyed recommended more screen time for preschoolers or toddlers. There are *no* such recommendations on optimum hours for screen use for older children. One of my contacts, a respected psychiatrist, recommends two to three hours per day or less. Families must figure it out and set boundaries. Rules and restrictions depend on how the child uses the "screen." The importance of person-to-person contact is so important, and most parents wisely restrict "screen time" to promote healthier development.

Outwitting and overruling your child is necessary. Children can be restricted in general from particular movies, reading material, TV, and computer sites with proper planning. They struggle to gain access, but too bad. However, children can be very sneaky and resourceful. Let it be said that protection is not always successful; if you will recall, successfully sneaking forbidden magazines or books at this age is something we all have done.

Now, how about those cell phones, and when I say cell phone, I will be referring to "smartphones." There may be a choice between a "smartphone," which has all the social media and computer access, and one without, known as a "flip phone." Non-smartphones may be unavailable at some point, if not already. One contact mentioned the availability of smartphones with built-in limitations for young children. Who knows what technology will bring in this area? A survey reported in Panda Security cited the average age to get a cell phone is ten. Of children under six, twenty-five percent have cell phones and half spend up to twenty-one hours per week on them. In that survey, forty percent of parents waited until middle-school age eleven to thirteen, and thirty-three percent waited until high school. Other surveys of parents report that the average age to begin cell phone use is between ten and twelve. All the difficulties with "screen time" are with the smart cell phone, but in addition, the device is expensive and children have to keep track of it. (5)

In the Pew surveys, 71% of parents feel smartphones might result in more harm than benefit. *Consumer Reports* (6) reported that six out of ten parents of children eight to twelve, give them a cell phone with 84% citing safety as a main concern and 73% keeping track of after-school activities. Pew reports that the average age to get the phone is twelve to thirteen. Bill Gates and Steve Jobs, both tech wizards, shared that they didn't give their kids smartphones until age fourteen.

### Deciding on Smartphones for Young Children

- Is there a genuine need (safety and convenience of communication) or is it just because everyone else has one?
- Is your child able to keep track of belongings?
- Can they be trusted not to use it during school hours, e.g. no texting in class?
- Can they be trusted not to post inappropriate content nor share personal information with strangers?
- Do they understand the cost for use and app charges?

Once you decide to entrust your child with a cell phone, you can set rules for usage and consequences for excessive use/costs. You can set passwords, track, and control the cell phone use using the apps mentioned above.

In this section about Independence, we must not forget that relationships depend on face-to-face communication, so overuse can take away from these opportunities. Human interaction in the family should be encouraged, such as conversation and game-playing. This section has not mentioned books, which are a source of enjoyment for many school-aged kids. Books are non-interactive, but, as they delve into more detail than is typical of a screen, they are excellent sources of learning!

Children's use of the cell phone will include calling friends to chat or make plans, which are good exercises in communication and friendship-building. In the old days, they could use the family phone but had to share. Now they have their own phone.

---

**CHOICE POINT**

**When to provide a "smartphone?" Based on normal development, ten to twelve seems to be a good age to trust a child with a "smartphone" if the child meets maturity criteria. Clearly written limitations and understandings are frequently part of a "contract."**

---

**Handling Homework**

Homework is a central issue leaving opportunities for succeeding in doing things on one's own. Unfortunately, homework frequently becomes a battleground. This subject was covered in the chapter on relationships, as it can be a strain. But also keep in mind that it is a mastery issue. "I can do things on my own." The converse is children who ask for excessive help. Your judgment will be when the child is not trying and to force the issue. Children can do (most of) their homework on their own, and it is important that parents stay out of it. But if an assignment is very difficult, parents pitch in. The dreaded science project is one that practically insists on parental input. One of my readers recalled her embarrassment when her daughter insisted on doing a science project on the durability of nail polish brands. Being doctors, the parents felt this project was excessively trivial!

Some children won't let parents help, even if they need it. They want to do it themselves. Helping your child to accept help when needed is a maturity issue. Their Self-Concept can be strengthened by finding another source of mastery—such as sports or art—to help a child realize that skills are not all the same. Maturity is knowing weakness as well as strength.

Below is a graph that may help you organize your approach to help your child with homework.

## SUCCESSFUL PARENTAL HOMEWORK HELP

| | Too Strict / Not Helpful / Negative / Critical / Perfectionistic | Too Laid Back / Unrealistic / No Effect / | Just Right / Realistic / Motivational |
|---|---|---|---|
| **Environment** | Tense | Nonchalant | Relaxed, Comfortable |
| **Parent Approach** | Admonish, Embarrass, Threaten | Over praising for no real reason | Encouraging |
| **Parent's Behavior** | Yelling, Scolding, Threatening | Cheerleading, False Statements of Praise, Blame the teacher if child struggles | Patient, Supportive, Proper Acknowledgement |
| **Child's Reaction** | Humiliated, Fearful, Guilt-ridden | Confused, Unsure of Reality | Positive, Hardworking |
| **Child's Mindset** | Negative, Lacks Self-Worth and Confidence, Angry | Lacks Motivation, Over Confident | Focused, Resilient, Confident, Can-Do |

## Extra-Curricular Activities

Your children will most likely be enrolled in some lessons and activities to develop mastery in other areas. Dance, piano, art, as well as baseball, soccer, tennis, and others are excellent avenues for your child's development of mastery. Finding that right activity which the child likes, helping them stick with it, and then successfully demonstrate their skills in recitals and games are part of building a healthy sense of mastery, and of course adding to their Self-Concept.

---

**CHOICE POINT**

**Many decisions are needed when it comes to which activity to pick, when to change course, how long to pursue, etc.**

---

## Cell Phones and Independence

The previous section discussed how cell phone use can affect families. The phone is a tool for Independence as well. Independence/Separation is involved when a child is apart from the family, and they may need to communicate. To review briefly, the issue of maturity for a child is essential; you know when children are capable of respecting property, and when they will show enough responsibility to handle it carefully. If a child is independent enough to take public transportation, it is certainly needed. It's a great tool, and a privilege which can be withdrawn for poor behavior.

## Latch-Key Kids

Many children take care of themselves alone at home for a few hours when they return from school and parents are at work. Be aware of differences in how your state defines age rules. For example in Georgia, children eight or older can be left alone (lest the Child and Family Services intervene); Hawaii and Idaho have no age limitations, and Illinois law is that no child under fourteen can be left alone as of 2021.

"Latch-key" kids are commonplace these days. A 2017 report from the American Academy of Child and Adolescent Psychiatry estimated that over 40% of children are left home alone at some time (rarely overnight) (7). They give no age limits but rather guidelines as to the child's maturity, knowledge of safety procedures, trustworthiness regarding computers (no pornography), and limitations on friends in the house. In an earlier report, 14% of children twelve and younger spend at least an hour home alone after school. Most of these children lived in neighborhoods where neighbors were present and could watch out for the children. Children from high-income homes usually went to after-school programs, so expense is a consideration (8). Your child's reasonableness, good judgment, and willingness to be responsible are key features for the decision, along with their agreement to "check in." Available neighbors can be a good asset. Visits from friends would be strictly limited and based on your good judgment.

While on the subject of friends in unsupervised homes, this is a big danger point. Children in school can be irresponsible when friends are available and there is no adult supervision. They will explore liquor cabinets. I'm speaking from personal experience here! They took the cupboard doors off the hinges as I had a lock on the handles. They can sneak forbidden items, or engage in forbidden activities with the help of their peers. This problem is even bigger with adolescents who "live for" the opportunity to gather in unsupervised settings. The stakes become bigger with drugs and sex in the mix.

## Sleepovers and Camp

Opportunities for your child to operate totally independent of you and with other adult supervisors come during these years. It starts with sleepovers at friends' houses and extends to sleepover camp. These are pivotal experiences for a child, and sometimes parents and kids can benefit from a break. Conquering fears and the possibility of a midnight call to come and get the child are part of the process. Work is required to find a good camp, label and pack clothes, and help your child overcome their fears. Then comes the joyous task of dragging them home from a camp, in tears having to leave new friends. I still remember those camp songs—"Sarasponda" and the like.

Choosing when to pick a camp for your child is a big one. Information from the American Camp Association and others gives some "tell-tale signs" that your child is ready. Most campers start when they are eight or nine years old, but some mature six- and seven-year-olds are eager to go, and some eleven- to twelve-year-olds aren't ready yet.

## Is Your Child Ready for Sleepover Camp?

1. Child can handle hygiene, such as showering by themself
2. They are requesting it
3. Your child likes sleepovers away from home
4. Your child is interested in trying and learning new things and can successfully navigate new situations (9).

---

**CHOICE POINT**

**When is it time to schedule these events for your child? Depending on your child's maturity and willingness to face the unknown, and when you think a separate experience would be beneficial would be your guide. My opinion for a week-long camp would be no younger than eight or nine, based on changes in cognitive maturity that occur by that time. Your choice of camp depends on so many factors like friends going, types of activities, and resources. Hope for no calls from camp!**

---

## Allowance

Financial independence is a goal in your child's future. The issue of allowance has come up previously. What chores are to be done and how often? How much to pay your child? And how free are they to spend it? You'll need to decide: which expenses will you expect them to cover? Lunch? Movies? Junk food? As children learn to value money, starting around six or seven or so, an allowance can be a good incentive for developing good work habits, cooperative, and polite behavior. Depending on the age of the child, peer group, the expenses the child is expected to cover, and the chores a child has, a family can supply an allowance of $5 to $20 a week. A dollar a day seems reasonable for a child of eight in a regular middle-class family. Whatever is negotiated should be paid on "payday." Many families came to me for therapy owing their child allowance. I insisted they pay up on the spot, and if they didn't have enough cash, issue a signed IOU, which I provided. An agreement is an agreement.

Your child's use of money is often a subject of argument. Many parents hate to see their child spending their allowance on junk food or things they see as worthless. My opinion is that the child has earned the money and it is theirs to spend as they like unless it's on dangerous items like spray paint or fireworks! Some parents insist they put some aside in savings accounts. I disagree with this strategy as it deprives the child of making their own decisions and in my opinion is an overreach of parental control. Free spending may not develop some good habits of "saving up," but the independence of the child is better able to flourish.

Children can earn extra money doing odd jobs around the house or in the neighborhood. Mowing the lawn, babysitting, or shoveling the walk may be paid outside of regular allowance. Since kids don't deliver papers any more they have to invent "side hustles." Enterprising children will mow neighbors' lawns and set up lemonade stands. Your encouragement of and participation in such "business" is a great opportunity for teaching about finance, working together, and having fun.

With allowance, children will have the option to "save up" for a future purchase, which is an important life skill. Also, your child *should not* be able to "borrow in advance" in order to have that "saving up" experience. It is a major lesson in maturity to wait for an anticipated purchase until one can afford it. Saying "no" to a child begging for a loan is not easy, but you have to hold the line to teach this very important trait. Remember the "marshmallow study" testing self-control in Chapter 4?

---

**CHOICE POINT**

**How much to pay your child for what type of work, and what, if any, restrictions they might have on spending is the hallmark "labor/management" negotiation.**

---

### Cultures & Their Independence and Individualism

The identity of the child is growing in this age and is of course the product of the culture. Because of the individualism typical of Western (WEIRD, as discussed in Chapter 16) culture, children will wish to be free of parental influence over their decisions. They will want to make career choices for themselves, unless there is huge family influence, like a family business or they lack confidence. In the Majority culture where family togetherness is highly important, children may be less willing to combat family influence, or at least do it more respectfully. However, the Arab families I met in Bethlehem (Palestine/Israel, not Pennsylvania), had the usual battles over screen use, homework, and time with peers.

## SUMMARY OF SCHOOL-AGE STAGE
## (Chapters 23, 24, 25, & 26)

School Age is the stage where classroom achievement and peer relations contribute significantly to personality development. Handling school-related problems such as learning difficulties and behavior problems is necessary to ensure the maximum school success. Teachers are key partners. Mental health professionals may be needed to navigate these issues so that your child can achieve their potential. Children this age will contribute to the family with chores and can develop good work habits. Friendships develop over time and social skills are cultivated. The peer group becomes all-important. The ability to take ownership of one's own behavior and to suffer the consequences of poor decisions with shame and guilt brings a child in this stage much closer to adulthood. Children develop a sense of mastery with academic achievement and also develop talents and skills. Freedom from adult supervision comes gradually over these years, yet parents must still keep an eye out for "forbidden" materials, movies, and computer sites, and for friends over in their homes when they are not there.

Successful negotiation through this stage will yield a healthy confidence and also understanding of one's own weaknesses. They'll have the capacity to stand up for themselves, yet yield appropriately to others' wishes. Watching your child progress in academics, extra-curricular skills, and social relationships is a joy. Cheering for your child's team at those games and attending graduation is a privilege at this age. And then the stage is set for adolescence. And you'll need another book for that!

# SECTION V

Appendix

# Appendix A

## Discussion of the Issue
## of Physical Punishment

### The Author's Position about Physical Punishment for this Book

In various chapters, I've mentioned "physical punishment" as an option to modifying behavior, but I have not covered it in depth. My position comes from what I've learned in my own parenting, what I've studied from research and development experts, and how I've discussed the issue with numerous parents of children in my therapy practice. This issue remains controversial, and this Appendix is offered to provide latest findings and opinions. Then, you can decide which practices you feel are best to modify your child's behavior.

Old-fashioned techniques using an authoritarian model of parenting advising "spare the rod, spoil the child" have changed over the centuries to a system that relies on a variety of techniques—not just the "rod." While the use of corporal punishment—generally recognized as spanking—has been declining over the decades, it is still in use.

Parental judgment is important in determining which behaviors, if any, will deserve corporal punishment. First, there are dangerous behaviors such as the common act of a toddler running into the street without waiting for an adult's permission. In this instance,

I believe that a potentially life-saving spank that comes right after the infraction can emphasize the danger of getting hurt or God forbid, losing a limb or life. Same could be said for opening an oven, touching a cooktop, climbing dangerously, opening chemical products in cabinets, etc. Toddlers do not have the wherewithal to understand "no" at all times and often push the envelope.

I don't believe that spanking is appropriate for the child being annoying or throwing a tantrum, even in a public place. The response, instead, needs to be firm, calm with disciplinary actions of going home, sitting in a time-out, or not getting the object desired.

Then, there are some extreme behaviors that I believe are dangerous, harmful, potentially life threatening, or damaging to mental or physical health for pre-school or school-age children. These extreme behaviors have greater stakes than being annoying or making a mess. These behaviors are:

1. Playing with fire
2. Sex play beyond age six
3. Stealing
4. Lying with harmful intent
5. Causing intentional severe injury to other persons or animals
6. Use of drugs or alcohol

It's obvious that these behaviors can have dire consequences and need to be addressed in a manner that teaches the lesson and deters future acts. In my personal and professional experience, I have learned that physical punishment can be a helpful addition to parents' tools in stopping these dangerous behaviors. And it can be used in combinations with other punishments meant to deter the problem behavior. When physical punishment is used in the correct way, sparingly by a calm and self-controlled parent, the parent/child relationship can remain intact, and children's Self is not in danger of being negatively affected. My position has been to state that while physical punishment is NOT necessary, it can be a parents' choice, again when used correctly. That is the "gray area" that brings tremendous controversy in American society, in my social and professional circles, and in other cultures.

I am aware that there is the possibility that this book can be criticized if not outright rejected for my position that there is a "gray area" in this issue—that while physical punishment is not required, or even recommended, it can be elected by parents under certain circumstances. Because I firmly believe the importance of this issue and want to also emphasize how physical punishment can be detrimental to the child's Self if used inappropriately, I present my position, the research, and insight about this topic as this Appendix.

# DEFINITIONS OF PHYSICAL PUNISHMENT & PHYSICAL ABUSE

Before going further, it will be helpful to look at the definition of these terms.

> *Physical Punishment* has been defined as "the use of physical force with the intention of causing a child to experience bodily pain or discomfort, so as to correct or punish the child's behavior" (1).

> *Types of physical punishment include* spanking, hitting, pinching, squeezing, paddling, whipping/whupping, swatting, smacking, slapping, washing out a child's mouth with soap, making a child kneel on painful objects, forcing a child to stand or sit in positions that become painful over time, and other types.

> *Physical Abuse* is defined as physical punishment that causes a skin injury which lasts more than a few minutes (2). Behaviors that cause or risk physical injury are termed

*physical abuse* such as punching, beating, kicking, biting, burning, shaking, or otherwise harming. Medical and educational professionals are mandated to call authorities when child abuse is suspected.

In 1996, one study reported that corporal punishment that was severe enough to qualify as physical abuse occurred in up to 35% of middle-class US households (3).

The most popular choice among these techniques using physical pain or discomfort would seem to be spanking. In a commentary published in 2018 by the American Association of Pediatrics, the author defined "spanking" as the "non-injurious, open-handed hitting with the intention of modifying child behavior" (4). This punishment is differentiated from child abuse which, as mentioned above, physically injures a child.

## USE OF PHYSICAL PUNISHMENT – HOW MUCH, WHAT, & HOW?

### A Review of Research Surveys

Given that physical punishment is a technique available to parents, what proportion would favor its use? A fairly recent study in 2017 integrated twenty-five research articles to learn what American parents believe about the use of physical punishment. They found "widespread approval" of this technique. The main factors that influenced parents' endorsement is the belief that physical punishment is usually used and a necessary part of parenting (5).

As would be expected from survey results, use of physical punishment is fairly widespread in the US, and perhaps even more widespread in other non-Western countries because the authoritarian model of parenting is preferred there. A 2017 position statement from the American Psychoanalytic Association reports that approximately 65% of adults in the US approve of physical punishment and about 50% use it.

A 1992 study reported that 90% of North American families use spanking as a tool, and that same year, an article from the American Medical Association Journal (6) stated that 80% of parents spank children from kindergarten to third grade. Obviously, these figures aren't the same, but show that some use of physical punishment is used by a large percentage of parents.

Based on my experience, if you are in a group of parents and ask who has been spanked as a child, you will see the prevalence before your eyes. If you add the question if they thought they deserved it—you will most likely get a marked majority of yesses.

## THE CONTROVERSY – TO USE PHYSICAL PUNISHMENT OR NOT

### Input From My Friends, Colleagues, and Contacts

The use of physical punishment remains controversial. Again, while it is possible to raise a child successfully without *any* such physical punishment, many parents choose to use these techniques.

When I asked some contacts about their opinions, I heard different responses. Many of them gave examples of times when they were spanked for behavior that was dangerous and/or harmful, and they credited their parents for their good judgment. Likewise, I agreed based on the incident when at age ten, I played with fire.

However, one contact said a spank may be ineffective as it is over quickly and other punishments can be longer and more "painful." A couple of people noted the potential unintended consequences that children who see that problems can be solved by physical aggression might think that they should use physical means to solve their own problems. And a few of my contacts described experiencing overuse of physical punishment with predictable results of harm to family relationships.

My esteemed colleague, Dr. Deborah Matek, who was kind enough to critically read the manuscript and to write the Foreword, believes that the use of spanking is simply an ineffective deterrent

to the problem behavior and that non-physical negative consequences work better. Thus, she counsels against it.

## Governments Take Stands

Various governments have weighed in on this issue. The use of
corporal punishment in schools and in the home has been a subject
of policy-making and laws. As of 2018, nineteen states allowed it
in public schools.

The United Nations Convention on the Rights of the Child,
first established in 1989, created a document that there was an
"obligation of all state parties to … eliminate all corporal punishment" of children under eighteen. As of April 2022, 196 countries
signed the document. A few were unwilling, including the US,
which has signed but has not ratified this document. Internationally,
forty-nine countries have banned physical punishment in the home
and the school. That is, use of spanking is a criminal offense. The
US has not adopted this stance.

## Input from Medical Professionals

Some in the medical profession, like some governments and the
UN, would insist that ANY use of physical pain in teaching children
is wrong, harmful, and should be avoided entirely. For example, in
2016, the Centers for Disease Control and Prevention formally
came out with a policy asserting that any physical punishment is
child abuse and that it should be prohibited (7).

The American Psychoanalytic Association (APsaA) (followers
of Freud's theory) also "condemns" the use of physical/corporal
punishment in the discipline of children (8). It puts forth the
argument that spanking is a euphemism for hitting, and since
one is not allowed to hit one's spouse or a stranger, a spank is a
crime of assault.

Other professional associations have strongly criticized the use of physical punishment but are less emphatic in their opinions and give parents the option. In 2019, the American Psychological Association Council of Representatives adopted a <u>Resolution on Physical Discipline of Children by Parents</u> (9) which recommends that caregivers use alternative forms of discipline "based on negative effects of physical discipline." The position statement on physical punishment from the American Association of Pediatrics (Sege) strengthens its opposition to physical punishment, encourages pediatricians to eradicate its use, and notes that frequency of use has declined over the decades. Pediatricians are encouraged to discuss discipline techniques with parents and to encourage use of techniques other than physical punishment.

In a 2003 commentary in the American Medical Association's Journal of Ethics, the authors presented corporal punishment as a controversial strategy. They state that while some argue that it is never acceptable in any of its forms, others view it as a useful disciplinary tool provided it is used correctly—that is, infrequently and in children of appropriate age (pre-school or school-aged)—and not leave children with lasting injury (10).

The opinion that spanking is equivalent to child abuse puts parents who choose some manner of physical punishment in a difficult position. Are they child abusers? Criminals? Is all physical punishment so harsh as to cause negative consequences? Should they feel guilty?

In my opinion, the very strong statements by medical professionals against physical punishment leave them lacking credibility because most parents know that an occasional spanking that is applied while the adult is not angry and is in control of their emotions does not ruin a child. But while some organizations see any physical punishment as unacceptable, others seem to see the "gray area" whereby in certain circumstances, physical punishment can be appropriate. Thus, there are organizations that recommend discretion in the use of physical punishment, using it only when necessary, and encouraging the use of other tools. I am in full agreement with those statements.

## TOOLS FOR PUNISHING BEHAVIOR & THE CORRECT WAY TO SPANK

### Review of Options to Correct Behavior

Just so you have these in mind, let's review the many tools that are available to correct behavior available to parents that are set forth in this book. The phrase "let the punishment fit the crime" has been a mantra throughout this book. Remember to also reference Chapter 10 for more examples.

1.  Verbal corrections ("discussions")
2.  Deprivation of privileges (loss of favorite toy or pastime)
3.  Isolation (time out, grounding)
4.  Imposing unpleasant recourse (cleaning up messes, paying for damages)

### Alternatives to Spanking for Dangerous Behaviors

One of the factors that can enter into a decision to spank or not to spank is the child in question. Certain children are extremely sensitive to criticism much less a spank—and others are less so. And some seem unaffected by everything including a spanking! Temperament will play a role.

Dr. Deborah Matek presents some interesting interventions for those dangerous behaviors discussed earlier. She counsels against spankings, period, as she feels they are ineffective. She suggests the following interventions that "fit the crime."

- **Fire-Setting** – Have the child view videos of burned buildings, visit people who have been severely burned, and donate allowance to Red Cross.
- **Stealing** – Give their allowance to the victim and do chores for penance.
- **Lying** – Have a day when nothing the child says is believed.
- **Exploitative sex play or deliberately hurting others** – Deny visits of children who are younger and/or have all visits supervised in the open room with no options for private moments.

While I think these interventions are truly appropriate and potentially very effective, I remain in favor of having spanking as an additional tool. Again, punishments can be combined.

## Proper Spanking Protocol

If the misbehavior is determined to deserve a spanking, here is the recommended procedure. The most effective manner to deliver physical punishment with children older than toddlers involves:

1. If there are two parents, they agree that a spanking is needed (in the case of a single parent, one is, of course, enough).
2. Prepare a calm environment where adults are not angry or expressing anger during the punishment.
3. Express the seriousness of the offense and why they are getting a spanking.
4. Deliver the punishment with an open-handed spank on bare flesh (or covered with a thin piece of clothing for privacy), usually the buttocks, judiciously delivering an amount of pain just significant enough to communicate the importance of the incident.

5. Discuss the infraction with the child again. With toddlers who run into the street, a spanking right after the incident is needed to allow for their limited memory and language.

6. Remember:

- Spanking impulsively or in anger is not the way it's done.
- Overuse of physical punishment can indeed harm the parent-child relationship by introducing fear.
- Overuse of spanking means that parents use spankings to correct mild infractions such as a messy room or sassy talk, or use it frequently in combination with other punishments.

Again, children can be raised successfully without any physical punishment. But sometimes that type of punishment may be chosen by parents. In my opinion, the judicious use of physical punishment—never in anger, in certain circumstances where dangerous behavior is involved, and not severe enough to cause injury—is NOT the same as overuse or abuse. _It is also highly important to state that if the child's dangerous behavior continues, seeking professional mental health assistance would be advisable._

## Research on the Effects of Spanking/Problems

Research has played a role in the developing policies on physical punishment. The policies from the American Association of Pediatrics (Sege) and the American Psychological Association (APA) draw heavily on studies of families where such punishment is used. The Pediatrics commentary cites a large national study conducted in twenty large US cities and noted that children who were spanked more than twice a month were more aggressive in subsequent surveys. The author of the study cited an increased risk of more aggression in school and an increased risk of mental health disorders and cognitive problems in children who were spanked; the only positive effect of physical punishment was that it stopped the target behavior quickly (Gershoff).

Other studies are reported where levels of chronically high cortisol levels are related to physical punishment. This relationship reflects the presence of toxic stress. These studies have been correlational in nature, however, and there is a problem with that type of research. When measures of two variables seem to occur together (in this case aggressive behavior in children and use of physical punishment), one variable is commonly assumed to cause the other. This erroneous thinking is all over science. Researchers have to be careful not to assume causal relationships. "Correlation does not imply causation" is a rule of thumb.

How can these results from correlational studies be explained? In a ground-breaking article in 1968, Richard Q. Bell challenged the then-current theory that the basic model of socialization is the action of a parent on a child. He felt that one-way direction was too limited to understand the complexity of the process. He cited data from human and animal studies that showed the effects of inborn factors in children on parent behavior. In other words, it wasn't just the type of parent choosing the socialization strategy, but rather the type of personality or style of a child helped to determine how parents would respond in correcting behavior. "A correlation does not indicate a direction of effect" or "correlation does not imply causation," as the research mantra states. And he concluded that the effect of children on their parents' behavior needs to be considered as an important aspect of parenting (11).

Let's consider this issue more deeply. You have learned in Chapter 4 about the presence of temperament, the inborn qualities of personality style and activity level. The infants who were described as "difficult" tended to grow to have personality qualities such as intensity of emotion as well as persistence. With this combination, these children would be expected to have behavioral issues and hence to require parental intervention to correct them. The most aggressive, intensive, and headstrong of those children might lead parents to choose physical punishment to try to "stop" that behavior. Following this reasoning, parents' choice of physical punishment may not "cause" more aggression or behavior problems in children, but rather the aggression/emotionality in the child would be more likely to "cause" the choice of physical punishment.

However, more recently, some researchers did studies which were not correlational in nature but where one factor was controlled to imply causation. Spanking can't be *introduced* as an experimental technique for ethical reasons, but *reduction* of spanking can.

A 1991 study compared two groups of parents. One group received instruction to avoid spanking and use other techniques. The other did not receive any instructions (12). The group that showed a reduction in harsh discipline was followed by significant reductions in children's aggression. This finding would seem to prove that physical punishment leads to more aggressive behavior in children.

Following that finding, in 2002, Gershoff reviewed twenty-seven studies, and found that regardless of many factors, use of physical punishment was associated with more aggressive behavior (Gershoff).

Research in this area implies that the use of physical punishment is either ineffective or causes poor behavior/outcomes in children, and you might be persuaded never to use that technique again. And yet, you may wonder why I still think it can be a useful tool. The jury is still out in the case of research.

Diana Baumrind (you may remember her research on authoritative versus authoritarian family structure in Chapter 8) has questioned the value of all that research. Like her, you may have wondered what type of parents were included in the researchers' groups. So, who is included in the studies? Families that spank exclusively or families that spank rarely, or those in between?

> **NOTE**
>
> A study is only as good as the groups which constitute the subjects, and those families who use physical punishment only rarely (like you, perhaps) would not necessarily be included in the study.

In 2002, Baumrind argued that Gershoff's findings did not evaluate "normative" corporal punishment. She felt that Gershoff's information, because it included "harsh and inept" parenting, did not justify a blanket injunction against mild to moderate disciplinary spanking (13).

Certainly, those parents whose emotional make up leads them to excess anger and impulsive actions would be counseled to avoid any corporal punishment. Cited in the Sege commentary, parents who have a history of trauma, who have been physically punished themselves, and who suffer from depression, economic challenges, partner violence, and substance abuse tend to prefer physical punishment. Baumrind states, "The fact that some parents punish excessively and unwisely is not an argument, however, for counseling all parents not to punish at all." You can evaluate on your own situation by situation, whether you are 1) able to judge the seriousness of the misbehavior by agreement with other adults, and 2) able to self-control enough to use physical punishment in the recommended manner.

## Counseling Parents in "Gray Area"

Here is one last note on how I came to develop my thinking in this "gray area" policy. As a child psychologist, I had the opportunity to work with many different families of different cultures, practices, and races who had various child-raising beliefs. During my work with Black American families at Cook County Hospital, I learned that, frequently, there was a cultural repertoire of punishment that relied almost exclusively on physical punishment (sometimes with belts, or extension cords that they called "switches"). For fear of insulting them or making them feel as though they had to defend themselves, I did not ask them to totally reject their style. Rather, I supported their wish to correct their child's behavior but asked them to save the "big punishments" for the "big problems" (such as stealing, lying, fire play, etc.) and to "let the punishment fit the crime." They began to understand my explanation as to why using spanking as an "everyday" punishment lost its effectiveness on correcting behavior. They understood completely and did not feel undermined nor insulted. I offered them other techniques such as grounding and loss of privileges. Over the two and a half decades I worked there, I witnessed a change in overall strategies with children "being on punishment," meaning "sent to their room" or "grounded" versus using spanking as everyday behavioral corrections.

During our professional discussion on this topic, Dr. Matek shared another approach. In this setting, when she faced parents who relied exclusively on physical punishment, she asked, "How's that working for you?" And when the parent realized that it wasn't working, many times, they became open to new ideas and learned how they could benefit from instruction about other techniques to avoid physical punishment altogether.

In my private practice, I also worked with many families who were from middle-class backgrounds with child-rearing techniques characterized by restraint, thoughtfulness, and attention to the child-parent relationship. They occasionally spanked their children when they thought it best. To tell them that their spanking was equivalent to child-abuse was laughable. A friend who attended a parent training session told me that the moderator asked those parents who had experienced spanking as a child to raise their hands. Almost all did. When the moderator asked those who had NEVER been spanked to raise their hands, two did—and the moderator added, "You no doubt deserved one!"

# CONCLUSION

This section is *not* meant to be a cheerleader for parents who choose physical punishment on occasion nor to diminish parents who choose alternative methods to change behaviors, but rather a means to ease off on the anxiety and criticism of those who do. True child abuse is damaging, reprehensible, and illegal. Certainly, parents who abuse need to be stopped. We can all get behind efforts to protect children, and professional organizations do great work here, but in my opinion, they can go too far. Parents who are careful and use physical punishment judiciously should have a tool to correct their children who engage in dangerous and harmful behaviors—which, when not stopped, could have seriously bad repercussions in their lives. And those parents should not have to feel like a "bad parent."

# Appendix B

## Examining Morality in Various Cultures

### CULTURAL ISSUES IN MORALITY

In a previous chapter, the issue of Morality was discussed from research, theory, and practical perspectives. There is a cultural aspect to Morality as well, and in that chapter, what we would call the "Western" approach prevailed (Western means the European lands and North America, where non-Western is everywhere else).

The fact that cultures have different rules, customs, and values is one that interests me, and I hope it interests you, too. Lest we be accused of being "ethnocentric," that is, focused on "our way" as "the right way," this Appendix was written to aid in cross-cultural understanding when it comes to matters of morality. All families use various practices to ensure that their children fit into their culture. This topic will cover "Moral Relativism," which means that there is not one absolute standard or code of behavior. It will also cover the opposite, Universalism, which supports that all cultures have the same moral code.

**Moral relativism** holds that judgments vary about what is morally important to humans across cultures. For example, not every culture holds that all persons are of equal value or that what is right or wrong is the same for any similar person in similar circumstances. Cultural practices or values, from not worshiping idols, to not remarrying if a husband dies, to veiling a face, are important on one side of the globe but not on the other side. **"Relativists"** see differences in moral precepts in various cultures and judge them all to be of equal value.

**Universalism** describes a theory that the same moral codes hold to be true across all cultures. An example to support this theory is the fact that major religions codify what is called in the Judeo-Christian tradition the "Golden Rule." "Treat others in the way you would like to be treated." The concept of respect for another's physical and psychological well-being, as well as upholding promises, may hold across cultures as an underlying tenet of the human race. The goal would be species-wide survival.

There may be some non-Western families in your social group from South Asia, East Asia, South America, or Arab lands whose child-rearing practices and teaching about morality and kindness may differ from your own. As covered in Chapter 16, anthropologists or social psychologists observe Western cultures as emphasizing individualism, independence, rights, and fairness. Non-Western cultures tend to emphasize group identity, interdependence, loyalty, obedience, authority, and fulfillment of role obligations.

Anthropologists have studied other cultures to learn about differences in group behavior. Most cultures promote kind and cooperative conduct. Anthropologist Margaret Mead in New Guinea (1) observed persons in some cultures to be cooperative, generous, and responsive to others' needs, and unconcerned about personal property. Other tribes were more aggressive, undisciplined, and lacking in cooperation (2).

There has been a fair amount of cross-cultural research on this topic to see if people in different countries think the same way. For the most part, there is great similarity in the development across cultures (3).

Research on thinking about morality is conducted through interviews of children and parents, however, research on positive social behaviors from a cross-cultural perspective has been studied by placing children from different cultures in laboratory situations and observing their behavior. One situation provides an opportunity to donate money earned to those in need. In one study, Chinese children showed more cooperative responses compared with American children who were more competitive (4).

Another scenario which gives children the opportunity to either cooperate or compete has yielded some interesting results. In a 1977 book, Mussen and Eisenberg-Berg summarized research by Millard Madsen and others in the early 1970s that showed a consistent pattern emerging whereby children reared in traditional rural subcultures with extended multi-generational families cooperate in an experimental setting more readily than children reared in modern urban subcultures with nuclear parents, children, and families. This is true for Mexican, Mexican American, African American, and Anglo/European American peers. In Australia, the indigenous persons living in traditional ways were more cooperative than the indigenous persons who became highly educated and Westernized and lived in urban settings.

Donation behavior has also been studied across cultures. In a slightly more recent study, researchers found that Chinese children showed more spontaneous sharing than did Indian children who tended to share when asked. Cultural beliefs underlie the sharing (5).

Beatrice Whiting and John W.M. Whiting (6) studied various cultures with controlled observations of children ages three to eleven years old in natural settings. They observed helping behaviors versus those seeking dominance or seeking help for themselves. They found children from Kenya, Mexico, and the Philippines showed more kindness than the group average on their measure of kindness behaviors. Children from Japan (Okinawa), US, and India scored lower. Their thinking was that the culture where children were more helpful was made up of more extended families; cultures with nuclear families raised more "egoistic children." More complex societies characterized by occupational specialization, caste, or social class (SES) systems appear to be less conducive to the development of kindness behaviors.

# CONCLUSION

While Westerners subscribe to a moral code based on the rights of the individual, other cultures may have different codes of behavior. But major codes of right/wrong, good/evil seem to have more in common than differences. It is helpful to keep that in mind when viewing those differences to avoid narrow-minded judgments.

Regarding kindness behaviors, researchers generally agree that in the extended families, children contribute more to the family in terms of task assignment and taking care of younger siblings related to the family's economic security, and thus develop the "kindness habit." Refer to Chapter 14 for more insight into developing "kind" children. This aspect may have more to say to parents in how best to raise children in any culture.

# Appendix C

## The Issue of Independence in Other Cultures: Family-Centered vs. Individualistic

### PARENTING VALUES ACROSS CULTURES

In writing about the topic of Independence, I came across material describing how families differ across cultures. Connections to family differ in terms of how close they live to one another, how frequently they communicate, and the importance of togetherness "rules." In Chapter 16, I described the differences between individualistic versus family-focused orientation. Anthropologists weigh in here with their analyses of how Western (European-based) families operate opposed to the rest of the world. When we Westerners raise kids, we may mistakenly assume that everyone else does it the same way.

I decided to provide more information about this issue to highlight how parents might approach this problem: "How to build independence without sacrificing connections." Because it is detailed, and a bit off the hands-on parenting topic, it forms this Appendix C.

Cross-cultural research may shed more light on parental values. Generally, Western (or European-American) parents are compared with those from the more family-oriented cultures and differences analyzed. Dr. Marie-Anne Suizzo, professor of psychology at the

University of Texas at Austin (1) analyzed questionnaires from 343 parents living in two Southwest US cities from four ethnic groups: Mexican American, African American, Chinese American, and Euro-American. The questions asked parents to identify goals important to them in raising their children. When all answers were put together, five goals were identified for two categories: 1) Group-Oriented and 2) Individual-Oriented.

In the **Group-Oriented Cultures (Interdependence),** family values consisted of:

1. **Tradition/Conformity** – Respect for elders, good manners
2. **Relatedness** – Marriage, friendships
3. **Group Harmony** – Kindness to others

For the **Individual-Oriented Cultures (Individualism),** family values consisted of:

1. **Power/Achievement** – Money, prestigious profession
2. **Self-Direction/Self-Reliance** – Thinking for oneself

The assumption of the researchers was that minority ethnic group parents in the US prefer the family cohesion, conformity, and interdependence values; whereas Euro-Americans prefer individualism.

Which goals would you select as most important? All four ethnic groups selected the following in order of importance:

1. Self-Direction
2. Harmony
3. Tradition
4. Relatedness
5. Power/Achievement

The ethnic groups *did not differ* in the order of preference they gave, but there were some differences.

- As predicted, Euro-Americans put less importance on Tradition than the three minority groups.
- African Americans attributed the highest importance to Tradition.
- Euro-Americans also attributed *less* importance to achievement and benevolence than the other groups.
- African Americans and Mexican Americans attributed *more* importance to Self-Direction than the other two groups.

Further analysis showed that the more education the mothers had, the *less* importance they put on tradition, power, and harmony, particularly in the Chinese American community. More education is generally associated with the middle class. These results and others show differences between the lower and middle socio-economic classes.

Looking at the data from the individual versus the group-oriented point of view, it appears that it supports the theory put forth by Turkish Scientist and Professor Cigdem Kagitcibasi. She found that both independence (Self) and Interdependence (emotional dependence on others) are basic human needs and must be met by parents.

Another study compared middle-class Western and Puerto Rican mothers' handling of certain tasks in infancy like self-feeding, toilet training, and sleep habits. Is this the beginning of "independence?" Would Individualism and Group Identity cultures show differences in this aspect of child-rearing? (2)

Results found that *both* Puerto Rican and Anglo (their word choice) mothers encouraged their infants to feed themselves, toilet themselves, and sleep by themselves, but that Puerto Rican mothers were *more* active in encouraging their infants to do things by themselves than the Anglo parents.

Anglo parents were inclined to let the child set the pace, and not to "rush" babies. Results showed while the end results were the same (i.e. accomplishment of tasks), their stated strategies were different. Puerto Ricans helped babies fit in with the society's expectations of "maturity." "Look what my baby can do!"

The Western parents tended to follow a child's lead or interest, paid more attention to the child's feeling of success, and avoided pressure or upset. "Look how proud my baby is!" Results were analyzed to show that Western parents focused more on building a sense of the person, and Puerto Rican parents focused more on accomplishment as defined by group membership, which translated to "success."

In addition to these cross-cultural experiments, anthropologists study independence in various cultures by observing how people train their young. In Chapters 13 and 14, research was discussed comparing rural and urban children on competition versus cooperation. Competition involves more individualism and self-orientation, and cooperation is more other-oriented. Independence training in the Mixtecan culture of Mexico for example begins by children getting simple tasks by age five and learning adult tasks gradually. Competition is not seen; cooperation is encouraged (3).

## More on How Western Culture differs from Non-Western

Child-rearing produces culture which of course includes the government. Governments differ across the globe. Western culture is associated with self-development and self-government. For a system like this to function, individuals must have qualities to allow them to 1) express opinions freely; 2) elect leaders; and 3) become leaders. Cultures with more authoritarian governments generally are associated with the Family-Oriented patriarchal systems. I'm not an expert on politics and culture, but it seems that there is a correlation, except for India, which is based on a family-oriented system, yet has a free press and contested elections. (I will take some liberties and note my observation that governments in family-oriented cultures are frequently painted with a "corruption" paintbrush. My interpretation is that leaders in authoritarian cultures are pressed to 1) hire family, even if they are not the best for the job, and 2) financially benefit the family. If they do not "come through" for their family, they may be put in a bad position.)

---

**ANECDOTE: FAMILY AND SERIAL KILLERS**

In a recent TV discussion program where a serial killer's life situation (typical loner) was described, a woman panelist with a Hispanic background jumped up and said, "Where was the family?" In Hispanic culture, the family would know everything about everybody's goings on—and thus would theoretically be able to prevent such disaster. With this discussion of how cross-cultural psychologists and anthropologists study the family and consequently child-rearing, we are setting the stage for a discussion of cultural differences.

---

## Family Differences:
## Independence Within Western Culture

Families within the Western geographic area (Europe, North America, and Australia) may differ in the degree to which Individualism and Self-Direction is valued. Mentioned previously in Chapter 16, there are degrees of emphasis on Individual development within the West. Families of various ethnicities may try to uphold their closeness traditions, as well as their family structure. The three types of family structures in the Western culture were also covered in Chapter 16 and included the Authoritarian, Authoritative, and Permissive models, which were described in the Baumrind analysis. However, in mainstream Western culture,

Individualism, Authoritative family structure, and less family closeness appear to prevail.

To review:

- **Authoritarian**-based families learn to defer to authority and may keep their own opinions under wraps. Chinese researchers noted "helicopter parenting" as primarily present in authoritarian-oriented families (4).

- **Authoritative**-based families display assertive yet respectful behavior, self-control, competition, striving, and future-focused behavior.

- **Permissive** families will raise children who bristle at limits placed on them by others.

Over-deferring to authority or resisting existing procedures in the workplace can be a challenge for those raised in Authoritative or Permissive environments! Having the confidence to express oneself starts in childhood. Children from Authoritative (controlled plus warmth) families are allowed to express themselves— sometimes seen as quite inappropriate by others looking in. The degree of expression and the dimension of respect will be key to whether the arguing is seen as "bratty" or "persuasive." For instance, if they are allowed to make important family decisions, they are developing over-confidence!

Religion has also been found to be a factor in developing independence with Catholic parents restricting their children more as they age; for example, when they start dating or driving. Lower socio-economic-status families are typically characterized more by Authoritarian structure (Mussen, et al).

## Some Personal Experiences with Cultural Differences

In my early twenties, I traveled around the world, and at one point, Asia. Two incidents of cross-cultural encounters stand out in my memory. In Japan, staying at a hostel, we (my girlfriend and myself—no, I didn't do this alone) befriended a Japanese student. There is an important building in Kyoto that we wished to visit. For some unknown reason, Japanese citizens were not allowed in. We tried to convince him that we would talk to those at the front desk and try to get him in. The poor guy panicked and said, "NO! NO!" and looked really fearful. We got the idea. Rules are not to be challenged. He defers to authority.

A second incident was in India. I was staying with a family that had a pretty big (but modest—no flush toilet) home. I was looking forward to having my own room, but at bedtime, several girls brought their (very light) beds into "my room" so I would not be lonely. Again, I got the picture. Japanese rules are pretty strict, and Indian people like togetherness. Families are very different from the "independence" and "individualism" that we espouse here in the US.

## Anthropological Research about WEIRD versus non-WEIRD

Anthropologists study culture in really big ways. A huge study (European Social Survey) described in the Henrich book (5) studied three traits, with data from thirty-six countries. They asked people questions about the following topics:

1. **Conformity and Obedience** – "It is important to behave properly."
2. **Individualism and Independence** – "Thinking up new ideas is important to me."
3. **Impersonal Fairness** – "Do you think most people would try to take advantage of you if they got the chance?"
4. **Impersonal Trust** – "Would you say most people can be trusted?"

Findings were that the longer people of that area were exposed to dictums of the Western Catholic Church that weakened the family systems, the weaker were inclinations toward conformity, the stronger motivation for individualism, and the greater belief in fairness and trust from others. Rather than seeing trustworthiness as coming only from the family, people that one didn't know were now seen as peers, and as such, generally trustworthy. This did not hold for areas under Orthodox Christianity.

These scientists went further and looked at differences in thinking styles, which were alluded to earlier in this section. Cultures can be characterized by different ways of approaching knowledge. Holistic thinkers look for relationships between items which may have an emotional component where analytical thinkers use rational rule-governed categories in their thinking. They saw a connection between intensive kinship cultures and the tendency to think in relational, not analytical terms. Analytical thinkers would process, "What is this information all about?" versus how relational thinkers process, "How will this information affect the people around me?"

Anthropologists also looked at conformity in the two different cultural styles. There is an experiment that tests whether university students in diverse countries would give their true opinion on a task requiring visual judgment or whether they would give a "wrong answer" by using the information from a previous person who was coached to give a wrong answer. This is, of course, devious, but results showed that those from *weaker* kin-based cultures are more willing to publicly contradict their peers and give the correct answer. They are less conformist. About 20% will give the incorrect answer in Western, low kinship intensity cultures to 50% with those with higher kinship values (6). What would you do if you heard someone give an answer which conflicted with your own?

---

## A NOTE ON SEMANTICS

The word "conformity" has somewhat of a negative connotation. Over the years, I have established friendly relationships with many people who are Arab. One of them suggested that "respect" instead of "obedience" may be an appropriate term for that tendency to follow another's lead. The "Majority" culture, growing up in a hierarchical family system, would be prone to "respect their elders."

---

Henrich also looked at charitable giving in the two cultures. Charitable giving depends on how one views the recipients. Researchers have some laboratory "games" where people give away money (or not) under various conditions. University students in sixteen cities around the world participated (not your average citizen, they admit). Those in areas where kin-based institutions were more intense contributed less money on average than others. Also, researchers looked at blood donations, which are anonymous and voluntary. Countries with the highest kinship rating donate almost no blood to strangers; countries with low rates of cousin marriage give forty donations per 1,000 people (Henrich). It is a different story when someone in your family needs blood! Kinship ties have influence, and in Majority cultures, charity may begin at home, as the saying goes.

Family structure in Asia was not changed by the MFP (Marriage and Family Plan). Henrich described a study by Talhelm which looked at Chinese families that worked communally on rice paddies versus those that did not. Apparently, you need a "village" to do the intensive irrigation and planting. Family structure would be assumed to be group-oriented. Over 1,000 Han Chinese students at six different universities were given tasks to measure 1) in-group favoritism; 2) self-focus; and 3) analytical thinking. Those who grew up in paddy regions were more likely to reward their friends more and punish them less than those growing up in other regions.

There was a greater self-focus and analytic thinking from the non-paddy region students. And the non-paddy region students' scores were typical of the Western undergraduates. Henrich concludes that knowing whether a person grew up in a communal culture determines several psychological features.

Pertaining as to the future of cultural differences, Henrich makes the point that kinship values are loosening with the increase in urbanization and modernization. Cultural change is an ongoing evolutionary process. Whether kinship ties were forcibly loosened as in the far past or whether the nature of the place of one's upbringing discouraged cooperation and self-development, Individualism seems to be increasing.

## Arab Family Values – A Case Study

We are still on the subject of "Independence," but in the interest of fully exploring important areas of human development, I am continuing to focus on "Interdependence." Yes, you wish your child to be independent, but how connected do you want your child to be to your family?

## Resources for Learning about the Arab Culture

To learn about how another culture looks at this issue, I have chosen to include a section on Arab culture. In a 2016 *Handbook of Arab American Psychology* (7), the authors stated that over a period of twenty-five years only 1% of studies focused on Arab culture. (Several books about Arab culture are available currently.) A book by Halim Barakat, published in 1993, is a chief source of information about the Arab family (8). However, several more recent books written by American professors are available, too (9), (10).

I have had the good fortune to befriend several persons of Arab descent. My connection to them has been through the Christmas Lutheran Church and at Dar al Kalima University in Bethlehem in the West Bank of Palestine, where for the past ten years, I have given lectures and in other ways participated in the community. Through personal conversations with them, in particular Raeda Mansour, Parish Nurse, traveling to that area of the world, and reading the books cited above, I would like to share what I've learned about how this culture views the issue of family closeness.

I've been fortunate to have as additional resources some educated Palestinian women living in the US who are practicing traditions. Dr. Iman Saca is a Ph.D. Anthropologist at St. Xavier University in Chicago, and her family remains in Bethlehem. She is married to a man also from Bethlehem who moved to the US. My friend, May Khoury and her family immigrated to Chicago when she was six years old; now she lives with her widowed mother. May was married to a professor at Dar al Kalima University who moved to Chicago in 2016 and died unexpectedly in 2019. Another friend is Rosana Thompson; her family was originally from Palestine, and they are now living in the US. She is the mother of two teen girls and is married to an American physician. Ameena Issa, from Nablus, is my Arabic teacher and a recent resident of the US.

## Research on Arab Cultural Values

A major source of data is a 1980 study which examined values of cultures worldwide, not just Europe. The Hofstede Cultural Dimension study (11) focused on analyzing IBM employees' responses to questionnaires from numerous cultures; six values were identified, and countries were ranked. Relative to other cultures, Arab responders ranked high on having hierarchical systems where inequalities were not challenged and high on conformity and tradition rather than change. Individualism was scored lower; on a scale measuring competitiveness and achievement for material success, they were in the middle. In another study (12) by an Arab scholar, two additional values were added to the questionnaire—Morality (nobility of character, high moral standards), and Hospitality (generosity). When Arabs were questioned, they noted that their most important values were Hospitality and Morality. In further discussion with my Arab friends, May emphasized Hospitality as very highly valued ("So true").

## Family Organization – Extended and Close

Arab culture is very family-oriented and maintains the Group Identity model. Individualism would be considered second to family loyalty. Barakat describes the Arab family as the center of Arab social organization. Its structure would fit Henrich's description of the cousin marriage type. Extended family includes grandparents, uncles, aunts, and cousins. All members generally cooperate to ensure the family's standing in the community. Businesses may be commonly owned and operated for the benefit of all and passed down from generation to generation.

In a 2004 book about various cultures, Negy describes several aspects that describe the importance of the family in the Arab world. He reports that Arabs think that raising children to be independent and self-sufficient is "cold" and uncaring; if children lack respect, the family is weakened. And in terms of values, materialism is *not* to be valued more than spirituality and caring for others (13).

As I mentioned, extended families are common and may live under the same roof. It is common for parents to build an extra floor on their residence for newly married or for aging parents. My friends in Bethlehem did so; their son and new wife moved to the new residence on the top floor, ready just in time for their wedding. At the same time, these parents are encouraging the couple to make decisions on their own—"encouraging independence"—as they have been coming to the parents perhaps a bit much for advice. This extended family arrangement may leave less room for independence or privacy, of course, depending on the personalities involved.

Over time, there have been changes in whether Arab families increasingly live in nuclear arrangements. Barakat reports that in the 1940s, 82% were in extended families, and in 1975 this number was lowered to 34% (Barakat). Certainly, economic circumstances play a role as more well-off families can afford housing.

Relatives may live in the same neighborhood, group together for celebrations and funerals, and expect a great deal from one another. Attendance at family events is a must, not an option. When they live together, families eat together. Contrast that with the busy schedules in the West, which don't allow for much togetherness at mealtime unless it is made a priority. (Well, there is that mandatory Sunday family dinner on the TV show *Bluebloods*.)

One of my contacts with Palestinian roots commented that people in the Arab culture often say that mental health professionals are not needed as the family tries to serve as the therapist. She acknowledges the family is a big support for those in distress but that professionals may be needed on occasion.

---

**NOTE ABOUT THERAPISTS**

**As a professional, I must stress that a family member cannot be a therapist—who by definition is someone with no relationship to the client. When there is a connection, the ethics are breached as if there is a "dual relationship" and psychotherapy is not possible. Families provide needed support, which is of course invaluable—just not "therapy."**

---

It is unheard of for single unmarried or divorced persons to live independently. One example my contacts gave was a young man who wanted "independence" and lived on his own in an apartment. According to my friends, he got lonely and missed the meals, and he returned home. Apparently, he did not explore the idea of roommates. When Western young adults leave home, they would not initially live alone but have roommates, and then there is no lack of company. Another contact faced living with her parents and siblings in a crowded home. She decided to buy a condo for herself and her two children, going against family wishes. "What would people think?" "It isn't safe without a man." (Apparently the two teenage sons living with her didn't count). The family came around eventually. She is currently trying to re-make her life in the US; her motivation was to "see what I could do by myself, without family interference."

As part of the Group Identity, family members are interdependent, maintain close relationships, and support each other. Family closeness was demonstrated to me in a sad incident. I mentioned before that my friend's husband died suddenly, early morning. I received a call from her mid-morning and gathered up food and flowers. By the time I got to her home around noon, her home was filled with people! Word had spread quickly, and all had dropped everything to be by her side. The guests—coming and going, and not just her immediate family—were a constant support to her and kept her company for days as she mourned and planned a funeral.

## Family Roles

Respect is expected for both parents, but the organization of the Arab family is patriarchal. This aspect was the first agreed on by my personal contacts. Fathers are in charge of members and are expected to be financial caretakers. The structure of the family is essentially authoritarian with father's word ruling. No discussion (much less, back talk) is generally allowed. There is, of course, much variation within this structure, and I have witnessed very patient and tolerant fathers whose children gave them arguments.

Mothers raise the children and support the role of the father. As women are educated and work outside the home and children become urbanized, fathers may now share responsibility and authority with others, especially the mother. But hierarchical relations remain with young subordinated to old, females to males. Note that my personal contacts are all highly educated, and have responsible jobs, but they describe patriarchy as definitely in force.

The women in Muslim-oriented countries have been frequently depicted as universally oppressed by a male-dominated culture.

However, a research article (14) found that the more women with small children emphasized religion in their lives, the more likely they were to be stay-at-home moms. When there were no children, Arab women were equally likely to work outside the home, and the degree of religion had no effect. Christian and Muslim women were equally represented in the sample.

Women living apart from their parents without a spouse is questionable; the incident described above with the woman buying her own condo shows the issue clearly.

Many Arabs have emigrated to the Western world, which may include Europe or Australia as well as North America (The WEIRD world). When that happens, family members keep in close contact. Phone calls are frequent. Children living abroad will travel at least once a year to visit family. Picture this happening in your family; how much communication would occur?

Person-to-person connections when possible are important. When I traveled to Palestine, I was part of the visits to relatives and neighbors—frequently on a Sunday. In fact, visits are the main form of entertainment in the evenings. People don't sit in front of the TV at night; they visit each other in their homes (and the TV may be on in the background).

## Financial Issues of Individualism versus Interdependence

We return to the issue of independence. Remember, you are helping your child to fit in successfully with the culture to which you belong, which means earning a living. In terms of financial independence, Arab families tend to handle children's financial independence in a different way from Western (WEIRD) families. Children live at home until they marry; parents will support them financially until either the end of college for middle-class families or until they marry. When adult children live at home, and they are working, they will contribute to the financial welfare of the household.

Unemployment is high in Bethlehem; perhaps two adults will be gainfully employed and will maintain the entire household. Charging adult children rent is unheard of (shocking!) in the Arab community. Financial help to the children when they marry is reciprocated when parents reach old age and require support from their children. One of my contacts notes that children are the 401K or the retirement plan for parents. Now, that is a real benefit! Think of the anxiety many Western families experience if income streams end or expenses become unbearable; the peace of mind and trust that one will be cared for if and when incapacitated cannot have a price tag.

Another positive in the group-oriented culture is in lessening the stress of workplace success. Rather than depending on the group, WEIRD individuals must "launch" into jobs and careers. But another downside of the WEIRD world is the possibility that a child may lack confidence and fail to "launch." Again, there is stress involved in the Individualism route. You can recall your own struggles in finding your place in the world of work—and see your child facing the same.

## Role of Parents in Decision-Making/Marriage

Respect for parents' opinions is high in Arab families. When a decision is contemplated by a family member, parents' opinions are sought. However, the competent women who were my sources clearly said they would *not* ask permission to make a decision, but would involve their parents in their decision process. On the other hand, the family is active in deciding whether a match is suitable. The potential groom has to demonstrate good financial habits, and a suitable place to live after marriage. Parents of the potential bride will tour the premises of the living space, and look at bank accounts.

Marriages will typically occur between the same lineage, sect, community, group, village, or neighborhood. This pattern happens in WEIRD couples, of course. However, in the Arab culture, kinship lines may be considered, and cousin-marriage (refer to information from Henrich's WEIRD book), is common. Genetic distance from cousin to cousin is taken into consideration as Arabs are aware that children from too-close relatives can have physical and mental defects. There is a prevalence of genetic kidney problems in the Palestinian community that relates to this problem. But it is still not unusual for persons with the same last name to marry. The ultimate family control of an individual would be the arranged marriage. Western adults might shudder at the thought of marrying someone they didn't love. But times have changed in the Arab world, and marriage is now an individual choice.

## Teaching Appropriate Behavior in Children

You get the picture of the family relationships as very strong. Children must be taught to fit in. Arab children misbehave like all children. When there are transgressions, physical punishment may be used, as well as "shaming" via scolding.

One might assume that in such a demanding family system, obedience would come early but this is not the case. I have observed Arab parents to be very lenient with their children's behavior—or misbehavior—until around age five or six. My friends agreed. If you go out to eat at a restaurant in an Arab community, you will witness children ages two to five running around, playing, making noise, and parents not interfering. And if parents request quiet, the child can successfully ignore them, and the parents will not persist. In contrast, Western parents—at least in the US—start the "listening" process at age two or three, with requests to "clean up toys" and warnings of punishments (usually time outs) if the child refuses. You may recall in an earlier chapter the incident when my granddaughter, age three, cried for a toy which her mother refused; she said, "I'll stop crying if you buy the toy." Be sure there was no toy as her mother held fast.

One episode illustrative of Arab socialization occurred at an Egyptian wedding I attended. A young boy around four or five was running around on the stage where a belly-dancer was performing. Weddings can be elaborate, and this was no exception. The boy was clearly disruptive to the dancer who moved to avoid running into him. His parents were seated nearby. The (US) wedding planner asked me, since he knew I worked with children, to "get that kid off the stage" as the bride and groom were about to have their first dance. I went to the mother at her table near the stage and asked her to help control him. She and I held the child's hands with a death grip while the child screamed and struggled to get free. The bride and groom had their dance; then we let him go. Of course, if the mother had not agreed, he would have been running wild, but we got the job done. The father was not involved at all!

School organization reflects cultural values, and is critical to children's acculturation. The educational process, at least up to secondary school, tends to be characterized by rote learning. Discussion where students' viewpoints are required is not promoted, and memorizing material is emphasized. Schools of course vary in this aspect. Respect for teachers would be emphasized as well.

This difference in respect has held up when students emigrate. One of my friends was on the faculty in a community college outside Philadelphia. Many of her students were from non-WEIRD countries; she commented on how respectful they were to the learning process and to her, unlike many US students. This sentiment was echoed in friends who taught in the American University in Sharjah, United Arab Emirates. They absolutely loved their hard-working and respectful students.

## Family Obligations to the Elderly

Caring for elderly parents is a privilege for Arab children, and unless the parents' physical problems require more than the family can bear, the seniors will live with their children. When children move abroad, parents can feel lonely. The church in Bethlehem provides a wonderful senior program to give social and activity options to older adults. One of the US contacts mentioned above lives with her mother, who has poor health but an engaging spirit. The other women are far apart from their mothers geographically, but communicate frequently.

In contrast, I will add my own Western input for caring for a parent, which may resonate with other readers. My mother did not want to be a "burden" to me and as such, saved enough money to move into a retirement community in Florida. She had originally moved there to be close to her brother and sister, so family was important to some degree. So, when she declined in health, she was cared for in this facility. I managed long-distance with visits every two months and hired a caregiver for special attention and communication with me. There was never a question about whether she would live with me and my family. This situation may be different for you, and your parent(s) may not be able to afford the type of facility nor see themselves as a "burden," but you get the picture.

## Dependence versus Independence

This information on Arab culture was presented in order to let you readers know how much family can be emphasized in other cultures. Perhaps, you are raising your child to fit into the Western manner of thinking and doing, which emphasizes individual independence. Each culture has its positives and negatives. Issues of isolation, loneliness, insecurity, and anxiety may accompany the Individualist model. On the other hand, in the family unity model, over-dependency may be a problem. In his book, Barakat cites another Arab author, Hisham Sharabi, who expresses the opinion that this Arab reliance on conformity can lead to a dependent attitude where persons look for leadership not in themselves but in others. Further, he suggests that Arab children may learn to avoid taking risks and trying new ways of doing things for fear of failure or guilt. Critical dissent and adventure may be discouraged by parents, who may be overprotective and restrictive. When I posed this issue to my contacts, they agreed and felt that deference in general can be a potential problem.

Cultures change of course, and Barakat makes the point that with economic, social, and political change, people change, and become de-socialized and re-socialized depending on what is required in the culture. People may feel more empowered to express and exert their own personal wishes whether or not the family approves.

Arab Anthropologist Suad Joseph, in a book about what he calls "Selving" suggests a way of looking at the issue that harks back to ideas promoted by the Turkish Anthropologist Cigdem Kagitcibasi (previous sections). He views persons in kin-oriented (Arab in his case) societies as "relational"—that is neither Individualist nor Group Identity, and he sees family relationships *shaping* a sense of Self but not denying persons their distinct initiative and ability to accomplish things on their own.

## CONCLUSION

In the above case study, I attempted to show Western parents that there are pluses and minuses in our manner of building independence and/or individualism in our children. Relational closeness does not have to suffer. Parents can build traditions that stress family obligation without taking away a sense of competence, or confidence. By showing you the different ways, perhaps there is some aspect of the family identity that can help you structure your family to be both nurturant of the individual Self yet respectful of family membership.

# References

## CHAPTER 1
## HOW THE BRAIN GROWS AND HOW YOU HELP

(1) Descartes René, & Cress, D. A. (1993). *Meditations on first philosophy: In which the existence of god and the distinction of the soul from the body are demonstrated.* Hackett Publishing Company.

(2) (Locke, J., & Woolhouse, R. S. (2004). *An Essay concerning Human Understanding.* London: New York.

(3) Myers, D. G. (2014). *Psychology: Tenth edition in modules.* Worth Publishers

(4) Myers, D. G., & DeWall, N. C. (2014). *Exploring Psychology. 9th ed.* Worth Publishers.

(5) Ashwell, K. W. S. (2012). *The Brain Book: Development, Function, Disorder, Health.* Firefly Books.

(6) Eliot, L. (2000). *What's going on in there?: How the brain and mind develop in the first five years of life.* Bantam Books.

(7) Chugani, H. T. "A critical period of brain development: studies of cerebral glucose utilization with PET." Pubmed.org. Last modified 1998. Accessed June 29, 2022. https://pubmed.ncbi. nlm.nih.gov/9578992/.

(8) Kagan, J. (1972). *Cross-cultural perspectives on early development.* Eric Institute of Education Sciences. Retrieved June 29, 2022, from https://files.eric.ed.gov/fulltext/ED073855.pdf.

## CHAPTER 2
## INTELLIGENCE AND HOW TO INCREASE IT

(1) *National Center on Disability and Journalism.* NCDJ. (2021, August). Retrieved July 18, 2022, from https://ncdj.org/style-guide/

(2) Silverman, R. E. (1974). *Psychology 2nd ed.* Prentice-Hall.

(3) Kagan, J., & Moss, H. A. (1983). *Birth to Maturity: A Study in Psychological Development. 2nd Ed.*

(4) Sternberg, R. J. (1999). The theory of successful intelligence. *Review of General Psychology*, *3*(4), 292–316. https://doi.org/10.1037/1089-2680.3.4.292

(5) Blumenthal, A. L. (1975). A reappraisal of Wilhelm Wundt. *American Psychologist*, *30*(11), 1081–1088. https://doi.org/10.103 7/0003-066x.30.11.1081

(6) Beaujean, A. A., & Benson, N. F. (2019). The one and the many: Enduring legacies of Spearman and Thurstone on Intelligence Test Score Interpretation. *Applied Measurement in Education*, *32*(3), 198–215. https://doi.org/10.1080/08957347.2019.1619560

(7) Varon, E. J. (1936). Alfred Binet's concept of intelligence. *Psychological Review*, *43*(1), 32–58. https://doi.org/10.1037/ h0060709

(8) Roid, PH.D., & Gale, H. PH.D., (2003). Stanford-Binet Intelligence Scales. *SpringerReference*. https://doi.org/10.1007/ springerreference_180625.

(9) American Psychological Association. (2019, September). *Disability.* American Psychological Association. Retrieved July 18, 2022, from https://apastyle.apa.org/ style-grammar-guidelines/bias-free-language/disability.

(10) Pearson. (2014). *Wechsler Intelligence Scale For Children: Fifth edition.* WISC-V Wechsler Intelligence Scale for Children - Fifth Ed. Retrieved July 15, 2022, from https:// www.pearsonassessments.com/store/usassessments/en/ Store/Professional-Assessments/Cognition-%26-Neuro/ Gifted-%26-Talented/Wechsler-Intelligence-Scale-for-Children-%7C-Fifth-Edition-/p/100000771.html.

# CHAPTER 3
## CAN YOU RAISE A SMARTER CHILD?

(1) Flynn, J. R. (1984). The Mean IQ of Americans: Massive Gains 1932 to 1938. *Psychological Bulletin 95*, 29–51. Retrieved June 29, 2022, from http://www.iapsych.com/iqmr/olley2009.pdf.

(2) Sundet, J. M., Barlaug, D. G., & Torjussen, T. M. (2004). *The end of the Flynn effect?: A study of secular trends in mean intelligence test scores of Norwegian conscripts during half a century.* Intelligence. Retrieved June 29, 2022, from https://www.sciencedirect.com/science/article/abs/pii/S0160289604000522.

(3) *The Dutch Hunger Winter 1944-45.* Environment & Society Portal. (n.d.). Retrieved June 29, 2022, from https://www.environmentandsociety.org/tools/keywords/dutch-hunger-winter-1944-45

(4) Brown, A. S., Os, J. van, Driessens, C., Hoek, H. W., & Susser, E. S. (n.d.). Further Evidence of Relation Between Prenatal Famine and Major Affective Disorder. *American Journal of Psychiatry.* Retrieved June 29, 2022, from https://ajp.psychiatryonline.org/doi/pdf/10.1176/appi.ajp.157.2.190.00

(5) Luders, E., Narr, K. L., Thompson, P. M., & Toga, A. W. (2019, May 14). *Neuroanatomical correlates of intelligence.* Life, Earth & Health Sciences. Retrieved June 29, 2022, from https://eurekamag.com/research/054/578/054578163.php.

(6) Talge, N. M., Neal, C., & Glover, V. (2007). Antenatal maternal stress and long-term effects on child neurodevelopment: How and why? Journal of Child Psychology and Psychiatry, 48(3-4), 245–261. https://doi.org/10.1111/j.1469-7610.2006.01714.x.

(7) Kinsella, M. T., & Monk, C. (2009). Impact of maternal stress, depression and anxiety on fetal neurobehavioral development. *Clinical Obstetrics & Gynecology*, 52(3), 425–24. https://doi.org/10.1097/grf.0b013e3181b52df1.

(8) Kisilevsky, B. S., Hains, S. M. J., Jacquet, A., Granier-Deferre, C., & Lecanuet, J. P. (2004). Maturation of fetal responses

to music. *Developmental Science*, 7(5), 550–559. https://doi.org/10.1111/j.1467-7687.2004.00379.x.

(9) Flynn, J. R. (2012). Are We Getting Smarter?: Rising IQ in the Twenty-first Century.

(10) Marchman, A. M., Weisleder, V., Weisleder, A., & Fernald, A. (2015). Talking to Children Matters: Early language experience strengths processing and builds vocabulary. *Psychological Science*, 2143–2152.

(11) Hayes, S., Barnett-Holmes, B., & Roche, B. (2001). *Relational Frame Theory: A post-Skinnerian Account of Human Language and Cognition*. Springer Science and Business Media.

(12) A relational frame skills training intervention to increase general intelligence and scholastic aptitude. (2016). *Learning and Individual Differences 47*. Retrieved June 2022, from https://www.psychologytoday.com/sites/default/files/lind.diff_cassidy_roche_et_al_2016_0.pdf.

(13) Jaeggi, S. M., Buschkuehl, M., Jonides, J., & Perrig, W. J. (2008). Improving fluid intelligence with training on working memory. *Proceedings of the National Academy of Sciences*, *105* (19), 6829–6833. https://doi.org/10.1073/pnas.0801268105.

## CHAPTER 4
## EMOTIONAL AND BEHAVIORAL STYLE, INCLUDING ATTENTION DEFICIT HYPERACTIVITY DISORDER

(1) American Psychological Association. (2015). *American Psychological Association Dictionary of Psychology*, (2nd ed.).

(2) Rothbart, M. K. (2007). Temperament, development, and personality. *Current Directions in Psychological Science*, 16(4), 207–212. https://doi.org/10.1111/j.1467-8721.2007.00505.x.

(3) Wasson, D. L. (2019, October). *Galen*. World History Encyclopedia. Retrieved June 29, 2022, from https://www.worldhistory.org/Galen/.

(4) Cattell, R. (1987). Impulsiveness versus Reflectivity in Garrison, W, and F. Earls, Temperament and Child Psychopathology. *Developmental Clinical Psychology and Psychiatry*.

(5) Thomas, A., Chess, S., Birch, H. G., Hertzig, M. E., & Korn, S. (1963). *Behavioral individuality in early childhood.* New York University Press. https://doi.org/10.1037/14328-000.

(6) Chess, S., & Thomas, A. (1990). Continuities and discontinuities in temperament. *Straight and Devious Pathways from Childhood to Adulthood*, 205–220.

(7) Kagan, J., & Snidman, N. (2009). The Long Shadow of Temperament. *Harvard University Press.*

(8) Plomin, R., & Dunn, J. (1986). *The study of temperament: Changes, continuities, and challenges.* Lawrence Erlbaum Associates.

(9) Kagan, J., Snidman, N., & Arcus, D. M. (1992). Initial reactions to unfamiliarity. *Current Directions in Psychological Science, 1*(6), 171–174. https://doi.org/10.1111/1467-9566.ep10770010.

(10) Current Directions in Psychological Science 1. (1992), 171–74.

(11) Larsen, R. J., & Diener, E. (1987). Affect intensity and individual differences in characteristics: a review. *Research in Personality*, 1–39.

(12) Lou, H. C., Henriksen, L., & Bruhn, P. (1984). Focal cerebral hypoperfusion in children with dysphasia and/or attention deficit disorder. *Archives of Neurology, 41*(8), 825–829. https://doi.org/10.1001/archneur.1984.04050190031010.

(13) Rubia, K., Alegria, A. A., Cubillo, A. I., Smith, A. B., Brammer, M. J., & Radua, J. (2014). Effects of stimulants on brain function in attention-deficit/hyperactivity disorder: A systematic review and meta-analysis. *Biological Psychiatry, 76*(8), 616–628. https://doi.org/10.1016/j.biopsych.2013.10.016.

(14) Mischel, W., & Metzner, R. (1962). Preference for delayed reward as a function of age, intelligence, and length of delay interval. *The Journal of Abnormal and Social Psychology, 64*(6), 425–431. https://doi.org/10.1037/h0045046.

(15) Murray, J., Theakston, A., & Wells, A. (2016). Can the attention training technique turn one marshmallow into two? improving children's ability to delay gratification. *Behaviour Research and Therapy, 77*, 34–39. https://doi.org/10.1016/j.brat.2015.11.009.

## CHAPTER 5
## THEORIES OF PERSONALITY DEVELOPMENT
## THE "WHYS OF BEHAVIOR" & THE VALUE OF
## UNDERSTANDING YOUR CHILD

(1) A&E Networks Television. (2021, May 25). *Francis Galton.* Biography.com. Retrieved July 30, 2022, from https://www. biography.com/scientist/francis-galton.

(2) Vaillant, G. E. (2011). Involuntary coping mechanisms: A psychodynamic perspective. *Dialogues in Clinical Neuroscience, 13*(3). https://doi.org/10.31887/dcns.2011.13.2/gvaillant.

(3) Hall-Flavin, D. K. (2021, December). *What is Passive Aggressive Behavior? What are Some of the Signs?* Mayo Clinic. Retrieved July 5, 2022, from https://www.mayoclinic.org/healthy-lifestyle/ adult-health/expert-answers/passive-aggressive-behavior/ faq-20057901

(4) Adler, A. (1927). *The practice and theory of individual psychology.* Harcourt.

(5) Sullivan, H. S. (1953). *The interpersonal theory of psychiatry.* Norton.

(6) Erikson, E. (1963). Childhood and Society (Revised). Norton.


## CHAPTER 6
## THEORIES OF INTELLECTUAL (COGNITIVE)
## DEVELOPMENT

(1) Piaget, J., & Inhelder, B. (1969). *The Psychology of the Child.* Basic Books.

(2) Stuart-Hamilton, I. (1999). *Key ideas in psychology.* J. Kingsley Publishers.

(3) Smith I. D. (1968). The effects of training procedures upon the acquisition of conservation of weight. *Child development, 39*(2), 515–526.

## CHAPTER 7
## NURTURING THE LOVING AND EMOTIONALLY
## WELL-ADJUSTED CHILD

(1) Myers, D. G., & DeWall, C. N. (2014). *Exploring Psychology. 9th ed.* Worth Publishers.

(2) Fantz, R. (1961). The Origin of Form Perceptions. *Science 204*, 66–72.

(3) Golding, W. (1954). *Lord of the Flies.* Putnam.

(4) Bregman, R., Manton, E., & Moore, E. (2020). *Humankind: A Hopeful History.* Little, Brown and Company.

(5) Cassidy, J., Jones, J. D., & Shaver, P. R. (2013). Contributions of Attachment Theory and research: A framework for future research, translation, and policy. *Development and Psychopathology, 25,* 1415–1434. https://doi.org/10.1017/s0954579413000692.

(6) Waters, E., & Cummings, E. M. (2000). A secure base from which to explore close relationships. *Child Development, 71*(1), 164–172. https://doi.org/10.1111/1467-8624.00130.

(7) Sroufe, L. A., Coffino, B., & Carlson, E. A. (2010). Conceptualizing the role of early experience: Lessons from the Minnesota Longitudinal Study. *Developmental Review, 30*(1), 36–51. https://doi.org/10.1016/j.dr.2009.12.002.

(8) Klaus, M. H., & Kennell, J. H. (1976). *Maternal-infant bonding: The impact of early separation or loss on Family Development.* Mosby Co.

(9) Benoit, D. (2004). Infant-parent attachment: Definition, types, antecedents, measurement and outcome. *Paediatrics & Child Health, 9*(8), 541–545. https://doi.org/10.1093/pch/9.8.541.

(10) Lorenz, K. (1981). *The Foundations of Ethology.* Springer.

(11) Suomi, S., & Leroy, H. (1982). In memoriam: Harry F. Harlow (1905-1981). *The American Journal of Primatology,* 319–342.

(12) Harlow, H. F., & Zimmermann, R. R. (1959). Affectional response in the infant monkey. *Science, 130*(3373), 421–432. https://doi.org/10.1126/science.130.3373.421.

(13) Harlow, H. F., & Harlow, M. (1966). Learning to Love. *American Scientist*.

(14) Rheingold, H. L. (1956). The modification of social responsiveness in institutional babies. *Monographs of the Society for Research in Child Development*, *21*(2), 1. https://doi.org/10.2307/1165614

(15) Spitz, R. A., & Wolf, K. M. (1946). Anaclitic Depression. *The Psychoanalytic Study of the Child*, *2*(1), 313–342. https://doi.org/10.1080/00797308.1946.11823551.

(16) Holmes, J. (2014). *John Bowlby and attachment theory* (2nd ed.). Routledge.

(17) Greenberg, M. T., Cicchetti, D., Cummings, E. M., Main, M., & Solomon, J. (1993). Procedures for identifying infants as disorganized/disoriented during the Ainsworth Strange Situation. In Attachment in the preschool years: Theory, research, and intervention. (pp. 121–160). Essay, University of Chicago Press.

## CHAPTER 8
## DEVELOPING A SECURE ATTACHMENT
## AND HEALTHY EMOTIONAL EXPRESSION

(1) Wolff, M. D., & Ijzendoorn, M. van. (1997). Sensitivity and attachment: A meta-analysis on parental antecedents of infant attachment. *Child Development*, *68*(4), 571–591. https://doi.org/10.1111/j.1467-8624.1997.tb04218.x.

(2) Fox, N. (1989). Infant temperament and security of attachment: a new look. *International Society for Behavioral Development*.

(3) Huft, E. C., & Dworetzky, J. (1996). *Study guide to accompany introduction to child development* (6th ed.). West Pub. Co.

(4) Schaffer, H. R., & Emerson, P. E. (1964). The development of social attachments in infancy. *Monographs of the Society for Research in Child Development*, *29*(3). https://doi.org/10.2307/1165727.

(5) Ding, Y.-hua, Xu, X., Wang, Z.-yan, Li, H.-rong, & Wang, W.-ping. (2014). The relation of infant attachment to attachment

and cognitive and behavioural outcomes in early childhood. *Early Human Development, 90*(9), 459–464. https://doi.org/10.1016/j. earlhumdev.2014.06.004.

(6) Sroufe, L. A., Coffino, B., & Carlson, E. A. (2010). Conceptualizing the role of early experience: Lessons from the Minnesota Longitudinal Study. *Developmental Review, 30*(1), 36–51. https://doi.org/10.1016/j.dr.2009.12.002.

(7) Sears, W., & Sears, M. (2001). *The attachment parenting book: A commonsense guide to understanding and nurturing your baby.* Little, Brown.

(8) Baumrind, D. (1966). Effects of authoritative parental control on child behavior. *Child Development, 37*(4), 887–907. https://doi.org/10.2307/1126611.

(9) Maccoby, E. E., & Martin, J. A. (1983). *Handbook of Child Psychology Vol 4: Socialization, personality, and social development* (4th ed.). Wiley.

(10) Fletcher, A. C., Steinberg, L., & Sellers, E. B. (1999). Adolescents' well-being as a function of perceived Interparental consistency. *Journal of Marriage and the Family, 61*(3), 599–610. https://doi.org/10.2307/353563.

(11) Sullivan, H. S. (1997). *The Interpersonal Theory of Psychiatry.* Norton.

(12) Damon, W. (1979). *The social world of the child.* Jossey-Bass Publishers.

## CHAPTER 9
## USING POSITIVES TO DEVELOP WORK HABITS

(1) Leijten, P., Gardner, F., Melendez-Torres, G. J., van Aar, J., Hutchings, J., Schulz, S., Knerr, W., & Overbeek, G. (2019). Meta-analyses: Key parenting program components for Disruptive Child Behavior. *Journal of the American Academy of Child & Adolescent Psychiatry, 58*(2), 180–190. https://doi.org/10.1016/j.jaac.2018.07.900.

(2) Lysakowski, R. S., & Walberg, H. J. (1981). Classroom reinforcement and Learning: A quantitative synthesis. *The Journal of Educational Research, 75*(2), 69–77. https://doi.org/10.1080/00220671.1981.10885359.

(3) Akin-Little, K. A., Eckert, T. L., Lovett, B. J., & Little, S. G. (2004). Extrinsic reinforcement in the classroom: Bribery or best practice. *School Psychology Review, 33*(3), 344–362. https://doi.org/10.1080/02796015.2004.12086253.

(4) Speaks, S. (2012, May 10). *Watson, Pavlov, Thorndike, Skinner and the development of behaviorism.* Owlcation. Retrieved July 13, 2022, from https://owlcation.com/social-sciences//Cognitive-Development-in-Children-from-Watson-to-Kohlberg.

(5) Premack, D. (1959). Toward empirical behavior laws: I. Positive Reinforcement. *Psychological Review, 66*(4), 219–233. https://doi.org/10.1037/h0040891.

(6) Lasure, L. C., & Mikulas, W. L. (1996). Biblical behavior modification. *Behaviour Research and Therapy, 34*(7), 563–566. https://doi.org/10.1016/0005-7967(96)00013-7.

(7) Furnham, A. (1999). Economic socialization: A study of adults' perceptions and uses of allowances (pocket money) to educate children. *British Journal of Developmental Psychology, 17*(4), 585–604. https://doi.org/10.1348/026151099165492.

(8) Abramovich, R., Freedman, J., & Pliner, P. (1991). *Journal of Economic Psychology, 12*(1).

(9) (2012, May 14). *Wall Street Journal.*

(10) Miltenberger, R. G. (2016). *Behavior Modification: Principles and Procedures* (6th ed.). Cengage Learning.

(11) Fattu, N. A., Mech, E. V., & Auble, D. (1955). Partial reinforcement related to "free" responding in extinction with pre-school children. *The Journal of Experimental Education, 23*(4), 365–368. https://doi.org/10.1080/00220973.1955.11010525

(12) Jenkins, W. O., & Stanley, J. C. (1950). Partial reinforcement: A review and critique. *Psychological Bulletin, 47*(3), 193–234. https://doi.org/10.1037/h0060772.

CHAPTER 10
WHEN POSITIVES DON'T WORK –
THE PRINCIPLES OF PUNISHMENT

NONE

CHAPTER 11
SELF/OTHER BALANCE and SELF-ESTEEM

(1) Myers, D. G. (2014). *Psychology in modules with updates on DSM-5* (10th ed.). Worth Publishers.

(2) Gesell, A., & Ilg, F. L. (1965). *The child from five to ten: (from the former clinic of Child Development School of Medicine at Yale University)*. Hamilton.

(3) Piaget, J. (1965). *The Child's Conception of the World*. Adams & Company

(4) Flavell, J. H., & Miller, P. H. (1998). Social Cognition. *Handbook of Child Psychology Cognition, Perception, and Language, 2*, 851–898.

(5) Selman, R. L., & Byrne, D. F. (1974). A structural-developmental analysis of levels of role taking in middle childhood. *Child Development, 45*(3), 803–806. https://doi.org/10.2307/1127850.

(6) Ashford José B, & LeCroy, C. W. (2013). *Human Behavior in the Social Environment: A Multidimensional Perspective* (5th ed.). Brooks/Cole, Cengage Learning.

(7) O'Connor, M. (1975). The nursery school environment. *Developmental Psychology, 11*(5), 556–561. https://doi.org/10.1037/0012-1649.11.5.556.

(8) O'Connor, M. (1977). The effect of role-taking training on role-taking and social behaviors in young children. *Social Behavior and Personality: an International Journal, 5*(1), 1–11. https://doi.org/10.2224/sbp.1977.5.1.1.

(9) Wayment, H. A., & Bauer, J. J. (2017). The quiet ego: Motives for self-other balance and growth in relation to well-being. *Journal*

*of Happiness Studies*, *19*(3), 881–896. https://doi.org/10.1007/s10902-017-9848-z

(10) Wayment, H., & Bauer, J. (2018). *Happy mind: Cognitive contributions to well-being*. SPRINGER INTERNATIONAL PU.

(11) *Erik Erikson*. Erikson Institute. (2022, June 17). Retrieved July 5, 2022, from https://www.erikson.edu/about/history/erik-erikson/.

(12) Bogels, S., & Melik, M. van. (2004). *Personality and Individual Differences*, *37*(8).

(13) Medinnus, G. R. (1965). Adolescents' self-acceptance and perceptions of their parents. *Journal of Consulting Psychology*, *29*(2), 150–154. https://doi.org/10.1037/h0021862.

(14) Saarni, C. (2010). *The development of emotional competence*. Guilford Press.

(15) Saarni, C. (n.d.). *Child Development*, *55*, 1504–1513.

(16) Gordon, T. (1974). *P.E.T.-- Parent Effectiveness Training. The Tested New Way to Raise Responsible Children*. Peter H. Wyden.

(17) Kubany, E Richard, D., Bauer, G and Muraoka, M. (1992) Adolescence, 27 (107).

## CHAPTER 12
## BUILDING TRUE SELF-ESTEEM
## & HEALTHY EXPRESSION OF EMOTIONS

(1) Twenge, J. M., & Campbell, W. K. (2003). "Isn't it fun to get the respect that we're going to deserve?" Narcissism, Social Rejection, and Aggression. *Personality and Social Psychology Bulletin*, *29*(2), 261–272. https://doi.org/10.1177/0146167202239051.

(2) Bushman, B. J., & Baumeister, R. F. (1998). Threatened egotism, narcissism, self-esteem, and direct and displaced aggression: Does self-love or self-hate lead to violence? *Journal of Personality and Social Psychology*, *75*(1), 219–229. https://doi.org/10.1037/0022-3514.75.1.219.

(3) Bandura, A. (1981). *Self-referent thought: a developmental analysis of self-efficacy*. Cambridge University Press.

(4) Gesell, A., & Ilg, F. L. (1946). *The child from five to ten.* Hamilton.

(5) Hall, C. S., Lindzey, G., & Campbell, J. B. (1998). *Theories of personality* (4th ed.). Wiley

(6) Lundholm, H. (1940). Reflections upon the nature of the psychological self. *Psychological Review, 47*(2), 110–126. https://doi.org/10.1037/h0062485.

(7) Rogers, C. (1951). *Client Centered Therapy.* Houghton-Mifflin.

(8) Berk, L. E. (2013). *Child Development* (9th ed.). Pearson.

(9) Elkind, D. (1994). *A sympathetic understanding of the child: Birth to sixteen* (3rd ed.). Allyn and Bacon.

## CHAPTER 13
## MORALITY AND KIND BEHAVIOR: INBORN OR TAUGHT?

(1) Killen, M. (2014). *Handbook of Moral Development* (2nd ed.). Psychology Press.

(2) Gesell, A., & Ilg, F. L. (1965). *The child from five to ten: (from the former clinic of Child Development School of Medicine at Yale University).* Hamilton.

(3) Haidt, J., & Kesebir, S. (2010). Morality. In S. T. Fiske, D. T. Gilbert, & G. Lindzey (Eds.), *Handbook of social psychology* (pp. 797–832). John Wiley & Sons, Inc.. https://doi.org/10.1002/9780470561119.socpsy002022

(4) Turiel, E. (2014). *Handbook of Moral Development: Morality: Epistemology, development, and social opposition.* (M. Killen & J. Smetana, Eds.)

(5) Gewirth, A. (1978). The golden rule rationalized. *Midwest Studies in Philosophy, 3,* 133–147. https://doi.org/10.1111/j.1475-4975.1978.tb00353.x.

(6) Manning, R., Levine, M., & Collins, A. (2007). The Kitty Genovese murder and the social psychology of helping: The parable of the 38 witnesses. *American Psychologist, 62*(6), 555–562. https://doi.org/10.1037/0003-066X.62.6.555.

(7) Franco, Z. E., Blau, K., & Zimbardo, P. G. (2011). Heroism: A Conceptual Analysis and Differentiation between Heroic Action and Altruism. Review of General Psychology, 15(2), 99–113. https://doi.org/10.1037/a0022672.

(8) Brosnan, S. F., & de Waal, F. B. (2003). Monkeys reject unequal pay. *Nature*, *425*(6955), 297–299. https://doi.org/10.1038/nature01963.

(9) Donaldson, Z. R., & Young, L. J. (2008). Oxytocin, vasopressin, and the neurogenetics of Sociality. *Science*, *322*(5903), 900–904. https://doi.org/10.1126/science.1158668.

(10) Harbaugh, W. T., Mayr, U., & Burghart, D. R. (2007). Neural responses to taxation and voluntary giving reveal motives for charitable donations. *Science*, *316*(5831), 1622–1625. https://doi.org/10.1126/science.1140738.

(11) Simner, M. L. (1971). Newborn's response to the cry of another infant. *Developmental Psychology*, *5*(1), 136–150. https://doi.org/10.1037/h0031066.

(12) Bloom, P. (2013). *Just Babies: The Origins of Good and Evil.* Crown.

(13) Hamlin, J. K., Wynn, K., & Bloom, P. (2007). Social evaluation by Preverbal Infants. *Nature*, *450*(7169), 557–559. https://doi.org/10.1038/nature06288.

(14) Decety, J., & Wheatley, T. (2017). *The Moral Brain: A Multidisciplinary Perspective.* MIT Press.

CHAPTER 14
HOW MORALITY DEVELOPS IN CHILDREN
AND WHEN THERE ARE LAPSES

(1) Piaget, J. (1997). The Moral Judgment of the Child. Simon & Schuster.

(2) Kohlberg, L. (1984). *Essays on moral development / the nature and validity of moral stages.* Harper & Row.

(3) Selman, R. L., & Byrne, D. F. (1974). A structural-developmental analysis of levels of role taking in

middle childhood. *Child Development*, *45*(3), 803–806. https://doi.org/10.2307/1127850

(4) DePalma, D. J., & Foley, J. M. (1975). *Moral development: Current theory and research*. Lawrence Erlbaum.

(5) Stams, G. J., Brugman, D., Deković, M., van Rosmalen, L., van der Laan, P., & Gibbs, J. C. (2006). The moral judgment of juvenile delinquents: A meta-analysis. *Journal of Abnormal Child Psychology*, *34*(5), 692–708. https://doi.org/10.1007/s10802-006-9056-5.

(6) Gottlieb, A., & DeLoache, J. S. (2017). *A world of babies imagined childcare guides for eight societies* (2nd ed.). Cambridge University Press.

(7) Staub, E. (1975). *To Rear a Prosocial Child: Reasoning, Learning by Doing, and Learning by Teaching Others*. Lawrence Erlbaum Associates.

(8) Whiting, B. B., Whiting, J. W. M., & Longabaugh, R. (1981). *Children of Six Cultures: A Psycho-cultural Analysis* (5th ed.). Harvard University Press.

(9) Kochanska, G., Gross, J. N., Lin, M.-H., & Nichols, K. E. (2002). Guilt in young children: Development, determinants, and relations with a broader system of standards. *Child Development*, *73*(2), 461–482. https://doi.org/10.1111/1467-8624.00418.

CHAPTER 15
## RELIGION AND SANTA CLAUS
## AS THEY RELATE TO MORALITY

(1) Bartkowski, J. P., Xu, X., & Levin, M. L. (2008). Religion and child development: Evidence from the early childhood longitudinal study. *Social Science Research*, *37*(1), 18–36. https://doi.org/10.1016/j.ssresearch.2007.02.001

(2) Galen, L. W. (2012). Does religious belief promote prosociality? A critical examination. *Psychological Bulletin*, *138*(5), 876–906. https://doi.org/10.1037/a0028251.

(3) Decety, J., Cowell, J. M., Lee, K., Mahasneh, R., Malcolm-Smith, S., Selcuk, B., & Zhou, X. (2015). The negative association between Religiousness and children's altruism across the world. *Current Biology, 25*(22), 2951–2955. https://doi.org/10.1016/j. cub.2015.09.056.

(4) Sabato, H., & Kogut, T. (2018). The association between Religiousness and Children's Altruism: The Role of the recipient's neediness. *Developmental Psychology, 54*(7), 1363–1371. https://doi.org/10.1037/dev0000526.

(5) Sabato, H., & Kogut, T. (2020). The development of prosociality among Christian Arab children in Israel: The role of children's household religiosity and of the recipient's neediness. *Developmental Psychology, 56*(8), 1509–1517. https://doi. org/10.1037/dev0000914.

(6) Bartkowski, J. P., Xu, X., & Bartkowski, S. (2019). Mixed blessing: The beneficial and detrimental effects of religion on child development among third-graders. *Religions, 10*(1). https:// doi.org/10.3390/rel10010037.

(7) Prentice, N. M., Manosevitz, M., & Hubbs, L. (1978). Imaginary figures of early childhood: Santa Claus, Easter Bunny, and the tooth fairy. *American Journal of Orthopsychiatry, 48*(4), 618–628. https://doi.org/10.1111/j.1939-0025.1978.tb02566.x.

(8) Woolley, J. D., Ma, L., & Lopez-Mobilia, G. (2011). Development of the use of conversational cues to assess reality status. *Journal of Cognition and Development, 12*(4), 537–555. https://doi.org/10.1080/15248372.2011.554929.

(9) Prentice, N., & Gordon, D. (1987). *Journal of Genetic Psychology, 148*(2).

(10) Anderson, C. J., & Prentice, N. M. (1979). Encounter with reality: Children's reactions on discovering the Santa Claus Myth. *Child Psychiatry and Human Development, 25*(2), 667–684. https://doi.org/10.1007/bf02253287.

(11) Woolley, J. (2020, January 6). *Is believing in Santa bad or good for kids?* UT News. Retrieved July 14, 2022, from https://

news.utexas.edu/2020/01/06/is-believing-in-santa-bad-o
r-good-for-kids/.

(12) Swanson, A. (2016, December). *What psychologists really think about you lying to your kids about Santa. The Washington Post.* Retrieved 2022.

## CHAPTER 16
## CONCEPTS OF INDEPENDENCE, SEPARATION
## & SOME CULTURAL DIFFERENCES

(1)  *Blue Bloods (official site) watch on CBS.* CBS. (2022, May 6). Retrieved 2022, from https://www.cbs.com/shows/blue_bloods/

(2)  Bradley-Geist, J., & Olson-Buchanan, J. (2014). Helicopter parents: An examination of the correlates of over-parenting of college students. *Education + Training, 56*(4), 314–328. https://doi.org/10.1108/et-10-2012-0096.

(3)  Triandis, H. (2001). *Individualism and collectivism: Past, present and future.* Oxford University Press.

(4)  Henrich, J. P. (2020). *The weirdest people in the world: How the west became psychologically peculiar and particularly prosperous.* Farrar, Straus and Giroux.

(5)  Kagitcibasi, C. (1997). *Family and Human Development across Cultures: A View from the Other Side.* Lawrence Erlbaum Associates.

(6)  Yan, Y., & Pan-Chang, K. (2021). Helicopter Parenting: Conceptions, Influence and Effects. *Journal of Psychological Science,* (3), 612–615.

(7)  Becker, S. O., & Woessmann, L. (2016). Social cohesion, religious beliefs, and the effect of Protestantism on suicide. *The Review of Economics and Statistics, 98*(2), 224–228.

(8)  Woessmann, L., Torgler, B., & Schaltegger, C. (2016). Suicide and religion: New evidence on the differences between Protestantism and Catholicism. *Journal for the Scientific Study of Religion, 53*(2), 316–340.

## CHAPTER 17
### EARLY INFANCY (0 to 3 Months)

(1) Schulze, P. A., & Carlisle, S. A. (2010). What research does and doesn't say about breastfeeding: A critical review. *Early Child Development and Care*, *180*(6), 703–718. https://doi.org/10.1080/03004430802263870.

(2) Iacovou, M., & Sevilla, A. (2012). Infant feeding: The effects of scheduled vs. on-demand feeding on mothers' wellbeing and Children's Cognitive Development. *European Journal of Public Health*, *23*(1), 13–19. https://doi.org/10.1093/eurpub/cks012.

(3) Thomas, T., Goodman, R., Jacob, A., & Grabher, D. (2021). Implementation of cue-based feeding to improve preterm infant feeding outcomes and promote parents' involvement. *Journal of Obstetric, Gynecologic & Neonatal Nursing*, *50*(3), 328–339. https://doi.org/10.1016/j.jogn.2021.02.002.

(4) Brazelton, T. B., & Sparrow, J. D. (2006). Touchpoints birth to 3: Your child's emotional and behavioural development (2nd ed.). Da Capo Lifelong.

(5) Weissbluth, M. (2021). Healthy Sleep Habits, Happy Child: A new step-by-step guide for a good night's sleep (5th ed.). Ballantine Books.

## CHAPTER 18
### MIDDLE INFANCY (4 to 9 Months)

NONE

## CHAPTER 19
### LATE INFANCY (9 to 15 Months)

(1) Hart, B., & Risley, T. R. (1995). *Meaningful Differences in the Everyday Experience of Young American Children*. Paul H. Brookes Publishing Co.

## CHAPTER 20
## DEVELOPMENT IN THE TODDLER YEARS
(15 Months to 3 Years)

(1)  Mussen, P. H., & Eisenberg, N. (1977). *Sharing and Helping: The Development of Prosocial Behavior in Children*. W.H. Freeman.
(2)  Reschke, K. (2019, January). *Who am I? Developing a sense of self and belonging*. ZERO TO THREE. Retrieved 2022, from https://www.zerotothree.org/resource/who-am-i-developing-a-sense-of-self-and-belonging/

## CHAPTER 21
## RELATIONSHIP BUILDING AND
## TEACHING ADAPTIVE BEHAVIOR

(1)  Rose V. L. (1998). AAP issues policy statement on parental discipline of children. *American family physician*, *58*(4), 1001.

## CHAPTER 22
## HANDLING MISBEHAVIOR

(1)  Sloat, S. (2018, December 18). *Is it bad to tell kids about Santa? survey results are mixed*. Inverse. Retrieved July 14, 2022, from https://www.inverse.com/article/51857-is-santa-real-survey-reveals.

## CHAPTER 23
## EDUCATION AND BRAIN GROWTH,
## INCLUDING LEARNING DISABILITIES & ADHD

(1)  World Health Organization. (2004). *International Statistical Classification of diseases and related health problems: 10th revision* (2nd ed.)
(2)  American Psychiatric Association Publishing. (2022). *Diagnostic and Statistical Manual of Mental Disorders* (5th ed.).

## CHAPTER 24
## PHYSICAL CARE, RELATIONSHIPS,
## AND COMMUNICATION/SCREEN TIME

(1) Rennicke, C. (2020, December 30). *Let's stop saying no all the time and try a yes day instead.* Let Grow. Retrieved July 14, 2022, from https://letgrow.org/yes-day/.


## CHAPTER 25
## ELEMENTS OF A HEALTHY SELF & MORAL VALUES

NONE


## CHAPTER 26
## MOVING TOWARD INDEPENDENCE

(1) Auxier, B., Anderson, M., Perrin, A., & Turner, E. (2020, December 17). *Parenting children in the age of screens.* Pew Research Center: Internet, Science & Tech. Retrieved 2022, from https://www.pewresearch.org/internet/2020/07/28/parenting-children-in-the-age-of-screens/

(2) *The Common Sense Census: Media use by tweens and teens.* Common Sense Media. (2019). Retrieved July 14, 2022, from https://www.commonsensemedia.org/research/the-common-sense-census-media-use-by-tweens-and-teens-2019

(3) *Top Apps For Parents To Monitor Children's Mobile Use.* Android Hits. (n.d.). Retrieved July 14, 2022, from https://www.androidhits.com/top-apps-parents-monitor-childrens-mobile-use.

(4) American Academy of Pediatrics. (n.d.). Retrieved July 14, 2022, from https://www.aap.org/

(5) *When should kids get smartphones? (Survey) - Panda Security.* Panda Security Mediacenter. (2020, October 13). Retrieved 2022, from https://www.pandasecurity.com/en/mediacenter/panda-security/when-should-kids-get-smartphones/

(6) *Consumer Reports.* Pew Research Center. (n.d.). Retrieved July 14, 2022, from Pewresearch.org

(7) *Home Alone Children.* American Academy of Children & Adolescent Psychiatry. (2017, October). Retrieved July 14, 2022, from https://www.aacap.org/AACAP/ Families_and_Youth/Facts_for_Families/FFF-Guide/ Home-Alone-Children-046.aspx.

(8) *Latchkey children statistics unlocked. The Washington Times.* (2000, April 13). Retrieved July 14, 2022, from https://www.washingtontimes.com/news/2000/ apr/13/20000413-011102-8484r/.

(9) *What's the best age for camp?* American Camp Association. (2018, December 5). Retrieved July 14, 2022, from https:// www.acacamps.org/campers-families/parent-blog/ whats-best-age-camp.

## APPENDIX A
## DISCUSSION OF THE ISSUE OF PHYSICAL PUNISHMENT

(1) Gershoff, E. T. (2008). *Report on physical punishment in the United States: What research tells us about its effects on children.* Report on Physical Punishment in the United States: What Research Tells Us About its Effects on Children | Office of Justice Programs. Retrieved July 14, 2022, from https://www.ojp.gov/ncjrs/virtual-library/abstracts/ report-physical-punishment-united-states-what-research-tells-us

(2) Kairys, S., Alexander, R., & Block, R. (2002). When inflicted skin injuries constitute child abuse. *Pediatrics, 110*(3), 644–645. https://doi.org/10.1542/peds.110.3.644.

(3) Graziano, A. M., Hamblen, J. L., & Plante, W. A. (1996). Sub-Abusive violence in child rearing in middle-class American families. *Pediatrics, 98*(4), 845–848. https://doi.org/10.1542/ peds.98.4.845.

(4) American Association of Pediatrics. (2018). Retrieved July 14, 2022, from www.aap.org.

(5) Chiocca, E. M. (2017). American parents' attitudes and beliefs about corporal punishment: An integrative literature review. *Journal of Pediatric Health Care*, *31*(3), 372–383. https://doi.org/10.1016/j.pedhc.2017.01.002.

(6) McCormick, K. F. (1992). Attitudes of primary care physicians toward corporal punishment. *The Journal of the American Medical Association*, *267*(23), 3161–3165. https://doi.org/10.1001/jama.1992.03480230053027

(7) Fortson, B. L., Klevens, J., Merrick, L. K., & Alexander, S. P. (2016). *Preventing child abuse and neglect: A technical package for policy, Norm, and programmatic activities*. Division of Violence Prevention, National Center for Injury Prevention and Control, Centers for Disease Control and Prevention.

(8) *Position Statement on Physical Punishment*. American Psychoanalytic Association. (2021). Retrieved July 15, 2022, from https://apsa.org/sites/default/files/CorporalPunishment.pdf).

(9) *Impact of Physical Discipline on Children May Be Harmful in the Long Term, According to APA Resolution*. American Psychological Association. (2019). Retrieved July 14, 2022, from https://www.apa.org/news/press/releases/2019/02.

(10) Isganitis, E., & Kamei, R. (2003). Spare the Rod and Save the Child, Commentary. *Faith-Based Decisions: Parents Who Refuse Appropriate Care for Their Children, Commentary 1*. Retrieved 2022, from https://journalofethics.ama-assn.org/article/faith-based-decisions-parents-who-refuse-appropriate-care-their-children-commentary-1/2003-08.

(11) Bell, R. Q. (1968). A reinterpretation of the direction of effects in studies of socialization. *Psychological Review*, *75*(2), 81–95. https://doi.org/10.1037/h0025583.

(12) Rubin, K., & Pepler, D. (1991). *The development and treatment of childhood aggression*. Routledge & CRC Press. Retrieved July 14, 2022, from https://www.routledge.com/ The-Development-and-Treatment-of-Childhood-Aggression/ Rubin-Pepler/p/book/9781138876026.

(13) Baumrind, D., Larzelere, R. E., & Cowan, P. A. (2002). Ordinary physical punishment: Is it harmful? Comment on Gershoff. *Psychological Bulletin*, *128*(580), 602–611. https://doi. org/10.1037/0033-2909.128.4.580.

## APPENDIX B
## EXAMINING MORALITY IN VARIOUS CULTURES

(1) *Margaret Mead*. Encyclopædia Britannica. (n.d.). Retrieved July 15, 2022, from https://www.britannica.com/biography/ Margaret-Mead

(2) Mussen, P. H., & Eisenberg, N. (1977). *Sharing and Helping: The Development of Prosocial Behavior in Children*. W.H. Freeman.

(3) Gibbs, J. C., Basinger, K. S., Grime, R. L., & Snarey, J. R. (2007). Moral judgment development across cultures: Revisiting Kohlberg's universality claims. *Developmental Review*, *27*(4), 443–500. https://doi.org/10.1016/j.dr.2007.04.001.

(4) Domino, G. (1992). Cooperation and competition in Chinese and American children. *Journal of Cross-Cultural Psychology*, *23*(4), 456–467. https://doi.org/10.1177/0022022192234003.

(5) Rao, N., & Stewart, S. M. (1999). Cultural influences on Sharer and recipient behavior. *Journal of Cross-Cultural Psychology*, *30*(2), 219–241. https://doi.org/10.1177/0022022199030002005.

(6) Whiting, B. B., Whiting, J. W. M., & Longabaugh, R. (1981). *Children of Six Cultures: A Psycho-cultural Analysis* (5th ed.). Harvard University Press.

APPENDIX C
THE ISSUE OF INDEPENDENCE
IN OTHER CULTURES:
FAMILY-CENTERED VS. INDIVIDUALISTIC

(1) Suizzo, M. (2007). Parents' goals and values for children. *Journal of Cross-Cultural Psychology*, *38*(4), 506–530. https://doi.org/10.1177/0022022107302365

(2) Schulze, P. A., Harwood, R. L., Schoelmerich, A., & Leyendecker, B. (2002). The cultural structuring of parenting and Universal Developmental tasks. *Parenting: Science and Practice*, *2*(2), 151–178. https://doi.org/10.1207/s15327922par0202_04.

(3) Mussen, P. H., & Eisenberg, N. (1977). *Sharing and Helping: The Development of Prosocial Behavior in Children*. W.H. Freeman.

(4) Yan, Y., & Pan-Chang, K. (2021). Helicopter Parenting: Conceptions, Influence and Effects. *Journal of Psychological Science*, *3*, 612–615.

(5) Henrich, J. P. (2020). *The WEIRDest People in the World: How the West Became Psychologically Peculiar and Particularly Prosperous*. Farrar, Strauss, and Giroux.

(6) Reynolds, D. (2016). *The Cambridge Companion to Modern Arab Culture* (Reprinted). Cambridge University Press.

(7) Amer, M. M., & Awad, G. H. (2016). *Handbook of Arab American Psychology*. Routledge

(8) Barakat, H. (2007). *The Arab World: Society, Culture, and State* (7th ed.). University of California Press.

(9) Nydell, M. K. (2018). *Understanding Arabs: A Contemporary Guide to Arab Society* (6th ed.). Intercultural Press, an imprint of Nicholas Brealey Publishing.

(10) Harb, C. (2003). *Culture and self: Values, self-construals and life satisfaction in the UK, Lebanon, Jordan and Syria*. American University of Beirut.

(11) Hofstede, G. (2001). *Cultures and organizations: Comparing values, behaviors, institutions, and organizations across nations* (2nd ed.). Sage Publications.

(12) Ghazal, J. (2004). *Journal of Marriage and Family, 66*

(13) Negy, C. (2009). *Cross-cultural psychotherapy: Toward a critical understanding of diverse clients.* Bent Tree Press.

(14) Joseph, S. (2005). *Intimate selving in Arab families: Gender, self, and identity.* Syracuse Univ. Press.

# Index

**A**

Active listening, 155
Activity rewards sequence, 122
Adaptive behavior, toddlers, 260–262
    cheating, choice point, 297–298
    choices, independent functioning, 302–303
    dangerous behaviors, 290
    extracurricular activities, 303
    going along with group, 302
    independence, separation, 300–304
    lying, 297
    morality, kindness, 295
    physical punishment, 289–291
    privileges, advance notice and, 286–288
    property damage, aggressive behavior, 288
    religious training, choice point, 298–299
    Santa dilemma, choice point, 299–300
    school, group care environment, 300–301
    self development, defense mechanisms choice points, 292–294
    sex play and, 290–291
    stealing, shoplifting, 296–297
    tasks/chores choice point, 303–304
    time outs, 289
Adaptive behaviors
    late infancy, 248–249
    middle infancy, 243–244
    preschool, limit testing, 281
    school age, 322–324
Addams, Jane, 35
Adler, Alfred, 71–72, 146, 254, 307
Agency, gaining mastery, 214–215
Ainsworth, Mary, 98
Allowance
    choice point, 323
    financial socialization, work habits, 125–128
    independence and, 212, 342–345
    school age, choice point, 323
Allport, Gordon, 44
Altruism, 176–177
American Academy of Pediatrics (AAP), 284
American Association of Pediatrics, 358
American Medical Association, *Journal of Ethics*, 355

American Medical Association
Journal study, 353
American Psychoanalytic
Association (APsaA), 354
American Psychological
Association (APA), 358–359
American Psychological
Association Council of
Representatives, 355
Ancient principles, Eastern healing
techniques, 42–43
Animal studies, 95–97, 178
Arab culture. *See also* culture, cross-
cultural differences
behavior teaching, 384–385
case study, 377
dependence *vs.* independence,
386–387
elder care, obligations, 385–386
family organization, 379–381
family roles, 381–382
financial independence, 382–
383
independence *vs.* group
identity, 380–381
learning resources, 377–378
marriage decision-making,
383–384
research, 378–379
school organization, 385
therapists and, 380
Attachment
animal studies, 95–97
attachment parenting, 103–104
bonding *vs.*, 94–95
caregivers, maternal
deprivation and, 97, 101

defined, 94
disorganized-insecure, 99, 100
indiscriminate *vs.* discriminate,
97
in infancy, 94, 97–100
infant temperaments and,
101–102
insecure avoidant, 99, 100
insecure resistant, 99
institutional settings, infants
and, 98
love nurturing and, 90–91
personality development and,
102–103
secure attachment, 99, 103–
104
separation/stranger anxiety,
late infancy, 247–248
Strange Situation Test and, 98
stranger anxiety and, 97
types, 99–100
Attention Deficit Disorder
(ADD), Attention Deficit
Hyperactivity Disorder
(ADHD)
classroom modifications,
support, 50
delayed gratification, 53–54
diagnosis criteria, 48–50
emotional, behavioral
development styles, 47
home modifications, support,
51
impulsivity *vs.* self-control,
53–54
Marshmallow Test, 53–54
medications and, 51–52
PET scan, fMRI, 52–53

pre-school, 275–276
understanding, 53
Authoritarian model, 108–109,
349, 352, 372–373

**B**

Barakat, Halim, 377, 379–380, 386
Bartkowski, John, 201–203
Baumrind, Diana, 107–109, 360–
361
Behavior, internalized standards, 329
Behavior change, research, 117–118
Behavior charts
guidelines, 291
negative phrasing, 292
reading ability and, 292
specific behaviors, 292
targeted behaviors, 291–292
token reinforcers, 123–125
Behavioral management strategies,
concepts, 115
Bell, Richard, 359
Berk, Laura, 167
Binet, Alfred, 22–24
Bloom, Paul, 179
Bonding vs. attachment, 94–95
Bowlby, John, 97, 98
Brain chemistry studies, 178–179
Brain development, 3
brain activity measurement, 14
brain structures, fetus,
6 weeks-9 months
gestation, 11–12
critical periods, prenatal
experiences, 15–16
early infancy, theory, 229–230

enhancement, adult training,
games, 38–39
glucose and, 14
homeschooling and, 37
infants, toddlers, 32–34
intelligence advancement and,
30–32
mother's health, prenatal
planning, 10
nature vs. nature debate, 4–5,
42–43
neural development, prenatal
through 4-5 months
gestation, 9–10
neurogenesis, nervous system
building blocks, 5–9
parental attitudes and, 40
prenatal, 30–32
preschool, 274–275
preschoolers, Early Childhood
Education, 34–36
role of experience learning,
13–14
school age children, 36–38,
308–309
socio-economic-status (SES)
and, 33
synaptogenesis, 12–13, 231
Brain development, theory, 229–230
Brain maturation, 231–232
Brain structures, fetus, 6 weeks-9
months gestation, 11–12
Brazelton, T. Berry, 235, 241, 243,
246
Bregman, Rutger, 91–92
Bribes vs. rewards, 125
Bullies, 321

Buss, Arnold, 47
Byrne, Diane, 185
Bystander effect, moral psychology,
176

# C

Caregivers, maternal deprivation,
attachment, 97, 101
Cattell, Raymond, 45
Cause-and-effect reasoning, 256
Centers for Disease Control and
Prevention, 354
Charitable activities
culture, cross-cultural
differences, 376
morality, kind behavior, 366,
375
school age, 331
Charitable activities, choice point,
331
Cheating, choice point, 297–298
Chess, Stella, 45–46
*Childhood and Society* (Erikson), 75
Childproofing, 248–249
Chores, choice point, 332
Chumship, 110–111
Cognitive development. *See*
intelligence (cognitive)
development
Conscience development, 308
Cortisol levels, correlational
studies, 358–359
Crane, Richard, 35
*Cross-Cultural Perspectives on Early
Childhood* (Kagan), 15

Culture, cross-cultural differences
Anglo, Puerto Rican, 370–371
Arab culture, 377–386
author's personal experiences,
373–374
charitable giving, 376
childrearing, government,
371–372
childrearing procedures,
government, 371–372
competition *vs.* cooperation,
371
conformity, semantics, 375–
376
education and, 371
family structure, Asia, 376–377
goals, preferences, 369–370
Henrich, 374, 376–377
Hofstede Cultural Dimension
study, 378–379
individual *vs.* group-oriented,
368–371
parenting values, 368–371
Suizzo analysis, 368–369
WEIRD *vs.* non-WEIRD,
anthropological research,
374–377
western cultures, independence,
family structures, 372–373
western *vs.* non-nonwestern,
independence, 212, 216–
217

# D

Dangerous behaviors, 137, 290
Dangerous/forbidden activities,
NO!, 248–249

Descartes, René, 4
Differences, 173–174
Disabilities, 25–27, 307–312, 309–312
Discipline, self-control, 117, 130–131
Disorganized-insecure attachment, 99, 100

**E**

Early infancy (0-3 months)
brain development, theory, 229–230
brain maturation, 231–232
building loving relationships, 237–238
choice points, 229–230, 238–239
feedings, on-demand/cue-based vs. scheduled, 235
independence/separation, nuclear family, 239
morality, kindness, 238–239
oral stage, 230
parental anxiety and, 229
physical care, breastfeeding advantages, 233–234
Piaget, 231
synaptogenesis, 12–13, 231
temperament, 232–233
trust/mistrust establishment, 230–231
Eastern healing techniques, ancient principles, 42–43
Ego, secondary processes, 64–65
Egocentric stages, Piaget, 145–146

Electrolytes, ions, 8
Emerson, Peg, 102
Emotional, behavioral development styles
ancient principles, Eastern healing techniques, 42–43
human/child development studies, origins, 43–45
Industrial Revolution and, 43–45
nature vs. nurture, 4–5, 42–43
nine personality dimensions, 45–46
Pavlov and, 44
temperament, 41–47
temperament, longitudinal effects, 46–47
three personality styles, 45–46
Emotional expressions, socialization, 327–328
Emotion(s). See also self-esteem, healthy expression of emotions
active listening and, 155
emotional dependence, 219
emotional disturbance, 106
emotional intelligence, 104–105, 112
expression of feelings and, 104
parent's, 155–158
school age, socialization, 327–328
tantrums, meltdowns, 267–268
Empathy, sympathy, 180–181
Erikson, Erik, 75–76, 94, 150, 230, 256, 308
European cultures, 20

Extended multi-generational families, 366

Extracurricular activities, 303, 340–341

Extreme behaviors, consequences, 350–351

**F**

Feeding, 235, 257

Flynn Effect, IQ tests, 29–30, 36

Formal education, 309

Fox, Nathan, 101–102

Francis, L., 195

Freud, Sigmund, 115, 146, 172, 186, 230, 255, 274, 277, 308, 328

    ego instincts, 63

    instincts, drives, 62

    instincts, life *vs.* death, 62–63

    libido, 62

    non-Freudian theorists, 70–76

    psychoanalysis and, 61–62

    psychological defenses, 67–70

    psychosexual development, 65–67

Friends, popularity, 320–322

Friendship, 110–111, 281, 320–322

Functional Magnetic Imaging (fMRI), 53

Future personality development, attachment, 102–103

**G**

Galen (Greek physician), 43

Galton, Francis, 60

Gender separation, 321

Genetic epistemology, 77

Genius, 19, 25

Genovese tragedy, 176, 183, 190

Gershoff, Elizabeth, 359, 360

Gesell, A., 195, 196, 233

Glucose, 14

Going along with group, 302

Golding, William, 91

Gordon, David, 204

Government policy-making, laws, 354

Grandma's Rule, 123, 264–265, 285–286, 323

Gray area policy, child-raising beliefs, 361–362

Group school experiences, choice point, 270

Guilt, guilt by association, 329–330

Guilt, shame

    autonomy *vs.*, 75–76

    initiative *vs.*, 76

    school age, 329–330

    toddlers, 256, 269

**H**

Haidt, Jonathan, 173, 178

Hall-Flavin, Daniel, 68

Hamlin, J.K., 179

Handbook of Arab American Psychology, 377

Harlow, Harry, 96

Head Start programs, 16–17, 34–35

Healthy self building, self-concept, 325–327

Henrich, Joseph, 217, 221–223, 374, 376–377, 379

Hofstede Cultural Dimension study, 378–379

Hollow threats, 133

Homeschooling, 37

Homework, 339–340

Human/child development studies, origins, 43–45

*Humankind: A Hopeful History* (Bregman), 91, 177

Humiliation, respect, 133–134

# I

The *id*, 63–64

I-messages, You-messages, 155–158

Impulsivity *vs.* self-control, delayed gratification, 53–54

Incentives, reward *vs.* punishment, 120–122

Independence
agency, gaining mastery, 214–215
allowance and, 212
autonomy, 220
collective, 220–221
competence, 220
culture, western *vs.* non-nonwestern, 212, 216–217
cultures, competing concepts, 218–220
emotional dependence, 219
family, nuclear *vs.* extended, 218
family closeness, relatives, 212–213
financial, 212

group identity/collectivism, cultural emphasis, 217, 221

independent *vs.* dependent ability, 220

individualism, cultural emphasis, 217

initial separation, birth/early infancy, 213–214

majority *vs.* minority World, 218

Marriage and Family Plan (MFP), 221–223

marriage rules, Roman Catholic Church, 221–222

object permanence and, 215

parental anxiety, helicoptering and, 216

parenting and, 211–214

physical separation and, 212

relatedness, 220

relational, 220–221

self-determination theory, 220

separate *vs.* independent *vs.* individualist, 219

separate *vs.* interdependent *vs.* self-decisions *vs.* respect, 219

separation milestones, 214–215

WEIRD (Western, Educated, Industrialized, Rich, and Democratic), 217, 221–222, 345

Independence, separation
allowance, choice point, 342–345
checking in, 334–335
cultures independence, individualism, 345

extra-curricular activities, choice point, 340–341
homework, 339–340
homework, parental help, 340
latch-key kids, 341–342
latch-key kids, American Academy of Child and Adolescent Psychiatry estimate, 341–342
parental supervision, 333–334
peer groups, social development and, 334
safety, choice point, 335
school and, 333
screen time, American Pediatrics recommendation, 337
screen time, computers, internet use, 336
sleepovers/camp, choice point, 342
smartphones, 338–339, 341
smartphones, *Consumer Reports*, 338
smartphones, Panda Security survey, 338
smartphones, Pew surveys, 338
Independence/separation, nuclear family, 239
Indiscriminate *vs.* discriminate, 97
Individual Education Plan (IEP), 311, 315
Individual Psychology Theory (Adler), 71–71
Industrial Revolution, 43–45
Industry *vs.* inferiority, 76

Industry/competence *vs.* inferiority, 308
Infractions, theft, intentional harm, 195
Insecure avoidant attachment, 99, 100
Insecure resistant attachment, 99
Instincts, drives, 62
Instincts, life *vs.* death, 62–63
Intelligence (cognitive) development
Binet and, 22–24
defined, 19–22
environment adaptation and, 20–21
European cultures, 20
learning disabilities, parental advice, 26–28
measurement of, 20–21
mental age, IQ, 22–26
numbers of, 21
Piaget, 77–83
Sternberg three elements, 20
success, positivity and, 27
tests, 20–26
Wechler tests, 26
Intelligence, advancement of
Flynn Effect, IQ tests, 29–30, 36
genius, 19, 25
individual differences, 18–19
nutrition and, 30–31
prenatal development, 30–32
Intelligence Quotient (IQ), 22–26, 29–30, 36
Interpersonal Theory of Psychiatry, Sullivan, 73–75

*Isn't it Fun to Get the Respect That We're Going to Deserve?* (research study), 161

# J

Joseph, Suad, 387

# K

Kagan, John, 15, 21, 27
Kagitcibasi, Cigdem, 218, 220–221, 370, 387
Kohlberg, Lawrence, 183–185, 188, 295

# L

Language
  body, 121
  development, 33–34, 83, 309, 347–348
  disability, 26
  disrespectful, foul, 109, 130, 327
  emotional, 105, 156
  written, 375
Latch-key kids, 341–342
Late infancy (9-15 months)
  adaptive behavior, choice point, 248–249
  attachment, separation/ stranger anxiety, 247–248
  childproofing, 248–249
  dangerous/forbidden activities, NO!, 248–249
  independence, 251
  language development, 247–248
  morality, kindness, 250
  motor development, 246–247
  self-esteem building, 250
  sleep/feeding, 246
  stimulating toys, 247
Lattimer, Agnes, 248
Learning disabilities, 25–27, 307–312
Learning disabilities, parental advice, 26–28
Libido, 62
Life training, natural consequences, 119
Locke, John, 4, 15
*Lord of the Flies* (Golding), 91
Love, nurturing
  agape, 90, 91
  Ancient Greeks, 89–90
  attachment and, 90–91
  defined, 89–90
  eros, 89
  philos, 90, 91
  philosophical views, 91–92
  unconditional, 90
Loving relationships
  assumptions, stereotypes, 93
  ingredients, 92–93
  limit setting and, 93–84
  respect and, 93
Luther, Martin, 34
Lying, 297

# M

Maccoby, E.E., 107

Magnetic Resonance Imagery (MRI), 14

Marriage and Family Plan (MFP), 221–223

Marriage rules, Roman Catholic Church, 221–222

Marshmallow Test, 53–54

Martin, J. A., 107

Mary Crane Center, 35

Matek, Deborah, 353, 356–357, 361

Material rewards, choice point, 319

Mead, Margaret, 365

Medical professionals input, 354–356

*Meditations on First Philosophy* (Descartes), 4

Mental Age (MA), 22–24

Mental age, academic tests, 309

Mental age, IQ, 22–26

Middle infancy (4-9 months)
  building healthy self, 244
  building loving relationships, 242–243
  games, communication, 243
  group caregiving, choice point, 245
  independence, separation issues, 245
  morality, kindness, 244–245
  physical care, feeding, 240
  problematic interactions, 243
  sleep, wake routines, 241
  sleep deprivation, parents, 242
  sleep-training, 241–242
  teaching adaptive behavior, 243–244
  teething, 240

Mischel, Walter, 54

Montessori, Maria, 34

Moral development, lapses
  apologies, reparations, 196–197
  autonomous morality, 183
  concrete operations, conventional morality, 184
  conscience, religion, 186–187
  family helping behaviors, 190
  generosity principles, 194
  history, study of, 182–187
  infraction, intentional harm, 194–196
  justice, fairness, 185–186
  juveniles, reasoning skills, 186
  kind children characteristics, 191
  moral behavior progression, children, 187
  moral reasoning measures, Kolberg, 188
  moral transgressions, 192–193
  parental control and, 188
  parents as role models, 188–190
  Piaget, 182–183
  post-conventional, complex thinking, 184–185
  preoperational morality, 183
  psychological factors, family affects, 187–188
  religion, moral transgressions and, 192–193
  sexual behavior, 196

shoplifting, theft, 194–195
*The Moral Judgment of the Child*
    (Piaget), 182
Morality, kind behavior, 328–331
    age-based, 172
    altruism and, 176–177
    animal studies, 178
    brain chemistry studies, 178–
        179
    bystander effect, moral
        psychology, 176
    characterstics, other, 191–192
    concepts, 171–175
    cross-cultural research, 365–
        366
    cultural issues, 364–366
    differences, 173–174
    donation behavior, 366
    empathy, sympathy, 180–181
    extended multi-generational
        families, 366
    Genovese tragedy, 176, 183,
        190
    infant studies, 179–180
    inherent *vs.* learned, 177–178
    internal standards, 172
    lapses, 194
    Mead research, 365
    modern psychology and,
        175–176
    moral psychology and, 176
    necessary components, 180
    prosocial concepts, 172
    relativism *vs.* universalism,
        364–365
    religion and, 177
    Turiel forms of, 17

Morality, kindness, 295
Morality, religion
    faith *vs.* religion, 199
    imaginary cultural icons, Santa
        Claus, 203–206
    religion, family and, 200–201
    religion role, 198
    research insights, 201–202
Mother's health, prenatal planning,
    10
Myelin sheath, 8–9, 11, 30

# N

Nature *vs.* nature debate, 4–5,
    42–43
Negy, C., 379
Neural development, prenatal
    through 4-5 months gestation,
    9–10
Neurogenesis, nervous system
    building blocks, 5–9
    brain, lower *vs.* higher, 5, 9
    electrolytes, ions, 8
    myelin sheath, 8–9, 11, 30
    nerve impulses, electrical
        activity, 7–9
    neurons, 5
Non-Freudian theorists, 70–76

# O

Oedipal complex, 146, 277
Oral stage, early infancy, 230
Organized religion, choice point,
    329–330

## P

Parental supervision, 333–334

Parenting
  attachment parenting, 103–104
  attitudes, brain development
    and, 40
  authoritative, 108
  Baumrind's styles, 107–109
  cultural differences, 109
  culture, cross-cultural
    differences, 368–371
  independence and, 211–214
  learning disabilities, advice,
    26–28
  parent techniques study results,
    138–139
  parent-child conflict, 152–153
  parent-child relationship,
    135–138
  parent's emotions and, 155–
    158
  permissive, 108–109
  punishment, discipline
    techniques study results,
    138–139
  role models, 160
  uninvolved parents, 109
  work habits development,
    128–129

Pavlov, Ivan, 44

Personality development
  ego, secondary processes,
    64–65
  history of study, 59–61
  the *id*, 63–64
  personality parts, 63–65
  personality theories and, 59–60
  personhood, 59
  Pleasure Principle and, 63–64
  psychological defenses, 67–70
  psychosexual development
    stages, 65–66
  superego, 65

Philos, 90

Physical punishment, 289–291
  American Association of
    Pediatrics, 358
  American Medical
    Association, *Journal of
    Ethics*, 355
  American Medical Association
    Journal study, 353
  American Psychoanalytic
    Association (APsaA), 354
  American Psychological
    Association (APA), 358–
    359
  American Psychological
    Association Council of
    Representative, 355
  authoritarian model, 349
  author's position, inputs, 350–
    351, 353–354
  Baumrind on, 360–361
  Centers for Disease Control
    and Prevention, 354
  correct behavior options *vs.*,
    356–357
  extreme behaviors,
    consequences, 350–351
  government policy-making,
    laws, 354
  gray area policy, child-raising
    beliefs, 361–362

Matek input, approaches, 353, 356–357, 361

medical professionals input, 354–356

punishment, physical abuse definitions, 351–352

research surveys review, 352–53

spanking, corporeal punishment, 349–351

spanking, protocol, 357–358

spanking research, effects of spanking/problems, 357–361

types, 351

United Nations Convention on the Rights of the Child, 354

Piaget, Jean, 19, 172, 215, 231, 255, 274, 277, 308

assimilation, accommodation, 78–79

cognitive stages, 80–82

egocentric stages, 145–146

genetic epistemology, 77–78

Play-dates, 321

Pleasure Principle, 63–64

Plomin Robert, 47

Positron Emission Tomography (PET), 14, 52

Power, sense of, 307

Premack Principle, 123

Prentice, Norman, 204–205

Preschool (3-6 years)

attention, 275–276

brain development, 274–275

choices, agency, 283–284

communication tips, choice point, 282–283

development theorists, 273–724

effective praise, verbal coaching, 284

feeding, choice point, 276

friendship, 281

Grandma's Rule, 285–286

language, systematic learning, 274–275

natural consequences, 284–285

Oedipal complex, 277

relationship building, 277–281

rules, 282–283

sibling relationships, 280–281

skill games, choice point, 280

sleeping, 276–276

teaching adaptive behaviors, limit testing, 281

temperament, 275

toilet training, 276

tyrannical behavior, power differences, 277–280

Preschool For All Initiative, 35

Privileges, advance notice, 286–288

Property damage, aggressive behavior, 288

Property damage reparations, 136

Psychological defenses, 67–70

acting out, 69

anticipatory anxiety, fearfulness, 70

healthy defenses, 70

immature, 68–69

intellectualization, 69

neurotic, 69–70

passive-aggressive behavior,
  68–69
projection, 68
psychotic, 68
reaction formation, 69
repression, 69
sublimation defense, 70
suppression, 70
Psychosexual development stages,
  Freud, 65–67
Punishment, discipline principles
  child's temperament and, 132
  cortisol levels, correlational
    studies, 358–359
  dangerous behaviors, 137
  discipline, self-control, 117,
    130–131
  discomfort, consequences and,
    130–131
  hollow threats, 133
  humiliation, respect and,
    133–134
  incentives, reward *vs.*
    punishment, 120–122
  infractions, theft, intentional
    harm, 195
  parent techniques study results,
    138–139
  parent-child relationship and,
    135–138
  physical punishment, 135–138
  property damage reparations,
    136
  reminders, warnings, 133
  severity of punishment, 130–
    132
  socialization strategy, Bell, 359

STOP, START behaviors and,
  119, 133
strategies, isolation/time outs,
  135–136
strategies, withdrawal of
  privileges, 134–135
Punishment, physical abuse
  definitions, 351–352

**Q**

Quiet ego concept, balance, 147

**R**

Receptive visual, expressive
  language transfer, 310
Relationship building, 259–260
Relationship building, parents, 317
Relationship building, school,
  317–318
Religion. *See* morality, religion
Religious training, choice point,
  298–299
Reminders, warnings, 133
Resistant child, 99, 100
Rogers, Carl, 166
Romantic relationships, 148

**S**

Saarni, Carolyn, 154
*Santa Claus and the Tooth Fairy
  for the Jewish child and parent*
  (Prentice, Gordon), 204
Santa dilemma, choice point,
  299–300

Schaffer, Rudolf, 101
School age (6-12 years)
  allowance, choice point, 323
  behavior, internalized
    standards, 329
  brain development, 308–309
  bullies, 321
  charitable activities, choice
    point, 331
  chores, choice point, 332
  communication tips, 328
  concrete operations, 308
  conscience development, 308
  developmental theorists,
    307–308
  emotional expressions,
    socialization, 327–328
  formal education, 309
  friends, popularity, 320–322
  gender separation, 321
  group care environment,
    300–301
  guilt, guilt by association,
    329–330
  healthy self building, self-
    concept, 325–327
  Individual Education Plan
    (IEP), 311, 315
  industry/competence vs.
    inferiority, 308
  learning disabilities, 309–312
  learning disabilities diagnosis,
    choice point, 312
  material rewards, choice point,
    319
  mental age, academic tests, 309
  morality, 328–331

  organized religion, choice
    point, 329–330
  physical care, 316
  play-dates, 321
  receptive visual, expressive
    language transfer, 310
  relationship building, parents,
    317
  relationship building, school,
    317–318
  self/other balance, 320
  sense of power, 307
  sleeping, 316
  teaching adaptive behavior,
    322–324
  temperament, ADHD choice
    point, 312–315
School age children, 36–38, 308–
  309
Screen time, computers, internet
  use, 336
Screen time, smartphones, 338–
  339, 341
  American Pediatrics
    recommendation, 337
  Consumer Reports, 338
  Panda Security survey, 338
  Pew surveys, 338
Sears, Bill, 103
Sears, Martha, 103
Secure attachment, 99, 103–104
Self development, defense
  mechanisms choice points,
  292–294
Self-esteem, healthy expression of
  emotions
  blame and, 159, 160

cognitive modeling, 163
 defensiveness, 160
 error acknowledgment, 159–160
 metacognition and, 165
 parental role models, 160
 recognition of Self, milestone, 167–168
 resilience, resilient Self, 161–162
 safety, 163–164
 self-concept, who am I?, 165–166
 Self-Esteem movement, 161
 semantics, 166
 skills, child's capacity, 163–165
Self-esteem
 self-other balance, 72–73
 active listening, validation of emotions, 155
 aggression and, 153–154
 competition and, 149
 components, meaning of Self, 143
 defensiveness and, 150–151
 egocentric stages, Piaget, 145–146
 emotion and, 153–158
 I-messages, You-messages, 155–158
 Oedipal complex and, 146
 outward *vs.* inward expression, 153–154
 parent-child conflict and, 152–153
 parent's emotions and, 155–158

quiet ego concept, balance, 147
 romantic relationships, 148
 self-acceptance, 150
 Self-system, Sullivan, 150
 social environment and, 150–151
 understanding others, 143–147
Self-Esteem movement, 161
Self-identity growth, 266–267
Self/other balance, 320
Self-system, Sullivan, 150
Selman, Robert, 185
Separation/stranger anxiety, 97, 247–248
Severity of punishment, 130–132
Sexual behavior
 development stages, Freud, 290–291
 moral development, lapses, 65–67
 psychosexual development stages, 65–66
 sex play, 290–291
 toddlers, sex play, 290–291
Sharabi, Hisham, 386
Sleep, 316
 consistency, 257
 deprivation, parents, 242
 sleep-training, 241–242
 wake routines, 241
Sleepovers/camp, choice point, 342
Socialization strategy, Bell, 359
Socio-economic-status (SES), 33
Spanking, 349–351, 357–361
Spanking research, effects of spanking/problems, 357–361

Stealing, shoplifting, 296–297
Sternberg, Robert, 20
Sternberg three elements, 20
STOP, START behaviors, 119, 133
Strange Situation Test, 98
Suizzo, Marie-Anne, 368–369
Suizzo analysis, 368–369
Sullivan, Harry, 72–75, 110, 150, 160, 230, 250, 256, 293
Superego, 65
Synaptogenesis, 12–13, 231

**T**

Tantrums, meltdowns, 267–268
Tasks/chores choice point, 303–304
Temperament
    early infancy, 232–233
    emotional, behavioral development styles, 41–47
    emotional, behavioral development styles, longitudinal effects, 46–47
    infant, attachment, 101–102
    preschool, 275
    punishment, discipline principles and, 132
    school age, ADHD choice point, 312–315
    toddlers, 256
Thomas, Alexander, 45–46
Three personality styles, 45–46
Time outs, 289
    angry, physical child, 264
    initiating, 262–263

Toddlers (15 months-3 years)
    anal possessiveness, 255
    autonomy vs. shame/doubt, 256
    brain maturation, 256
    cause-and-effect reasoning, 256
    developmental theorists on, 255–256
    egocentrism, 255
    emotional expression, tantrums/meltdowns, 267–268
    feeding, 257
    Freud, 255
    Grandma's Rule, 264–265
    group school experiences, choice point, 270
    guilt, 269
    healthy self building, positive self, 266–267
    independence, separation, 269–270
    isolation, time outs, 260–265
    morality, kindness, 268–269
    natural consequences, 261
    negative consequences, 261–262
    parent-child interactions, 256
    physical punishment, 265–266
    Piaget, 255
    praise, 261
    relationship building, 259–260
    self development, defense mechanisms choice points, 292–294
    self-identity growth, 266–267

sleep consistency, 257
stimulation, brain maturation,
    256
supervision of, 255
teaching adaptive behavior,
    260–262
temperament, 256
toilet training choice point,
    258–259
Token reinforcers, behavior charts,
    123–125
Trust vs. mistrust, 75
Trust/mistrust establishment,
    230–231
Turiel, Elliot, 173

**U**

Uninvolved parents, 109
United Nations Convention on the
    Rights of the Child, 354

**V**

Valliant, George, 67
Van Ijzendoom, Marinus, 101
Vygotsky, Lev, 83

**W**

Washington Post, 205
Wechler tests, 26
WEIRD (Western, Educated,
    Industrialized, Rich, and
    Democratic), 217, 221–222,
    345, 374–377

Weissbluth, Marc, 241, 242
Western cultures, independence,
    family structures, 372–373
Western vs. non-nonwestern,
    independence, 212, 216–217
Whiting, Beatrice, 190, 366
Whiting, John, 190, 366
Wolff, Marianne, 101
Wooley, Jacqueline, 205
Work habits, development
    activity rewards sequence,
        system, 122
    allowance, financial
        socialization, 125–128
    attitude adjustment,
        disciplinarian, 118
    behavior change research,
        control groups, 117–118
    bribes vs. rewards, 125
    concepts, behavioral
        management strategies,
        115
    discipline, self-control and,
        117, 130–131
    historical examples, 123
    incentives, reward vs.
        punishment, 120–122
    life training, natural
        consequences, 119
    parental attention, 128–129
    partial reinforcement and, 129
    praise and, 121–122
    Premack Principle, 123
    responsibility and, 116–117
    socialization and, 116
    STOP, START behaviors, 119

token reinforcers, behavior
    charts, 123–125
training types, reasons, 119–
    120
Wundt, Wilhelm, 20

## Y

Yale Clinic of Child Development,
    172
Yokum, Barbara, 206